Praise for
Just Keep Buying

"*Just Keep Buying* is the ideal combination of thoughtful and actionable. Maggiulli not only uses evidence to guide his suggestions, but he is also among the best at boiling everything down into ideas that are easy to understand and apply."

—James Clear, #1 *New York Times* bestselling author, *Atomic Habits*

"The first time I read Nick Maggiulli's writing I knew he had a special talent. There are lots of good data scientists, and lots of good storytellers. But few understand the data and can tell a compelling story about it like Nick. This is a must-read."

—Morgan Housel, bestselling author, *The Psychology of Money*

"Nick Maggiulli clearly delights in flouting the received wisdom about how people should manage their money. The end result is a book that's full of both aha moments and practical takeaways. As a fellow writer about personal finance, I felt a creeping sense of jealousy in what I was reading. Nick takes the tired topics of how to save and invest well and managed to make them utterly fresh and even quite a bit of fun."

—Christine Benz, Director of Personal Finance, Morningstar

"Nick has a genuine gift—while he uses rigorous empirical evidence to make his case, he manages to tell the story in such a way to keep the reader's attention and give them practical, actionable advice. He also has just enough of a mischievous streak to challenge some long-held assumptions about investing, but in a manner that makes the empirical data a fresh, interesting story. Investors, new and old, will benefit from Nick's practical approach to investing."

**—James O'Shaughnessy, Founder and Chairman, OSAM LLC;
bestselling author, *What Works on Wall Street***

JUST KEEP BUYING

Every owner of a physical copy of this edition of

JUST KEEP BUYING

can download the eBook for free direct from us at Harriman House, in a DRM-free format that can be read on any eReader, tablet or smartphone.

Simply head to:

ebooks.harriman-house.com/justkeepbuying

to get your copy now.

JUST KEEP BUYING

Proven ways to save money and build your wealth

Nick Maggiulli

HARRIMAN HOUSE LTD
3 Viceroy Court
Bedford Road
Petersfield
Hampshire
GU32 3LJ
GREAT BRITAIN
Tel: +44 (0)1730 233870

Email: enquiries@harriman-house.com
Website: harriman.house

First published in 2022.

Hardback ISBN: 978-0-85719-971-3
Paperback ISBN: 978-0-85719-925-6
eBook ISBN: 978-0-85719-926-3

British Library Cataloguing in Publication Data
A CIP catalogue record for this book can be obtained from the British Library.

CONTENTS

HOW TO USE THIS BOOK

I HAVE WRITTEN THIS book in a way to optimize the use of your time. While you are free to read it in order, you may find it more useful to jump around to the chapter that best fits where you currently are in your wealth-building journey.

The book is divided into two sections—saving and investing. Saving will cover all the aspects of saving money including: how *much* to save, how to save *more*, how to spend money guilt-free, and so forth. Investing will cover the many facets of putting your money to work including: *why* you should invest, *what* you should invest in, *how* often you should invest, and much more.

I wrote the book in this way so that you could quickly find the information you need and put it to use. If you don't need help saving money, then skip that chapter. Trust me, I won't mind. I'd rather you find something valuable than stop reading altogether.

Lastly, for those who want a quick summary of the book's key ideas and practical takeaways, you can find this at the end of the book in the conclusion.

INTRODUCTION

My late grandfather was addicted to gambling on horse races. When I was a kid we used to go to the Los Angeles County Fair and watch thoroughbreds with names like Magnificent Marks and Jail Break gallop around the track. What I saw then as a form of mild entertainment I later learned was a lifelong struggle for my grandfather.

His addiction started with horse racing but eventually progressed to card games. Blackjack. Baccarat. Pai Gow. You name it, he had played it. I had never heard of some of these games, but my grandfather knew them well. And he bet like it too. $25 a hand. $50 a hand. Sometimes $75 a hand. Sizeable sums of money to throw away on gambling at cards.

You have to understand that my grandfather was retired and living with his mother (my great-grandmother) at the time. She paid for his food and housing. When he initially retired at age 55, he started getting $1,000 a month from his pension. Seven years later, he began receiving Social Security for an additional $1,200 a month.

However, despite having $2,200 a month in income and almost no costs, he died in May 2019 with no assets to his name. Throughout his 26-year retirement, he gambled it all away.

But what if my grandfather had taken just *half* of his monthly retirement income (money he was going to gamble away anyways) and invested it in the U.S. stock market? What would have happened then?

He would have died a millionaire.

He would have been able to gamble throughout his retirement with half his money, and still build wealth because of the growth of the other half invested in stocks.

This is true even though a sizeable chunk of his investments would have been made during one of the worst decades in U.S. stock market history (2000–2009). That wouldn't have mattered. By continually investing his money month after month, my grandfather could have counteracted his worst financial habits and built wealth. And though you probably don't have a severe gambling addiction, by following this philosophy, you can build wealth as well.

A few years before my grandfather's passing, I stumbled upon this idea almost by chance. An idea that consists of only three words. An idea that could make you rich.

Just. Keep. Buying.

This is the mantra that changed my life.

Growing up, I had no concept of wealth or how to build it. I didn't know that the word summer could be used as a verb ("I *summer* in the Hamptons"). I didn't know what dividends were. Heck, most of my life I thought Sizzler and Red Lobster were high-end restaurants.

And though my parents were hard workers, both dropped out of college and never learned about investing. As a result, I didn't either. In fact, it wasn't until I went to college that I truly understood what a stock was.

However, learning about investing wasn't enough to solve my financial problems. Because, despite getting a great education, my financial life after college was fraught with uncertainty and stress. I questioned nearly every financial decision I made.

What should I invest in?

Am I saving enough?

Should I buy now or wait it out?

My neuroticism around money followed me into my mid-20s. I was now supposed to be a full adult, embarking on my career, and in control of my life. Yet, I couldn't quiet that little voice in the back of my head. My uncertainty around money haunted me.

So I started reading everything I could get my hands on about money and investing. I trolled online forums, read every Berkshire Hathaway letter to shareholders, and dug through the footnotes of obscure books on financial history. This helped, but I still felt unsure about what to do next.

Then, in early 2017, I decided to start blogging about personal finance and investing. I was going to force myself to figure this stuff out.

Shortly thereafter, I saw a YouTube video from Casey Neistat that changed everything.

The video, titled "3 words that got me to 3 MILLION SUBS," discussed how Neistat grew his channel to three million subscribers using three words of advice given to him by fellow YouTuber Roman Atwood—Just. Keep. Uploading. Though Neistat was talking about how to build a YouTube following, I immediately saw the connection to investing and building wealth.

In the weeks prior to seeing that video, I had been doing some analysis on the U.S. stock market when I discovered something profound. To build wealth it didn't matter *when* you bought U.S. stocks, just that you bought them and kept buying them. It didn't matter if valuations were high or low. It didn't matter if you were in a bull market or a bear market. All that mattered was that you kept buying.

Combining this insight with Neistat's YouTube advice, Just Keep Buying was born. It's a philosophy that can transform your finances… if you let it.

I am talking about the continual purchase of a diverse set of income-producing assets. When I say income-producing assets, I mean those assets that you expect to generate income for you far into the future, even if that income isn't paid directly to you. This includes stocks, bonds, real estate, and much more. However, the specifics of the strategy are not critically important.

It's not about *when* to buy, *how* much to buy, or *what* to buy—just to keep buying. The idea seems simple because it is simple. Make it a habit to invest your money like you make it a habit to pay your rent or mortgage. Buy investments like you buy food—do it often.

Formally this approach is known as dollar-cost averaging (DCA), or the regular purchase of an asset over time. The only difference between DCA and Just Keep Buying is that Just Keep Buying has the psychological motivation built in.

It is an *aggressive* investment approach that will allow you to build wealth with ease. Think of it like a snowball rolling down a hill. Just keep buying and watch that ball grow.

In fact, Just Keep Buying is easier to follow today than at any point throughout history.

Why is that?

Because if you had implemented this advice just two decades ago, you would have racked up some hefty fees and transaction costs along the way. At $8 per trade in the 1990s, Just Keep Buying would've gotten very expensive, very fast.

But things have since changed. With free trading on many major investment platforms, the rise of fractional share ownership, and the availability of cheap diversification, Just Keep Buying has an edge like never before.

Today you can purchase a single share of an S&P 500 index fund and have every person in every large public corporation in America working to make you richer. And if you buy international index funds, the rest of the world (or most of it) will be working for you as well.

For a trivial sum, you can own a small piece of the future economic growth of much of human civilization. Economic growth that will allow you to build wealth for decades. This isn't just my opinion either—it is backed by over a century's worth of data that transcends geography and asset class.

Of course, Just Keep Buying is only the beginning of your financial journey. Despite its simplicity, I know that it's not sufficient to answer every question that you will have along the way. That's why I have written this book.

In the pages that follow I will answer some of the most asked questions in personal finance and investing. Each chapter will address one topic in-depth and provide actionable takeaways that you can start using in your financial life right away.

Most importantly, the answers to these questions will be based on data and evidence, rather than belief and conjecture. This means that some of my conclusions will go against mainstream financial advice. Some of them may even shock you.

For example, in the pages that follow I will explain:

- Why you need to save less than you think.
- Why credit card debt isn't always bad.

- Why saving up cash to buy the dip isn't a good idea.
- Why you shouldn't buy individual stocks—and why it has nothing to do with underperformance.
- Why a big market correction is usually a good buying opportunity.

And much more.

My goal isn't to be controversial, but to use data to search for the truth, wherever it may be.

Ultimately, *Just Keep Buying* is a book illustrating the proven ways to save money and build your wealth. By following the strategies here, I will show you how you can act smarter and live richer.

We begin by asking, "Where should you start?" In the first chapter, I will demonstrate whether you should focus on saving or investing based on your current financial situation.

1. WHERE SHOULD YOU START?

Why saving is for the poor and investing is for the rich

When I was 23 years old I thought I knew the answer to building wealth. Keep your fees low. Diversify. Hold for the long term. I had heard this kind of advice many times from investing legends such as Warren Buffett, William Bernstein, and the late Jack Bogle. While this advice wasn't incorrect, it made me focus on all the wrong things financially as a recent college graduate.

Despite having only $1,000 in my retirement account at the time, I spent hundreds of hours analyzing my investment decisions over the next year. I had Excel spreadsheets filled with net worth projections and expected returns. I checked my account balances daily. I questioned my asset allocation to the point of neurosis.

Should I have 15% of my money in bonds? Or 20%? Why not 10%?

I was all over the place. They say that obsession is a young man's game. I learned this truth all too well.

But despite my intense fixation on my investments, I spent no time analyzing my income or spending. I would regularly go out to dinner with coworkers, buy rounds and rounds of drinks, and then Uber home. Spending $100 in a night was easy in San Francisco, where I lived at the time.

Think about how foolish this behavior was. With only $1,000 of investable assets to my name, even a 10% annual return would have only earned me $100 in a year. Yet, I was regularly blowing that same $100 every time I went out with friends! Dinner + drinks + transportation and my year's investment returns (in a good year) were gone.

Forgoing just *one night* of partying in San Francisco would've made me the same amount of money as *one year* of investment growth at the time. Can you see why my financial priorities were so messed up? All the Buffett, Bogle, and Bernstein in the world wouldn't have made a difference.

Compare this to someone with $10 million in investable assets. If they were to see just a 10% decline in their portfolio, they would lose $1 million. Do you think they could save $1 million in a year? Highly unlikely. Unless they have a very high income, their annual savings just can't compete with the regular fluctuations in their investment portfolio. This is why someone with $10 million has to spend a lot more time thinking about their investment choices compared to someone with only $1,000.

These examples illustrate that what you should focus on depends on your financial situation. If you don't have much money invested, then you should focus on increasing your savings (and investing it). However, if you already have a sizable portfolio, then you should spend more time thinking about the details of your investment plan.

More simply: saving is for the poor and investing is for the rich.

Don't take this statement too literally. I use the term poor (and rich) in both an absolute and relative sense. For example, as a recent college graduate partying in San Francisco, I definitely wasn't poor on absolute terms, but I was poor *relative to my future self.*

Using this frame of mind, it is much easier to see why saving is for the poor and investing is for the rich.

If I had known this at age 23, I would have spent more time developing my career and growing my income instead of questioning my investment decisions. Once I had a bigger nest egg, then I could have fine-tuned my portfolio.

How do you know where you are on what I call the Save-Invest continuum? Use this simple calculation as a guide.

First, figure out how much you expect to comfortably save in the next year. I say "comfortably" because this should be something that you can achieve with ease. We will call this your *expected savings.* For example, if you expect to save $1,000 a month, your expected savings should be $12,000 a year.

Next, determine how much you expect your investments to grow in the next year (in dollar terms). For example, if you have $10,000 in investable assets and you expect them to grow by 10%, that means you are expecting $1,000 in investment growth. We will call this your *expected investment growth.*

Finally, compare the two numbers. Which is higher, your *expected savings* or your *expected investment growth?*

If your *expected savings* are higher, then you need to focus more on saving money and adding to your investments. However, if your *expected investment growth* is higher, then spend more time thinking about how to invest what you already have. If the numbers are close to each other, then you should spend time on both.

Regardless of where you currently are in your financial journey, your focus should shift from your savings to your investments as you age. To demonstrate this, consider someone who works for 40 years while saving $10,000 a year and earning a 5% annual return.

After one year, they will have invested $10,000 and have earned a $500 return on this investment. At this point their annual change in wealth from savings ($10,000) is 20 times *greater than* their annual change in wealth from investing ($500).

Now fast forward 30 years. At this point they will have $623,227 in total wealth and will earn $31,161 from this sum in the next year (at the same 5% annual return). Now their annual change in wealth from savings ($10,000) is three times *less than* their annual change in wealth from investing ($31,161).

You can visualize this transition in the following plot, which shows their annual change in wealth broken out by type.

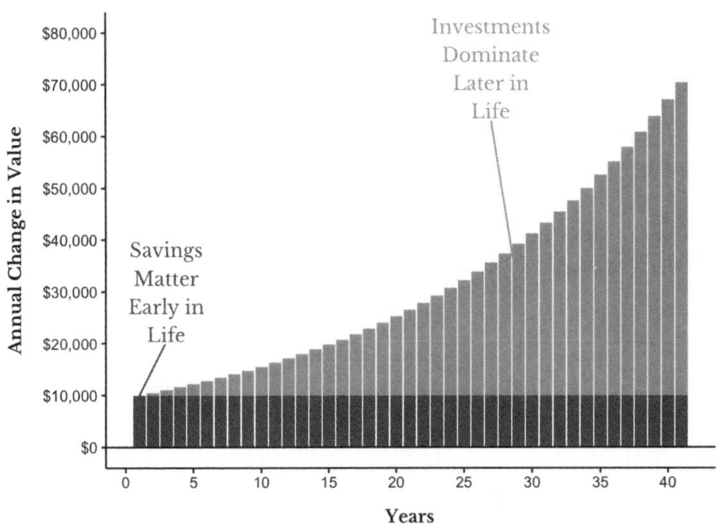

As you can see, in the first few decades of working, most of their annual change in wealth is being generated by their yearly savings (the darker gray bar). However, in their final few decades, it is their investments (the lighter gray bar) that contribute far more to their yearly growth.

This shift is so pronounced that, by the end of their working life, nearly 70% of their total wealth has come from investment gains, not annual contributions!

This is why the Save-Invest continuum is so important for determining where your financial attention will get its best return today.

At the extremes, it's obvious. If you have no investable assets, then you need to focus on saving. And if you are retired and can no longer work, you should spend more time on your investments.

For everyone else, the question of where to spend your time

is a bit harder. This is why there are two parts to this book. The first is about saving (the first stage of the Save-Invest continuum) and the second part is about investing (the second stage on the continuum).

To start things off, let's look at the right way to think about saving.

I.
SAVING

2.
HOW MUCH SHOULD YOU SAVE?

It's probably less than you think

IF YOU EVER go fishing in the streams of southern Alaska you will see hundreds of Dolly Varden char swimming in the clear waters. What you won't see is much for them to eat. Well, at least most of the year. But starting in the early summer, the salmon arrive.

From the moment the char encounter their egg-filled prey, they erupt into a gluttonous feeding frenzy that leaves their bellies ready to explode.

"They are totally egg-crazed," says Jonny Armstrong, a David H. Smith Conservation Research Fellow at the University of Wyoming. "Their stomachs are packed with eggs. They are beaten up and scratched from duking it out with salmon."

Once the salmon are gone, many of the char stay behind

despite having no consistent food source. "If you do the energy calculations and the amount of food in the watershed most of the year, you quickly see they shouldn't be able to survive there year-round," says Armstrong. "But they do."

How do the char withstand such conditions? As Armstrong and his colleague Morgan Bond discovered, when food is scarce the char shrink their digestive tracts in order to use less energy. When the salmon arrive, their digestive organs grow to twice their normal size.[1]

In biology this concept is called *phenotypic plasticity*, or the ability for an organism to change its physiology in response to its environment. Not only is phenotypic plasticity useful for understanding how plants, birds, and fish change based on their surroundings—it can also be useful when determining how much money you should save.

The Problem with Most Savings Advice

When you Google "how much should I save" you will get over 150,000 results. Look through the top 10 and you will see this sort of advice:

"Save 20% of your income."

"10% of your income should go to savings, but work up to 20%, then 30%."

"Have 1x your income saved by age 30, 2x your income saved by age 35, and 3x your income saved by age 40."

These articles share the same flawed assumptions. First, they assume that income is relatively stable over time. Second, they assume that people at all income levels have the ability to save at the same rate. Both of these assumptions have been disproven by academic research.

First, data from the Panel Study of Income Dynamics (PSID)

suggests that incomes are becoming less stable, not more stable, over time. Researchers utilizing this data found that "the estimated trends in family income volatility show a 25 to 50 percent increase" from 1968 to 2005.[2]

This makes logical sense as the gradual shift from one-income households to two-income households means that the typical family doesn't have to worry about one person losing their job anymore, but two people losing it.

Second, the biggest determinant of an individual's savings rate is the level of their income. This fact has been broadly established within the financial literature.

For example, researchers at the Federal Reserve Board and the National Bureau of Economic Research estimated that earners in the bottom 20% saved 1% of their income annually while earners in the top 20% saved 24% of their income annually.

In addition, their estimates show that those in the top 5% of earners saved 37% annually while those in the top 1% saved 51% of their income each year.[3]

Similarly, two economists at UC Berkeley found that savings rates were *positively correlated with wealth* in every decade in U.S. history from 1910 to 2010, with the exception of the 1930s.[4]

This is why savings rules like "save 20% of your income" are so misguided. Not only do they ignore fluctuations in income, but they also assume that everyone can save at the same rate, which is empirically false.

This is where the Dolly Varden char and phenotypic plasticity come in. Instead of consuming the same number of calories throughout the year, the char change their caloric intake (and their metabolism) based on how much food is available.

We should do the same thing when it comes to saving money.

When we have the ability to save more, we should save more—and when we don't, we should save less. We shouldn't use static, unchanging rules because our finances are rarely static and unchanging.

I experienced this personally after seeing my savings rate drop from 40% while living in Boston to only 4% during my first year in NYC. My savings rate plummeted because I changed careers and stopped living with roommates when I moved to New York.

If I had vowed to always save 20% of my income no matter what, then I would have been absolutely miserable during my first year in NYC. And that's no way to live.

This is why the best savings advice is: **save what you can**.

If you follow this advice, you will experience far less stress and far more overall happiness. I know this because people worry enough about money as it is. According to the American Psychological Association, "regardless of the economic climate, money has consistently topped Americans' list of stressors since the first Stress in America™ survey in 2007."[5]

And one of the most common financial stressors is whether someone is saving enough. As Northwestern Mutual noted in their 2018 Planning & Progress Study, 48% of U.S. adults experienced "high" or "moderate" levels of anxiety around their level of savings.[6]

The data is clear that people are worried about how much they save. Unfortunately, the *stress* around not saving enough seems to be more harmful than the act itself. As researchers at the Brookings Institute confirmed after analyzing Gallup data, "The negative effects of stress outweigh the positive effects of income or health in general."[7]

This implies that saving more is only beneficial *if* you can do it in a stress-free way. Otherwise, you will likely do yourself more harm than good.

I know this personally because, once I stopped saving money based on an arbitrary rule, I no longer obsessed over my finances.

Because I *save what I can,* I am able to enjoy my money instead of questioning every financial decision I make.

If you want to experience a similar transformation when it comes to saving money, then you first need to determine how much you can save.

Determining How Much You Can Save

Figuring out how much you can save comes down to solving this simple equation:

Savings = Income – Spending

If you take what you earn and subtract what you spend, what you are left over with is your savings. This means that you only need to know two numbers to solve this equation:

1. Your income
2. Your spending

I recommend calculating these numbers on a monthly basis given how many financial events occur monthly (e.g., paychecks, rent/mortgage, subscriptions, etc.).

For example, if you get paid $2,000 twice a month (after taxes), then your monthly income is $4,000. And if you spend $3,000 a month, then your monthly savings is $1,000.

For most people, calculating income is going to be easy while calculating spending is going to be much tougher since spending tends to fluctuate more.

In an ideal world, I would ask you to know where every dollar you are spending goes, but I also know how time consuming this is. Every time I read a book that told me to calculate my exact spending, I ignored it. Since I am assuming you will do the same, I have a far easier approach.

Instead of calculating every dollar you spend, find your *fixed* spending and estimate the rest. Your fixed spending is your monthly spending that doesn't change. This will include: rent/mortgage, internet/cable, subscription services, car payment, etc.

Once you add all these figures up, you will have a monthly fixed spending amount. After this, you can estimate your variable spending. For example, if you go to the grocery store once a week and spend about $100, use $400 as your monthly food estimate. Do the same thing for going out to eat, travel, etc.

Another tactic that has helped me better estimate my spending is putting all of my variable expenses on the *same* credit card (which I pay off in full at the end of the month). This won't maximize your rewards points, but it will make tracking your spending much easier.

Whatever you decide to do, at the end of this process you will know approximately how much you can save.

I recommend this approach because it's so easy to get lost worrying about not having enough money. For example, if you ask 1,000 American adults, "How much money do you need to be considered rich?" they will say $2.3 million.[8] But if you ask the same question to 1,000 millionaires (those households with at least $1 million in investable assets), the number increases to $7.5 million.[9]

We get richer yet still feel like we don't have enough. We always feel like we *could* or *should* be saving more. But if you dig into the data you will find a completely different story—you might be saving too much already.

Why You Need to Save Less Than You Think

One of the biggest worries for new retirees is that they will run out of money. In fact, there is overwhelming evidence that the opposite seems to be happening—retirees aren't spending enough.

As researchers at Texas Tech University stated, "Rather than spending down savings during retirement, many studies have found that the value of retirees' financial assets held steady or even increased over time."[10] The authors demonstrated that this occurs because many retirees don't spend more than their annual income from Social Security, pensions, and their investments. As a result, they never sell down the principal on their investments portfolios and, therefore, typically see their wealth *increase* over time.

This is also true despite required minimum distribution rules (RMDs) that force retirees to sell down a portion of their assets. As the researchers concluded, "[this] is evidence that retirees take required distributions and reinvest them in other financial assets."

What percentage of retirees *do* sell down their assets in a given year? It's only about one in seven. As the Investments & Wealth Institute reported, "Across all wealth levels, 58 percent of retirees withdraw less than their investments earn, 26 percent withdraw up to the amount the portfolio earns, and 14 percent are drawing down principal."[11]

The end result of this behavior is lots of money left to heirs. According to a study by United Income, "The average retired adult who dies in their 60s leaves behind $296k in net wealth, $313k in their 70s, $315k in their 80s, and $238k in their 90s."[12]

This data suggests that the *fear* of running out of money in retirement is a bigger threat to retirees than actually running out of money. Of course, it is possible that future retirees will have far less wealth and income than current retirees, but the data doesn't seem to support this either.

For example, based on wealth statistics from the Federal Reserve, millennials had roughly the same per capita wealth as Generation X, who had roughly the same per capita wealth as baby boomers *at the same age* and after adjusting for inflation.[13]

As the following chart illustrates, the per capita wealth of these generations seems to be following a similar trajectory over time.

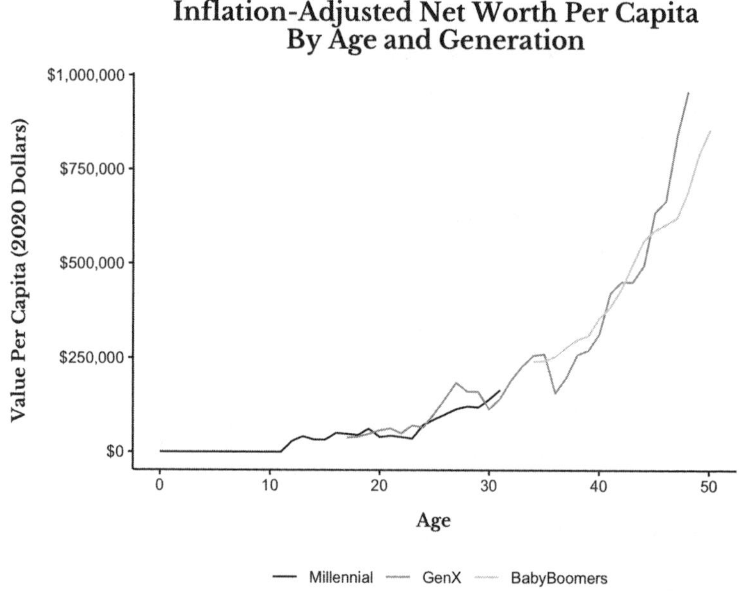

This is evidence that, on aggregate, millennials don't seem to be building wealth at a slower pace than prior generations. Yes, there are issues with the distribution of that wealth and how much debt some millennials have, but the overarching story isn't as dire as the media usually makes it out to be.

And on the Social Security front, things aren't as bleak as they seem either. Though 77% of workers believe that Social Security won't be there for them when they reach retirement, the complete elimination of benefits seems unlikely.[14]

The April 2020 report on the Actuarial Status of the Social Security Trust Fund concluded that there would be sufficient income to pay "79 percent of scheduled benefits" even after the Trust Fund runs out of money around 2035.[15]

This means that future retirees should still receive roughly 80% of their estimated benefits if the U.S. stays on its current course. This isn't an ideal outcome, but it is far better than the one so many have imagined.

Given the empirical research, the risk of running out of money for many current and future retirees remains low. This is why you probably need to save less than you think. Along with saving what you can, these comprise the two important answers to the question, "How much should you save?"

However, for those that need to save more, we turn to our next chapter.

3.
HOW TO SAVE MORE

The biggest lie in personal finance

THE CONVENTIONAL WISDOM in public health attributes rising obesity in the Western world to two factors: improper diet and lack of exercise. The theory goes that, in addition to eating more calorie-dense foods more often, we also burn fewer calories sitting at our desks than our ancestors did while hunting and foraging.

But when anthropologists studied the daily energy expenditure of the Hadza, a hunter-gatherer tribe living in Northern Tanzania, they were shocked at what they found. Yes, the Hadza were doing far more physical activity than your typical Westerner. Between the men hunting large animals and chopping down trees and the women foraging for food and digging through rocky soil, their lifestyles were quite active.

However, this physical exertion didn't translate into higher daily energy expenditure. In fact, after controlling for body size, the Hadza were burning roughly the same number of calories as their sedentary counterparts in the U.S. and Europe.[16]

What this research implies is that the human body will adjust its total energy expenditure over time based on physical activity. So, if you decide to start running one mile every day, you will burn more calories initially, but then it will level off. Your body will eventually adapt to this change in physical activity and adjust its energy expenditure accordingly.

This adaption is something that has been documented in the scientific literature for decades. For example, a review of all studies concerning exercise and fat loss from 1966–2000 found that increased physical activity did lead to more fat loss *in the short term*. However, "no such relationship was observed when the results from long-term studies were examined."[17]

This suggests that, despite the many documented health benefits of exercise, its effect on weight loss seems to be limited by human evolution. Though physical activity can have a moderate impact on weight, changes in diet seem to be more important.

Similar to the diet vs. exercise debate in the weight loss community, there is a two-sided debate going in the personal finance community over how to save more money. One faction believes that you should focus religiously on *controlling your spending*, while the other claims that you should *grow your income*.

For example, the control your spending faction might claim that making your coffee at home (instead of buying it at Starbucks) can save you up to $1 million over the course of your lifetime. On the other hand, the raise your income group may argue that it's far easier to earn extra income through a side hustle than to question your every spending decision.

Technically, both sides have valid points. Going back to our equation from the prior chapter, savings is defined as:

Savings = Income – Spending

Therefore, in order to *increase* your savings, you either have to increase your income, decrease your spending, or both.

But is one of these sides more correct?

The data suggests so. Similar to the effect of exercise on weight loss, cutting spending seems to have inherent limitations when it comes to saving more money.

To illustrate this, let's take a look at the Consumer Expenditure Survey which summarizes how much U.S. households spend on a variety of different categories. After breaking this data into five groups (quintiles) based on income, we can see that cutting spending isn't a feasible option to help many U.S. households save money.

For example, if you look at how much *after-tax* income the lowest 20% of earners spend on food, housing, healthcare, and transportation, it is evident that their income isn't sufficient for even the necessities.

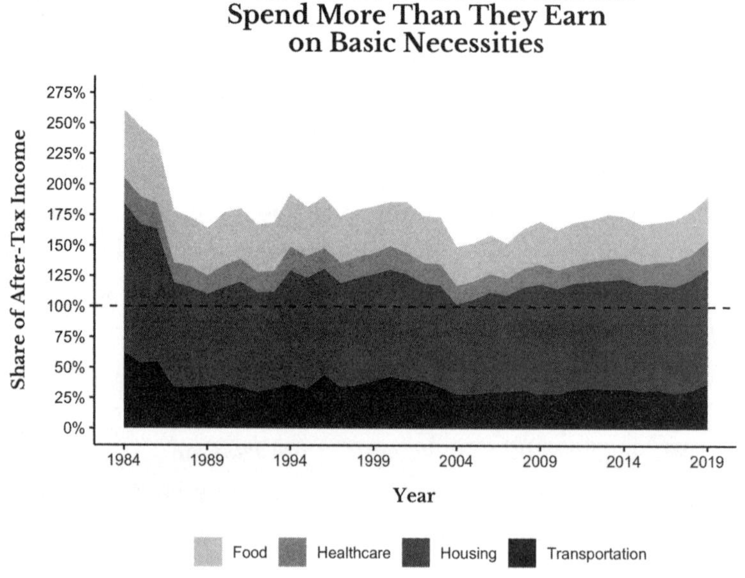

Going back to 1984, the bottom 20% of earners have consistently spent more than 100% of their take-home pay on these four categories. Note that this doesn't include spending on education, clothing, or any form of entertainment. Just the necessities eat up their entire paycheck and then some.

Considering that the average after-tax income of the bottom 20% of U.S. households was $12,236 in 2019, these households only had about $1,020 to spend each month. However, in 2019, their average *monthly* spending on food, healthcare, housing, and transportation was $1,947.

If we break this out by category, we see that they spend the following amount each month:

- Food: $367
- Healthcare: $238
- Housing: $960
- Transportation: $382

If you think any of these amounts are excessive, where do you think they could reasonably cut back? Frankly, I don't see much wiggle room.

Remember that these households only earn $1,020 a month while spending $1,947 a month (on average). This means that, in order for them to save money, they would need to cut their spending in half! This doesn't seem realistic to me, especially considering their already low level of spending.

But this logic also applies to households above the bottom 20% as well. For example, if we look at the next 20% of earners (the 20th–40th percentile of U.S. households), we see a similar story.

While this group of households earned $32,945 after taxes in 2019—nearly three times higher than the bottom 20%—they spent almost all of it on the necessities.

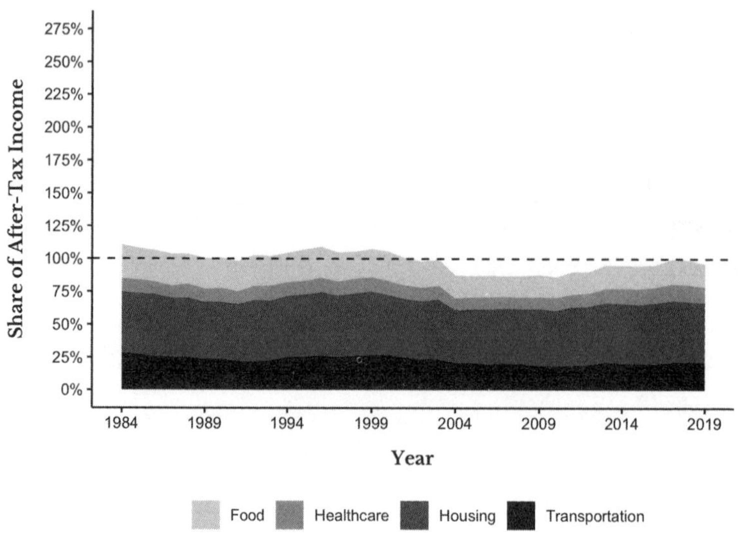

Once again, spending on the basics eats up most of their paycheck. However, when we look at the *absolute level* of spending for these households, a pattern starts to emerge.

While the average income of households in the 20th–40th percentile is nearly 200% higher than the average income of households in the bottom 20%, their total spending is only 40% higher. This illustrates a key point in the cutting spending vs. raising income debate:

Increases in income aren't followed by similar increases in spending.

Of course, you may know someone who has a high income and spends it all. I'm not saying these people don't exist. The important point is that the data suggests that these individuals are the *exception* to the rule. In aggregate, higher income households spend a smaller percentage of their income than lower income households.

We can see this most clearly when examining the *highest* 20% of earners among U.S. households. These households made $174,777 after tax in 2019, yet only spent about half of that on the necessities of food, healthcare, housing, and transportation in the same year.

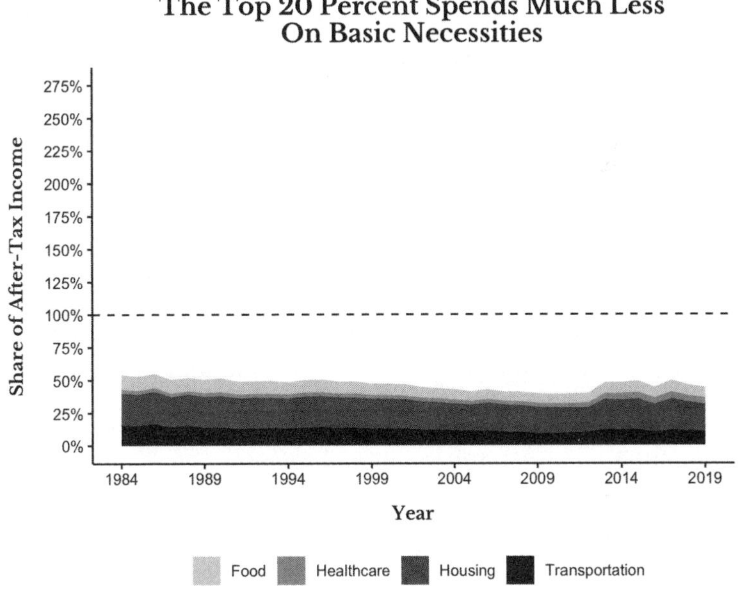

When compared to households in the bottom 20%, households in the top 20% spent 3.3 times more on basic necessities, yet had an after-tax income that was over 14 times higher!

Why doesn't spending go up proportionally with income? Because of something that economists call *diminishing marginal utility*. This is a jargonistic phrase, but its meaning is simple. It means that each additional unit of consumption brings about less benefit than the unit before it.

Personally, I call it *the law of the stomach*.

Imagine you are hungry and really craving some pizza. The first slice you eat is going to be amazing. From the first bite you will experience an eruption of flavor that will send pleasure signals directly to your brain. Compared to having no slices of pizza, having a single slice of pizza is wonderful.

But then you are going to have your second slice. Yes, it will still be very good, but it's not going to be better than the feeling of going from zero slices to one slice. The same can also be said about the third slice of pizza when compared to the second slice, and so forth.

Each additional slice will bring you less joy than the slice before. And, at some point, you will get so full that eating another slice of pizza will actually make you feel worse.

The same thing happens when it comes to spending money. You can see your income increase by a factor of 10, but it is unlikely that you will spend 10 times more on food, housing, or any other necessity as a result. While you might increase the quality of food and housing you consume, these higher-quality items are unlikely to cost 10 times more.

This is why it is so much easier for higher income households to save money—they don't spend on necessities at the same rate, relative to their income, as lower income households.

Yet much of the mainstream financial media won't acknowledge this. Instead, they continue to perpetuate the same lie about how to save more and get rich.

The Biggest Lie in Personal Finance

Read enough personal finance articles and you will find no shortage of advice on how to get rich or retire early. These articles will talk about having the proper mindset, setting goals, and following a system, but what they won't tell you is how the authors *actually* got rich.

Because if you dig deep enough into each of these articles, you will discover that the real way they got rich was high income, absurdly low spending, or both.

Yes, you can retire at 35 if you live in a trailer.

Yes, you can get rich if you work as an investment banker for over a decade.

But, no, you can't accomplish either of these on mindset alone. The fact is that all the expense tracking and goal setting in the world cannot make up for insufficient funds.

After examining the Consumer Expenditure Survey above, it is hard for me to argue otherwise. Yes, some percentage of U.S. households don't have the knowledge, habits, or mental framework to improve their financial situation. You can probably think of a few people like this from your personal life.

But, once again, these people are the *exception*, not the rule. While there are lots of individuals who are in financial trouble because of their own actions, there are also many others with good financial habits who just don't have sufficient income to improve their finances.

Empirical research from around the globe has demonstrated this beyond a reasonable doubt. For example, researchers at the London School of Economics released a paper titled, "Why Do People Stay Poor?" that illustrated how the lack of initial wealth (and not motivation or talent) is what keeps people in poverty.

The researchers tested this hypothesis by randomly allocating wealth (e.g., in the form of livestock) to female villagers in Bangladesh and then waited to see how that wealth transfer would affect their future finances. As their paper states:

> "[We] find that, if the program pushes individuals above a threshold level of initial assets, then they escape poverty,

> but, if it does not, they slide back into poverty... Our findings imply that large one-off transfers that enable people to take on more productive occupations can help alleviate persistent poverty."[18]

Their paper clearly illustrates that many poor people stay poor not because of their talent/motivation, but because they are in low-paying jobs that they *must* work to survive.

They are, in essence, in a poverty trap. This is a poverty trap where their lack of money prevents them from ever getting training or capital to work in higher-paying jobs. You might be skeptical of these findings, but similar things have been found by experimental researchers doing random cash transfers in Kenya as well.[19]

This is why the biggest lie in personal finance is that you can be rich if you just cut your spending.

And the financial media feeds this lie by telling you to stop spending $5 a day on coffee so that you can become a millionaire. However, these same pundits conveniently forget to mention that this is only possible if you are earning 12% annualized returns from your investments (something that is well above the market average of 8%–10% a year).

And even if you could get 12% annualized returns, you would need to earn these while holding a 100% stock portfolio and not panicking for *decades*. Easier said than done.

This is the same financial media who write stories about how people save money by making their own dish soap or reusing their dental floss. What really upsets me is how these examples are touted as *proof* that cutting spending can make you rich.

Just think about how condescending this message is to the typical household. The author of these posts might as well say, "The reason you aren't financially free is because you keep buying Tide Pods!"

You can already see the trick they are playing on us. They are taking these outlier cases and passing them off as normal. Yet, nothing could be further from the truth.

The most *consistent* way to get rich is to grow your income and invest in income-producing assets.

This doesn't imply that you can ignore your spending altogether. Everyone should do a periodic review of their spending to ensure that it isn't wasteful (e.g., forgotten subscriptions, unnecessary luxuries, etc.). But there is no need to cut your lattes.

If you want to save more, the main point is to tighten up where you can, then *focus on increasing your income.*

How to Increase Your Income

I will be the first to admit that increasing your income is going to be much harder than cutting your spending, at least initially. However, if you want a sustainable path to saving more and building wealth, it is the only option.

And the best way to increase your income is to find ways to unlock the financial value that is already inside you. I am talking about a concept called *human capital*, or the value of your skills, knowledge, and time. Your human capital can be thought of as an asset that you can convert into financial capital (i.e., money).

What are some good ways to convert human capital into financial capital? Here are five methods you should consider:

1. Sell Your Time/Expertise
2. Sell a Skill/Service
3. Teach People
4. Sell a Product
5. Climb the Corporate Ladder

Each one of these has pros and cons that we will discuss in the following sections, but all of them can be utilized to start increasing your income.

1. Sell Your Time/Expertise

As the old saying goes, "Time is money." Therefore, if you need to make more money, consider selling more of your time, or your expertise.

There are a variety of ways in which you can do this, but I recommend that you do research to find where your set of skills are put towards their best use. You may not make much from this initially, but as you develop expertise, you can start charging more.

The only downside to selling your time is that it doesn't scale. One hour of work will always equal one hour of income. Nothing more. As a result, you'll never get extremely wealthy by only selling your time.

There is nothing wrong with selling your time to start, but eventually you'll want to have income coming in that you *don't* have to work for. We will address this shortly.

Selling Your Time Summary

- **Pros**: Easy to do. Low startup cost.
- **Cons**: Time is limited. Doesn't scale.

2. Sell a Skill/Service

Now that we have discussed selling your time, this naturally segues into selling a skill or service. Selling a skill or service is developing a marketable skill and then selling it through a platform (likely an online one).

For example, you could advertise your photography services on Craigslist or do graphic design work on websites like Upwork. These are just a few examples of the hundreds of marketable skills that are being bought and sold online every day.

Selling a skill or service can earn you more income than selling your time because you can sell things that are not perfectly linked to your time. This is especially true if you can build a brand around your work and charge premium prices.

Unfortunately, similar to selling your time, selling an individual skill or service doesn't scale. You have to do the work for each service delivered. Yes, you could hire others who are similarly skilled to help out with the workload, but this brings additional complexities.

Selling a Skill/Service Summary

- **Pros**: Higher pay. Able to build a brand.
- **Cons**: Need to invest time to develop marketable skill/service. Doesn't scale easily.

3. Teach People

As Aristotle once said, "Those who know, do. Those that understand, teach."

Teaching (especially online) is one of the best ways to have scalable income. Whether you choose to do it through YouTube or a learning platform like Teachable, teaching something useful can be a great way to grow your pay.

Teaching online can either be done through pre-recorded, self-paced courses, or live cohort-based classes. While self-paced courses are more scalable, you can't charge as much as you can with a live course.

What can you teach? Anything that people are willing to pay to learn. Writing. Programming. Photo-editing. The list goes on.

The beauty of teaching people something is that you can also build a brand around it that you can market for many years to come. Unfortunately, this is also one of the difficulties of teaching online. Unless you are in a niche space, there are going to be lots of other people with their own courses teaching people as well. To compete with them, you are going to need to find a way to stand out.

Teaching People Summary

- **Pros**: Easily scalable.
- **Cons**: Lots of competition. Attracting students can be an ongoing battle.

4. Sell a Product

If teaching isn't for you, you could consider making a product that is beneficial to others. The best way to do this is to identify a problem and then build a product to solve it.

The problem could be emotional, mental, physical, or

financial in nature. Whatever you decide on, solving a problem through a product helps you create scalable value.

Why? Because you only need to create your product once, yet you can sell it as many times as you want. This is especially true for digital products that can be sold online an unlimited number of times with few additional costs.

Unfortunately, creating a product will require lots of upfront investment to build it and even more effort to market it to others. Products are not easy to do, but if you can find one that people like, you can earn income from it for an extended period of time.

Selling a Product Summary

- **Pros**: Scalable.
- **Cons**: Lots of upfront investment and constant marketing.

5. Climb the Corporate Ladder

Of all the ways to grow your income, climbing the corporate ladder is the most common and also the most despised. There is this prevailing attitude that working a 9 to 5 job is somehow less worthy than working for yourself or starting your own business or side hustle.

But, if you look at the data, a 9 to 5 is still the way that most people build wealth. In fact, the best chance that many Americans have of becoming a millionaire is through a professional degree (e.g., doctor, lawyer, etc.). As *The Millionaire Next Door* stated about a group of millionaires studied in the late 1990s:

> "As a group, [millionaires] are fairly well educated. Only about 1 in 5 are not college graduates. Many of [them]

hold advanced degrees. Eighteen percent have master's degrees, 8 percent have law degrees, 6 percent medical degrees, and 6 percent Ph.D.s."[20]

Not only are millionaires more likely to have followed a traditional education and career path, but they don't become millionaires overnight either. In fact, it takes 32 years for the typical self-made millionaire to gain their wealth.[21]

This is why I am a champion of a traditional career path for growing your income, especially to those who are younger or who lack experience. While a 9 to 5 will rarely make you filthy rich, learning how to work well with people and developing your skills can be one of the best things for your career development.

And even if you want to do your own thing eventually, being an employee first is the norm. This explains why the typical age of an entrepreneur is 40 years old.[22] By age 40 you have two things that most 22-year-olds don't have—experience and money. And where did that experience and money come from? A traditional career, likely working for someone else.

Climbing the Corporate Ladder Summary

- **Pros**: Gain skills and experience. Less risk around income growth.
- **Cons**: You don't control your time or what you do.

Regardless of how you try to increase your income in the future, all of the methods above should be viewed as *temporary* measures. I say temporary because, ultimately, your extra income should be used to acquire more income-producing assets.

That's how you really give your savings a boost.

To Save Even More, Think Like an Owner

Guess who's the richest NFL player in history? Tom Brady? Peyton Manning? John Madden? No, no, and no.

It's a guy by the name of Jerry Richardson. You've probably never heard of Richardson. Neither had I. But he is the only billionaire to ever play in the NFL.

How did Richardson make his money? Not by playing football.

Richardson was a good enough player. He was on the team that won the 1959 NFL Championship. But he built most of his wealth by opening up Hardee's fast food franchises across the U.S. Eventually he acquired enough capital to start the Carolina Panthers NFL franchise in 1993.

It was Richardson's ownership of business ventures that made him fabulously wealthy, *not* his labor income.

I want you to think about growing your income in the same way. Yes, selling your time, skills, or products is great and all, but it shouldn't be the end goal of your wealth-building journey.

The end goal should be ownership—using your additional income to acquire more income-producing assets.

Whether that means investing in your own business or in someone else's, you need to convert your human capital into financial capital to build long-term wealth.

And if you want to do this, you need to start thinking like an owner.

Now that we have discussed how you can *save* more money, let's turn our attention to how to *spend* money, guilt-free.

4.

HOW TO SPEND MONEY GUILT-FREE

The 2x Rule and maximizing fulfillment

ONE OF MY best friends was studying abroad in South America when he told me about one of his fellow classmates, James (not his real name), who had no concept of prices. I was initially confused by my friend's statement. "What do you mean he has no concept of prices?" I asked. My friend went on to explain:

> "When you sit down at a restaurant and open the menu you probably notice two things. First, you see what food items the restaurant has to offer. But, second, you also notice *the price* of these items. Maybe the difference in price between one entrée and another won't affect your final decision on what to eat, but at least you *acknowledge* that there is a price.

> The simplest way to know whether you acknowledge prices is to imagine how you might feel if you sat down at a restaurant where the menu had no prices."

My friend then went on to explain that his classmate James had no such notions. But, what James did have was his father's credit card.

Dinner? James covered it. Club admission? On James. Bottle service? James's treat. One time James even offered to charter a helicopter via his satellite phone to rescue everyone after they got lost while on an overnight hike to Machu Picchu. Thankfully, others in the group convinced James otherwise before reorienting themselves and finishing the hike unscathed.

James is an example of someone who had no guilt when it came to spending money. However, I've seen the other end of the spending spectrum as well.

I once had a coworker in San Francisco named Dennis (not his real name) who took frugality a bit too far. One thing Dennis used to do to save money was game the Uber app to try and avoid its dreaded surge pricing.

For those that don't remember, in the early days of Uber you weren't quoted a price for your ride, but a surge indicator of how much your ride would be expected to cost. So a 2x surge meant the fare was twice as high as it normally would be, and so forth. One of the other things that Uber used to do was require you to drop a pin of your location in the app. This pin told your driver where you were, but it also determined the surge price.

Dennis somehow figured out a glitch in the app where you could drop your pin into a low surge area, lock in the price, then move it back to your actual location for your driver to pick you up. Dennis showed us how he would drop his pin into the middle of the San Francisco Bay (where there was never a surge) before moving his pin back to his location and saving $5–$10 per ride.

I still have no clue how he figured out this early glitch in their system, but I warned him that Uber would fix it. Surely enough, they did.

On New Year's Eve 2015 Dennis tried the "Uber pin trick" while trying to get a ride home drunk at 2AM. The surge pricing indicated 8.9x the normal fare and he didn't want to pay it. Well, the trick failed.

The next day he got the bill for $264. I only know this because he eventually told the whole office how "Uber ripped him off" after he spent weeks fighting the charge. I don't think I've ever felt more happiness at someone else's misery in my life.

James and Dennis illustrate the extremes people can go to when it comes to spending money. Unfortunately, neither of these approaches is ideal. While James spent his money guilt-free, he did so frivolously. And while Dennis managed his money well, anytime he did spend it he was filled with anxiety.

Unfortunately, most of the personal finance community tends to side with Dennis over James. Whether they emphasize reducing your expenses or growing your income, their approach is typically based around one thing—guilt.

Between Suzie Orman telling you that buying coffee is equivalent to "peeing away $1 million" and Gary Vaynerchuk asking you whether you are working hard enough, mainstream financial advice is built upon sowing doubt around your decision-making.[23]

Should you buy that car?

How about those fancy clothes?

What about a daily latte?

Guilt. Guilt. Guilt.

This kind of advice forces you to constantly second-guess yourself and creates anxiety around spending money. And having more money doesn't easily solve this problem either.

A 2017 survey by Spectrem Group found that 20% of investors

worth between $5 million and $25 million were concerned about having enough money to make it through retirement.[24]

This is no way to live your life. Yes, money is important, but it shouldn't alarm you every time you see a price tag. If you have ever debated whether you could afford something even when you had sufficient funds, then the problem isn't you, but the *framework* that you are using to think about your spending.

What you need is a new way of thinking about how to spend money so that you can make financial decisions without worry. To do this, I recommend two different tips that, when combined, will allow you to spend your money 100% guilt-free. These are:

1. The 2x Rule
2. Focus on Maximizing Fulfillment

1. The 2x Rule

The first tip is what I call *The 2x Rule.* The 2x Rule works like this: Anytime I want to splurge on something, I have to take the same amount of money and invest it as well.

So, if I wanted to buy a $400 pair of dress shoes, I would *also* have to buy $400 worth of stocks (or other income-producing assets). This makes me re-evaluate how much I really want something because if I am not willing to save 2x for it, then I don't buy it.

I like this rule because it removes the psychological guilt associated with binge purchases. Since I know that my splurging will be accompanied by an equal-sized investment in income-producing assets, I never worry about whether I am spending too much.

How big does a purchase have to be for it to be considered a "splurge"?

This will vary from person to person and over time, but

whatever *feels* like a splurge to you, for all practical purposes, is one. For example, when I was 22 years old (and had far less wealth), spending $100 on a non-essential item was a splurge for me. Today it's probably closer to $400.

However, the exact amount is irrelevant. All that matters is the *feeling* that you get when you consider buying something. Whether you are spending $10 or $10,000, you can use The 2x Rule to overcome that feeling of guilt and enjoy your wealth.

More importantly, you don't have to invest your excess savings for The 2x Rule to work effectively. For example, if you buy something worth $200, you could *donate* $200 to a charity and have the same guilt-free effect.

Every extravagant dollar you spend on yourself could be matched with a charity dollar that goes to a worthy cause. Not only does this allow you to help others, but you won't feel bad when you spoil yourself.

No matter how you decide to use The 2x Rule, this is one simple tip that can help free you from the prison of purchase guilt.

2. Focus on Maximizing Fulfillment

The second tip I use to spend my money worry-free is to focus on maximizing my long-term fulfillment. Note that I said *fulfillment* and not happiness. The difference is important.

For example, running a marathon is probably a fulfilling experience, though it may not necessarily be a happy one. The exertion and effort required to complete a marathon does not typically create a sense of moment-to-moment happiness, but it can create a deep sense of accomplishment and fulfillment once the event is over.

This is not to say that happiness doesn't matter. Of course it does. The authors of *Happy Money: The Science of Happier Spending* found that spending money in the following ways was most likely to increase your overall happiness:[25]

- Buying experiences
- Treating yourself (on occasion)
- Buying extra time
- Paying upfront (e.g., all-inclusive vacations)
- Spending on others

These are all areas where having (and spending) more money *generally* means more happiness.

However, even these great tips are no panacea. You can buy the absolute best experiences and allow yourself all the free time in the world, but this does not guarantee that you will be fulfilled.

So, what can increase fulfillment?

This isn't an easy question to answer. In *Drive*, Daniel H. Pink proposes a framework for understanding human motivation that provides a great start. Pink discusses how autonomy (being self-directed), mastery (improving your skills), and purpose (connecting to something bigger than yourself) are the key components to human motivation and satisfaction.[26]

These same categories are also useful filters for deciding how to spend your money. For example, buying a daily latte may seem unnecessary, unless that latte allows you to perform at your best while at work.

In this instance, the daily latte is *enhancing* your occupational mastery and represents money well spent. You can use the same logic to justify purchases that would increase your autonomy or sense of purpose as well.

Ultimately, your money should be used as a tool to create the life that you want. That's the point. Therefore, the difficulty lies not in spending your money, but figuring out what you truly want out of life.

What kind of things do you care about?

What scenarios would you prefer to avoid?

What values do you want to promote in the world?

Once you figure that out, spending your money becomes easier and much more enjoyable. The key is to focus on the *framing* of the purchase rather than the purchase itself.

After all, it's not the purchase that makes you feel guilty, but how you justify that purchase in your head. And if you don't have a good reason to buy something, then you will probably feel bad about it later. You can lie to yourself all you want, but deep down you know the truth.

The easiest way to combat this is to ask yourself whether a given purchase will contribute to your long-term fulfillment. If the answer is "Yes," then make the purchase and stop beating yourself up mentally. But if the answer is "No," then you need to move on because there are other areas where your money would be better spent.

The Only Right Way to Spend Money

The only right way to spend money is the way that works for you. I know this sounds cliché, but it's backed by data as well.

Researchers at the University of Cambridge found that individuals who made purchases *that better fit their psychological profile* reported higher levels of life satisfaction than those who didn't. Additionally, this effect was stronger than the effect of an individual's total income on their reported happiness.[27]

This research suggests that your personality may determine what you enjoy spending money on. If this is true, then some of the common advice around optimal spending may need to be reconsidered.

For example, it has been well documented that people get

more happiness buying experiences over material goods.[28] However, what if this is only true for a subset of the population (e.g., extroverts)? If so, then we may be generating spending advice based on the 60%–75% of people who are extroverts to the dismay of introverts around the world.

This is why you have to go beyond the research to find what works best for you when it comes to spending money. The science of spending can only get so precise when it comes to predicting what will make someone happier.

Ultimately, you are the one that must figure out what you want out of life. Once you do, then spend your money accordingly. Otherwise you might end up living someone else's dream rather than your own.

Now that we have discussed some tips on spending your money guilt-free, let's move on to discuss the right way to spend a raise.

5.
HOW MUCH LIFESTYLE CREEP IS OKAY?

And why it's more than you think

IT WAS JANUARY 4, 1877 and the world's richest man had just died. Cornelius "The Commodore" Vanderbilt had amassed a fortune of over $100 million over the course of his lifetime as a railroad and transportation pioneer.

The Commodore was of the belief that splitting the family fortune would lead to ruin, so he left a majority of his wealth ($95 million) to his son William H. Vanderbilt. At the time of this bequest, $95 million was more money than was held in the entire U.S. Treasury.

The Commodore's decision not to split his empire proved right. Over the next nine years, William H. doubled his father's fortune to nearly $200 million through proper management of their railroad business. After adjusting for inflation, the $200 million Vanderbilt fortune would be worth roughly $5 billion in 2017 dollars.

However, William H.'s death in late 1885 would cultivate the seeds of folly that would lead to the fall of the House of Vanderbilt. Within 20 years no Vanderbilt would be among the richest people in America. In fact, "when 120 of the Commodore's descendants gathered at Vanderbilt University in 1973 for the first family reunion, there was not a millionaire among them."[29]

What caused the Vanderbilts' financial ruin? Lifestyle creep and lots of it.

Lifestyle creep is when someone increases their spending after experiencing an increase in income or as a way of keeping up with their peers.

For the Vanderbilts this meant dining on horseback, smoking cigarettes wrapped in $100 bills, and living in the most opulent mansions in New York City—all just to keep up with other Manhattan socialites. While your tastes may not be as extravagant as the Vanderbilts', their story illustrates how easy it is to increase your spending over time, especially after you've experienced an increase in income.

For example, imagine that you just received a raise at work and now you want to go out and celebrate. After all, you've worked hard and you deserve something nice, right? Maybe you want a new car, a better place to live, or you just want to dine out more often. No matter what you decide to do with your newfound cash, you've just fallen victim to lifestyle creep.

While many personal finance experts will tell you to avoid lifestyle creep at all costs, I am not one of them. In fact, I believe that *some* lifestyle creep can be very satisfying. After all, what's the point of working so hard if you can't enjoy the fruits of your labor?

But, where is that limit? How much lifestyle creep can you afford? Technically it varies based on your savings rate, but *for most people* the answer is around 50%.

Once you spend more than 50% of your future raises, then you start delaying your retirement.

It might seem odd that earning extra money without saving enough of it can force you to delay your retirement, but I will demonstrate why this is true. In fact, people with higher savings rates have to save *a larger percentage* of their future raises (if they want to retire on the same schedule) than people who have lower savings rates.

Once you understand why this is the case, then the 50% limit above will make a lot more sense.

Why High Savers Need to Save More of Their Raises

To start, imagine two different investors: Annie and Bobby. Both of them earn the same after-tax income of $100,000 a year. However, they save different amounts annually. Annie saves 50% of her after-tax income ($50,000) each year, while Bobby only saves 10% ($10,000). By definition, this means that Annie *spends* $50,000 and Bobby *spends* $90,000 a year.

If we assume that Annie and Bobby both want to spend the same amount of money in retirement as they did while working (lifestyle maintenance), then Annie will require less money to retire than Bobby because she lives on less money.

If we also assume that each investor needs 25x of their annual spending to retire comfortably, then Annie requires $1.25 million, while Bobby will require $2.25 million to retire. In chapter 9 we will discuss why a savings goal of 25x annual spending can lead to a comfortable retirement.

With a 4% real rate of return and no changes in their income/savings rates over time, Annie will be able to retire in 18 years while Bobby will take 59 years. Note that Bobby's retirement timeline of 59 years is unrealistic for most people, so he will probably have to increase his savings rate if he wants to retire on a more reasonable schedule.

Now, let's go 10 years into the future. After 10 years of saving (with a 4% inflation-adjusted return), Annie will have accumulated $600,305, while Bobby will have $120,061. They are both still on track to retire on their original schedules (i.e., Annie in eight years and Bobby in 49 years).

But, now let's say they both get a raise of $100,000 a year to increase their earnings to $200,000 annually (after tax). How much of this raise should Annie and Bobby save if they want to retire on their original schedule?

You might think, "Just save at their *original* savings rate," right? But if Annie saves 50% of her raise and Bobby saves 10% of his raise, this would actually *delay* their retirements.

Why? Because their retirement goal hasn't accounted for their *increase in spending* as a result of their raise.

If Annie is now making $200,000 a year and saving 50% of it ($100,000), by definition, she is *spending* the other 50% of it ($100,000) each year. Since her spending doubled from $50,000 to $100,000 after her raise, her spending *in retirement* must also double if Annie wants to maintain her new lifestyle.

This means that Annie now requires $2.5 million to retire instead of her original $1.25 million. However, because Annie saved for the prior ten years *as if* she only needed $1.25 million for retirement, she has to work longer to make up for this lower level of savings in her past.

With $600,305 invested and annual post-raise savings of $100,000 (at a 4% rate of return), Annie would reach her $2.5 million retirement goal over 12 years from now, instead of her original plan to retire eight years from now. Her lifestyle creep pushed back her retirement date. This is why too much lifestyle creep can be dangerous. It's the impact on your lifetime spending that matters.

If Annie wanted to retire on her original schedule, she would have to spend less than $100,000 a year. This implies that she has to save *more than* 50% of her raise. In fact, Annie would need to save 74% of her raise ($74,000) in order to retire on schedule in eight years. Therefore, Annie needs to save $124,000 a year in total ($50,000 original savings + $74,000 from the raise) until retirement.

And since Annie is saving $124,000 a year, it follows that she gets to spend $76,000 a year for the rest of her life. At this level of spending, Annie's retirement target would be $1.9 million instead of $2.5 million.

And what about Bobby? If he wanted to retire on schedule in 49 years' time after getting a $100,000 raise, he would need to save an additional $14,800 a year or 14.8% of his raise to do so. This gives him annual spending of $175,200 and a retirement target of $4.38 million, but still requires another *49 years* for him to reach retirement.

As I mentioned above, saving for a total of 59 years isn't realistic. As a result, Bobby should save 50% of his raise (or more) if he wants to retire within a more reasonable timeframe. I will explain why this is true in the following section.

More importantly, this thought experiment demonstrates why higher savers have to save an even larger percentage of their raises (compared to lower savers) if they want to keep their retirement date constant. This is why Annie (the high saver) has to save 74% of her raise while Bobby (the low saver) only has to save 14.8% of his raise to stay on schedule for retirement.

While this thought experiment is useful in this regard, it isn't useful for determining exactly how much of *your* raise you should save. Since most people tend to get many small raises throughout their career (instead of one big raise), we should simulate the impact of many small raises if we want to be more precise.

The next section does this and provides an exact measure of how much of your raise you should save.

How Much of Your Raise Should You Save?

After running the numbers, the most important factor in determining how much of your raise you need to save (to keep the same retirement date) is your current savings rate.

Differences in annual rate of return, income level, and income growth rate matter far less for this discussion. After testing all of these things, I found that savings rate was the most important.

Therefore, I have created the following table showing how much of your raise you need to save to have the same retirement date based on your current savings rate. This analysis assumes that you require 25 times your annual spending to retire, you get an annual raise of 3%, and your portfolio grows at 4% a year (all in inflation-adjusted terms).

Initial Savings Rate	How Much of Your Raise You Need to Save
5%	27%
10%	36%
15%	43%
20%	48%
25%	53%
30%	59%
35%	63%
40%	66%
45%	70%
50%	76%
55%	77%
60%	79%

For example, if you save 10% a year now and get a raise, then you need to save 36% of that raise (and each subsequent raise) in order to retire on the same timetable. If you save 20% now, then you need to save 48% of your future raises. If you save 30% now, then you need to save 59% of your future raises, and so forth.

What this really shows is that some lifestyle creep is okay! For the person saving 20% of their income now, they are allowed to spend half of their future raises without altering their retirement timeline. Of course, if they spend less than half of their future raises, they can retire sooner, but that is up to them.

Counter-intuitively, the lower your current savings rate, the more your lifestyle can creep without affecting your current retirement plan. Why? Because those people who save less, by definition, spend more (for the same level of income).

Therefore, when these low savers get a raise and decide to spend a portion of it, it changes their total spending (on a percentage basis) less than a higher saver who got the same raise and spends the same percentage of it. It is the impact of a raise on *spending* that disproportionately affects higher savers more than lower savers.

Why You Should Save 50% of Your Raises

Despite all the complicated theory, assumptions, and analysis shown above, I suggest that you save 50% of your raises simply because this is what will work for most people most of the time.

If we assume that the vast majority of savers have savings rates in the 10%–25% range, then the 50% limit is the correct solution based on my simulated data (see table above). And if your savings rate is currently below 10%, I can only assume that saving 50% (or more) of your future raises would be helpful to build your wealth.

More importantly, saving 50% of your raises is easy to implement and remember. Half is for you and half is for future you (in retirement).

Coincidentally, this idea is similar to *The 2x Rule* I wrote about in the prior chapter when discussing how to spend money without feeling guilty.

As a quick refresher, The 2x Rule states that before you buy something expensive, you should set aside a similar amount of money to buy income-producing assets. So, spending $400 on a pair of nice dress shoes means that you would also need to invest $400 into an index fund (or other income-producing assets).

This is the equivalent of a 50% marginal savings rate and just so happens to perfectly fit with the 50% limit on lifestyle creep highlighted above. So, go out and enjoy your raises—but remember, only half.

So far, we've been talking about spending money that you have. However, some purchases may require spending money that you *don't* have.

Let's now discuss whether you should ever go into debt.

6. SHOULD YOU EVER GO INTO DEBT?

Why credit card debt isn't always bad

I HAVE A PUZZLE for you.

In the desert, the vast majority of flowering plants fall into one of two categories—annuals and perennials. Annuals are plants that grow, reproduce, and die all within one season, while perennials are those that can live through multiple seasons.

But there's something odd about annuals that live in the desert—every year a portion of their seeds don't germinate. This is true even when the conditions for sprouting are optimal.

Why?

From the outside looking in this behavior doesn't make any sense. After all, why would a plant that lives in a harsh environment like the desert not take full advantage of good conditions when they present themselves?

The answer has to do with rainfall or, rather, *the lack* of rainfall. Since desert annuals require sufficiently wet conditions in order to sprout and grow, rainfall is what determines their survival. However, in an environment as unpredictable as the desert, dry spells sometimes occur.

If a desert annual were to sprout all of its seeds and then experience one of these extended dry spells, all of their offspring would die. That's game over for their lineage. As a result, some seeds remain dormant as a way of coping with an uncertain future.

This behavior, known as *bet hedging*, is a risk-reduction strategy that seeks to maximize an organism's long-term reproductive success. It's not about maximizing offspring in any one year, but *over time.*

While bet hedging is advantageous for organisms trying to maximize their reproductive fitness, it can also be used when determining whether you should ever take out debt.

Why Debt (Even Credit Card Debt) Isn't Always Bad

Debt. It's a topic that has been debated since biblical times. As Proverbs 22:7 states, "The borrower is slave to the lender."

However, is debt always bad? Or are only *some kinds* of debt bad? Unfortunately, the answer isn't so straightforward.

For example, if you had asked me years ago whether you should ever take out credit card debt, I would have given you the same answer as every other financial expert: "Under no circumstances."

But after spending more time studying how people use debt, I realized that this advice wasn't always right. Obviously, the high interest rates charged by credit card companies are something that should be avoided. But I know you already know that. Everyone knows that.

However, what you may not know is how credit cards can help reduce risk for some low-income borrowers. This is most easily demonstrated by what researchers have called *the credit card debt puzzle.* The credit card debt puzzle is the observation that some people hold credit card debt despite having the ability to pay it off from savings.

For example, imagine someone with $1,500 in their checking account who also has $1,000 in credit card debt. They could easily pay off that $1,000 debt and still have $500 in their checking account, but they don't. Their decision to hold onto their debt might seem irrational, but after taking a closer look, it's just a form of bet hedging.

Researchers Olga Gorbachev and María José Luengo-Prado discovered this when analyzing individuals who had both credit card debt and liquid savings ("borrower-savers"). What they found is that these borrower-savers tended to have different perceptions about their future *access* to credit than everyone else.[30]

In other words, people with both credit card debt and savings tend to be worried about whether they will have access to money in the future. As a result, they willingly give up some short-term reward (by paying interest on their credit cards) in order to reduce the long-term risk of not having sufficient funds. What seems foolish on the surface is actually a legitimate money management technique.

But this isn't the only reason why someone might take on high interest debt. In the book *Portfolios of the Poor,* the authors discovered, to their surprise, that some of the world's poorest people actually use debt *as a way to save money.*

For example, a woman named Seema, from the town of Vijayawada in southern India, took out a loan for $20 at a 15%

monthly interest rate despite having $55 in her liquid savings account. When she was asked why she did this, she stated:

> "Because at this interest rate I know I'll pay back the loan money very quickly. If I withdrew my savings, it would take me a long time to rebuild the balance."[31]

Seema, like many other poor borrowers around the world, used debt as a behavioral crutch to force herself to save money. From a purely mathematical perspective this might seem irrational. However, if you understand human behavior, it makes sense.

This is why labeling debt as *good* or *bad* misses the point. Debt, regardless of the type, is a financial tool like any other. If used properly, it can work wonders for your financial situation. If not, it can be harmful.

The difference depends on context. Though I don't expect you to ever take out credit card debt, it can be helpful for understanding *when* you should consider taking out debt in general.

When You Should Consider Debt

Though there are a lot of reasons why someone might consider taking out debt, the most useful ones tend to fall within two buckets:

1. To reduce risk.
2. To generate a return greater than the cost to borrow.

When it comes to reducing risk, debt can be used to provide additional liquidity, smooth cash flow, or decrease uncertainty.

For example, someone may choose *not* to pay off their mortgage early so that they can have more cash on hand in the event of an emergency. In this case, the optionality provided by holding debt can be worth more than the cost to hold it.

Debt can also be used to decrease uncertainty when locking in a payment stream into the future. For example, if you want to live in a particular area, taking out a mortgage can fix your cost of living for the next few decades. Because of that debt, you no longer have to worry about changing rents or housing security since your future payments are known and unchanging.

In addition to reducing risk, debt can also be utilized to generate a return *greater than* the cost of borrowing. For example, when it comes to paying for an education (student loan), starting a small business (business loan), or buying a home (mortgage), the cost of borrowing can be lower than the return it eventually generates.

Of course, the devil is in the details. If the difference between your expected rate of return and your cost to borrow is too small, then taking out debt could be a risky move. However, when the expected return is large, debt can change your life. One area where this is typically true is in higher education.

Why College is Worth It (Most of the Time)

Despite the rising costs of college, the lifetime earnings of college graduates exceed those of high school graduates by a sizeable premium.

According to a 2015 report from the Georgetown University Center on Education and the Workforce, the median annual earnings of high school graduates aged 25–29 was $36,000, compared to $61,000 for college graduates.[32] The annual difference in earnings is only $25,000, but over a 40-year career that adds up to $1 million.

This $1 million figure is what has been thrown around in the media as to what a bachelor's degree is actually worth. Unfortunately, this figure doesn't consider that you earn this money over time (the time value of money) nor the demographic differences of the people who tend to get bachelor's degrees.

For example, if we took a student who was about to attend Harvard and forced them not to attend any college whatsoever, they would likely earn far more than the typical person with only a high school degree.

When researchers controlled for these kinds of demographic factors, they found that the lifetime earnings premium for a college graduate (over a high school graduate) was $655,000 for men and $445,000 for women. Additionally, after adjusting for the time value of money (bringing future earnings to the present), the lifetime earnings premium of a college education was $260,000 for men and $180,000 for women.[33]

This means that, on average, men should be willing to pay up to $260,000 for a college education while women should be willing to pay up to $180,000. Of course, these amounts represent the break-even amount one should be willing to pay for a college education. Ideally, you would need to pay less than this to make it financially worthwhile.

In addition, these estimates are only on average. Since earnings vary so much *across* majors, the decision about whether college is worth it ultimately comes down to what major you choose. For example, the estimated difference in lifetime earnings between the lowest paying major (early childhood education) and highest paying major (petroleum engineering) was $3.4 million.[34]

Therefore, when determining whether getting a particular degree is worth the cost, you need to estimate how much it will increase your lifetime earnings and then remove any lost earnings from attending the program.

For example, let's assume you want to get an MBA because you think it will increase your annual earnings by $20,000 per year over the next 40 years (compared to not having an MBA). In that case the expected increase in your lifetime earnings would be $800,000.

The proper way to find the current value of these future earnings is to discount this payment stream by 4% per year. However, there is a simpler way to approximate this—divide the increase in lifetime earnings by two.

This will be roughly equivalent to a 40-year payment stream discount by 4% per year. I prefer this shortcut because you can now do the math in your head. Therefore, a $800,000 increase in lifetime earnings over 40 years is worth about $400,000 today.

Lastly, you should remove any earnings you would lose from attending school. So, if you are earning $75,000 a year and you want to get an MBA, you should remove $150,000 (two years of earnings) from the present value of the expected increase in lifetime earnings.

Putting it all together, today getting your MBA is worth:

($800,000/2) - $150,000 = $250,000

A quarter of a million dollars. This is the most you should be willing to pay for an MBA that earns you $800,000 more over your lifetime, assuming you currently earn $75,000 a year.

You can do this calculation for a different degree by using your own set of numbers and plugging them into the same equation:

Value of Degree Today = (Increased Lifetime Earnings/2) – Lost Earnings

While things like taxes and other variables can affect this calculation, it's still a simple way to check whether a degree is worth the cost.

If you run the numbers, you will see that going to college (and taking out debt to do so) is still worth it for most undergraduate and graduate programs.

For example, we know that the average public university student in the U.S. borrows around $30,000 to get a bachelor's degree.[35] We also know that the average *annual* out-of-pocket cost to attend a public four-year school is $11,800.[36] This means that, over a four-year period, the total cost (out-of-pocket cost plus debt) of attending a public university is $77,200 ($11,800 × 4 + $30,000).

For simplicity's sake, let's round this to $80,000 (or $20,000 per year). Assuming the lost earnings over four years would be $120,000 (or $30,000 per year), we can plug these numbers into our formula above:

$80,000 = (Increased Lifetime Earnings/2) – $120,000

Solving for the Increased Lifetime Earnings, we would rearrange the formula such that:

Increased Lifetime Earnings = ($80,000 + $120,000) × 2

Therefore:

Increased Lifetime Earnings = $400,000

This implies that lifetime earnings would need to increase by roughly $400,000 (or $10,000 per year) for the typical bachelor's degree at a public university to be worth it. While some undergraduate degrees may not be able to provide a lifetime earnings boost of this magnitude, many of them will.

This is why taking out debt to finance a degree is typically an easy decision. Unfortunately, when it comes to taking out debt to buy a home or start a small business, the calculus is less clear.

Of course, all of the above is only considering the financial cost of taking out debt, but there can be non-financial costs as well.

The Non-Financial Costs of Debt

Taking out debt can be much more than a financial decision. Empirical research has demonstrated that it can affect your mental and physical health as well, depending on *the type* of debt.

For example, research published in the *Journal of Economic Psychology* found that British households with higher levels of outstanding credit card debt were "significantly less likely to report complete psychological well-being."[37] However, no such association was found when examining households with mortgage debt.

Researchers at Ohio State echoed these findings when they reported that payday loans, credit cards, and loans from family and friends caused the most stress, while mortgage debt caused the least.[38]

On the physical health front, a study in *Social Science & Medicine* found that high financial debt relative to assets among American households was associated with "higher perceived stress and depression, worse self-reported general health, and higher diastolic blood pressure." This was true even after controlling for socioeconomic status, common health indicators, and other demographic factors.[39]

In all these studies, *non-mortgage, financial debt* was the culprit. Ideally, you should avoid this kind of debt, when possible.

However, this doesn't imply that other kinds of debt can't cause you stress. In fact, depending on your personality, you may want to avoid debt altogether.

For example, a survey of college students found that those with much thriftier attitudes around money expressed more concern about their credit card debt, regardless of the level of debt that they had.[40]

This suggests that some people will always have a strong

aversion towards debt even if they aren't in financial trouble. I know a few people who are like this. They paid off their mortgage when they didn't have to, simply for the peace of mind.

Though their decision wasn't optimal financially, it may have been optimal from a psychological point of view. If you happen to be debt-averse, then you may find it helpful to avoid all debt despite some of the benefits outlined above.

Debt as a Choice

After reviewing the literature on the financial and non-financial costs of debt, I have found that those who benefit the most from using debt are those who can *choose* when to take it. If you can use debt strategically to reduce risk or increase return, then you may be able to benefit from it.

Unfortunately, many of the households that currently utilize debt don't have this luxury. According to Bankrate, among the 28% of individuals who had an unanticipated expense in 2019, the average cost was $3,518.[41] This cost is significant and can explain why lower income households would need to take out debt to cover it.

More importantly, expenses like this are almost guaranteed to occur for every household at some point in the future. If we assume that the probability of having an emergency expense each year is 28%, then the probability of having *at least one* emergency expense over five years is 81%, and over ten years is 96%!

Unfortunately, those who rely on debt to cover an emergency expense can end up in a vicious cycle that is hard to escape. As LendingTree noted at the end of 2018, one-third of Americans were still in debt from a prior emergency expense that they couldn't cover.[42]

Though many of these households will find a way out of debt, a significant portion of them won't. As researchers at the Federal Reserve discovered, though 35% of U.S. households experience financial distress (i.e., severe debt delinquency) at some point in their lives, 10% of them account for roughly half of all distress events.[43] For a minority of households, debt isn't a choice but an obligation.

I highlight this point because if you are someone who is *considering* debt then you are more fortunate than you may realize.

Now that we have discussed debt generally, let's tackle the most common debt decision that most people make—should I rent or should I buy a home?

7. SHOULD YOU RENT OR SHOULD YOU BUY?

How to think about your biggest financial purchase

IN 1972 MY grandparents purchased their home in California for $28,000. Today it is worth around $600,000, or over 20 times what they paid for it. Even after adjusting for inflation, their home has increased in value by a factor of three. But in addition to their financial return, my grandparents also raised three children in that home, including my mother, and partially raised seven grandchildren there, including me.

I love that home. I've spent nearly all my Christmas Eves there. I remember eating stacks of my grandmother's delicious, peanut butter covered pancakes in the kitchen. I remember the permanent indentation in the couch where my grandfather would sit and watch television. I remember the bricks outside where I fell and slashed open my left eyebrow as a kid. Every time I look in the mirror I see the scar and am reminded of it.

Hearing stories like this it's easy to see why home ownership has been touted by so many over renting. Not only can a home help you build financial wealth, but it also can help you build social wealth as well by providing a stable foundation to raise a family. Some consider this *emotional* return on investment priceless.

But before we crown home ownership the winner in the renting vs. buying debate, we need to consider the many other costs of home ownership as well.

The Cost of Home Ownership

In addition to paying the mortgage, home ownership has an array of both one-time and ongoing costs. The one-time costs consist of the down payments and fees related to buying, while the ongoing costs consist of taxes, maintenance, and insurance.

The first time you buy a home you should expect to put down anywhere between 3.5%–20% of the home's purchase price. Saving up this much money can take time, but the next chapter will discuss the best way to do this.

After saving for your down payment there will also be closing costs which will be roughly 2%–5% of the home's value. These closing costs include: application fees, appraisal fees, origination/underwriting fees, and much more. While some sellers may cover these closing costs for buyers, this depends on your (or your real estate agent's) ability to negotiate.

Speaking of real estate agents, this is one of the other big costs of buying a home. Real estate agents typically charge a 3%

commission for every home they help buy/sell. In the event there are two real estate agents involved in the transaction (one for the buyer and one for the seller), that means 6% of the total value of the home will need to be paid in commissions.

In full, the one-time costs of buying a home can range anywhere from 5.5%–31% of the value of the home depending on the down payment, closing costs, and real estate agents employed. If we ignore the down payment, the transaction cost associated with buying a home ranges from 2%–11% of the home's value.

This is why buying a home usually only makes sense for people who will stay in it for the long term. The transaction costs alone can eat away any expected price appreciation if you buy and sell too often.

In addition to the one-time costs of buying a home, the ongoing costs can be significant as well. After paying for the home itself you will also need to pay property taxes, maintenance, and insurance. Fortunately, property tax and insurance are typically included in the monthly mortgage payment.

However, the size of these added costs will vary based on a handful of factors. For example, the taxes you pay on your home will be determined by where you live and the current tax law.

When the Tax Cuts and Jobs Act of 2017 raised the standard deduction, one of the primary benefits of being a homeowner (deducting mortgage interest) was effectively eliminated for many homeowners. This is one of many changes to the tax code (and future changes to come) that will affect the cost of homeownership.

When it comes to insurance, where you live and how much money you put down when you buy your home will determine how much you have to pay. Anyone who puts down less than 20% of their home's value typically has to pay for private mortgage insurance (PMI) in addition to homeowner's insurance. This will cost you anywhere from 0.5%–1% of your loan value annually. So if you have a $300,000 mortgage, you are looking at an additional cost of $1,500–$3,000 per year, or $125–$250 a month for PMI.

Lastly, the ongoing maintenance on a home can be considerable from both a financial and a time perspective. While the financial costs will vary depending on *where* you live and *when* your home was built, most experts recommend budgeting for 1%–2% of your home's value in annual maintenance costs. This means that on a $300,000 property, you should expect to spend anywhere between $3,000–$6,000 per year keeping it intact.

In addition to the explicit financial costs associated with maintaining your home, there are also significant time costs as well. I've heard far too many anecdotes from friends and family about how being a homeowner is like having a part-time job. Whether you are scheduling repairs or doing it yourself, home maintenance can take up more time than you might initially imagine.

This is one of the more overlooked costs of being a homeowner. Unlike being a renter, when things break, you, as the homeowner, have to fix them. Though some people will find joy in being the designated repair person around their home, many won't.

Whether we examine the one-time costs or the ongoing costs of homeownership, a home can be more of a liability than an asset at times. Of course, renters aren't immune from these financial costs—as they are likely already included in the monthly rent.

However, a renter and a homeowner experience these costs very differently from a risk perspective. Because a renter *knows* exactly what they will have to pay for the foreseeable future, while a homeowner doesn't. For example, the maintenance costs for a given property could be 4% of the home's value within a given year, or 0%. This is something that would affect a homeowner but would have no effect on a renter.

As a result, homeownership is generally more risky than

renting in the short term. Over the next year, the costs associated with being a homeowner are far more variable than the costs associated with being a renter. However, if we look over longer periods of time, this changes.

The Cost of Renting

The primary cost of renting (outside of the monthly rent payment) is long-term risk. This risk shows up in unknown future housing costs, instability in living situation, and ongoing moving costs.

For example, though renters are able to lock in the price they pay for housing for the next 12 to 24 months, they have no idea what they will be paying for housing a decade from now. As a result, they are always buying at the market price, which can fluctuate widely. Compare this to a homeowner who *knows* exactly what they will be paying for their housing into the future.

More importantly, when you are a renter your housing situation is far less stable from year to year. You might find a place you love only to have the owner raise the rent considerably, forcing you to move yet again. This housing instability can cause both financial and mental turmoil, especially for those trying to raise a family.

Lastly, given their housing instability, renters have to move far more often than homeowners do. I know this well since I have lived in eight different apartments across the U.S. since 2012 (about one a year). And while some of these moves were easy thanks to friends and family, some of them required movers and were far more costly.

No matter how you look at it, renters face long-term risks that many homeowners don't face. However, one risk that renters are unlikely to face is whether they will get a good return on their investment.

Housing as an Investment

When it comes to housing as an investment, unfortunately, the data isn't that promising. Robert Shiller, the Nobel Prize-winning economist, calculated the inflation-adjusted return on U.S. housing was "only 0.6% a year" from 1915–2015.[44] More importantly, most of that return came *after* the year 2000.

As the following chart illustrates, from the late 1800s to the late 1900s, U.S. housing was basically flat after adjusting for inflation.

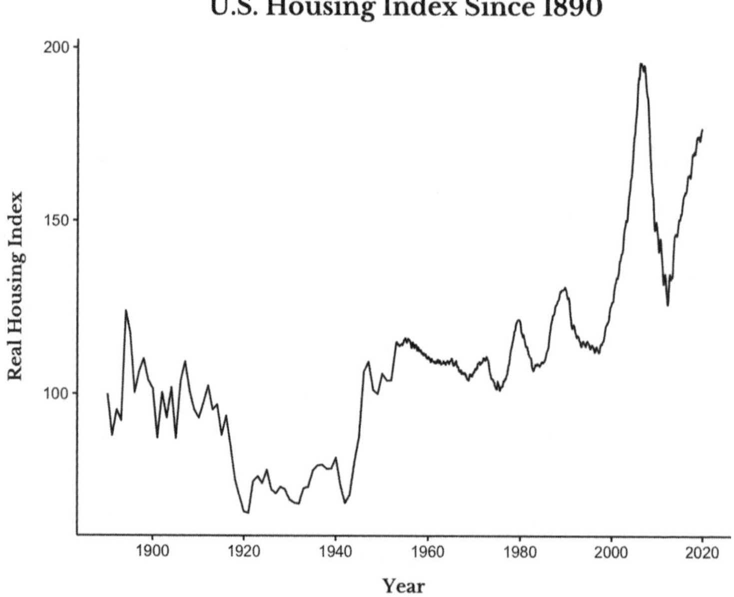

That is 100 years where U.S. housing saw no major changes in its inflation-adjusted value. The last few decades have seen increasing U.S. home prices, but I'm not confident that this trend will continue into the future.

Anytime you look at U.S. housing as an investment, you have to compare it to what an investment in another asset would have done over the same time period. This is known as the *opportunity cost* of the investment.

For example, my grandparents bought their $28,000 home and paid a $280 monthly mortgage from 1972 to 2001. Around 2001, their home was valued at around $230,000. But what if instead of buying that home, they had invested that money into the S&P 500?

If they had put $280 a month into the S&P 500 from 1972 to 2001, they would have had over $950,000 by 2001, after reinvested dividends. And this doesn't even include their down payment! Had they invested their down payment as well, they would have had over $1 million by 2001.

Despite my grandparents living in California, which has had one of the best multi-decade returns in U.S. real estate history, their house earned them roughly one-fourth of what a similar investment into a broad basket of U.S. stocks would have earned them.

Of course, holding U.S. stocks for three decades is much harder emotionally than paying off a mortgage. When you have a home, you don't get the price quoted to you daily and you probably won't ever see its value cut in half. However, this isn't true with U.S. stocks. In fact, from 1972–2001 there were three major market crashes (1974, 1987, and the DotCom bubble), and two of those crashes had declines of over 50%!

This is what makes housing a fundamentally different asset than equities or other risk assets. While your home is unlikely to crash in value, it's also unlikely to be your long-term ticket to wealth either. More importantly, even if you see your home price increase significantly, you can only extract that value if you sell and buy a cheaper home elsewhere, or if you sell and go back to renting.

Does this imply that you should rent forever and invest whatever money you would've spent on a home into other assets? Not necessarily. As I have stated previously, there are non-financial reasons to own a home that you need to consider. But, more importantly, there are societal reasons why you should consider home ownership as well.

Buying a Home Isn't About If, but When

Though your home is unlikely to be a stellar long-term investment, there are societal reasons why you should probably own one. According to the Survey of Consumer Finances, the home ownership rate in the U.S. was 65% in 2019.[45] And if you look at those households with higher levels of income and wealth, the homeownership rate only seems to increase.

For example, researchers at the U.S. Census Bureau found that in 2020, the homeownership rate was nearly 80% for those households with an income greater than the median income.[46] And my own calculations suggest that the homeownership rate is over 90% for those households with a net worth greater than $1 million in the Survey of Consumer Finances.

Why is homeownership so universal? In addition to government subsidies and cultural norms that promote homeownership, it is also the primary way that many U.S. households accumulate wealth.

Using 2019 data from the Survey of Consumer Finances, researchers found that housing represented "nearly 75 percent of the total assets of the lowest-income households... but for the highest income households that percentage was only 34."[47] No matter where you are on the income spectrum, your home is likely to be a source for building wealth, even if it isn't the optimal one.

More importantly, buying a home will probably be the biggest financial decision you ever make. And this decision is socially acceptable and critically important for so many other things in life. Housing determines what neighborhoods people live in, where their children go to school, and much more. If you decide to be a lifelong renter, that is fine—but you could be excluded from certain communities as a result.

This is why most people who can afford a home usually get one. Therefore, the more important question you need to be asking yourself isn't whether you should buy or rent, but *when* you should consider buying instead of renting.

When is the Right Time to Buy a Home?

The right time to buy a home is when you can meet the following conditions:

- You plan on being in that location for at least ten years.
- You have a stable personal and professional life.
- You can afford it.

If you can't meet all of these conditions, then you should probably be renting. Let me explain.

Given that the transaction costs of buying a home are 2%–11% of the home's value, you will want to ensure that you stay in the home long enough to make up for these costs. For practical purposes let's choose the middle of this range and assume that the transaction cost of buying a home is 6%. Using Shiller's estimate for real U.S. housing returns of 0.6% per year, this means it would take ten years for the typical U.S. home to appreciate enough to offset this 6% transaction cost.

On a similar note, if you plan to stay in an area for ten years but your personal or professional life isn't stable, then buying a home may not be the right choice. For example, if you buy a home while you are single, you may end up needing to sell it and upgrade to a larger home if you decide to build a family. In addition, if you are always changing jobs or your income is highly variable, then taking out a mortgage may put your finances at risk. Either way, instability makes it more likely that you will pay more in transaction costs in the long run.

This is why mortgages work best when you are better able to predict your future. Of course, the future is never certain, but the more insight you have about how your future will look, the more likely you can buy a home with ease.

What makes buying a home even easier is if you can afford it. This means being able to provide 20% as a down payment and keeping your debt-to-income ratio below 43%. I chose 43% because that is the maximum debt-to-income ratio you can have for your mortgage to be considered qualified (i.e., lower risk).[48] As a reminder, the debt-to-income ratio is defined as:

Debt-to-Income Ratio = Monthly Debt / Monthly Income

So if you plan to have a $2,000 mortgage and you currently have monthly gross income of $5,000, then your debt-to-income ratio would be 40% ($2,000/$5,000), assuming you have no other debt payments. Of course, if your debt-to-income ratio is lower, then that's even better.

Additionally, you don't have to put down 20% when you buy your home, but you *should be able to.* This distinction is important. Having the ability to put down 20% shows that you have the financial responsibility to save sufficient cash over time.

Therefore, if you can put down 20% but choose not to, you will probably still be fine. I understand that putting all that cash into an illiquid investment such as house can be risky in the short term. However, putting down more means you can generally afford a more expensive (and likely bigger) home.

If you are deciding whether you should save up and get a bigger home or get a starter home and then transition later, I recommend waiting for the bigger home. Given the transaction costs, it's probably better to wait to buy something a little outside of your budget than to buy a starter home and then sell it within a few years.

I know this sounds risky, but when you buy a home, the riskiest part is in the first few years. As time goes on, your income will likely grow with inflation, but your mortgage payment won't.

My grandparents experienced this firsthand after their mortgage payment was cut in half (in real terms) due to the high inflation of the 1970s. They were paying half as much for housing in 1982 as they had a decade prior. A renter wouldn't have had that benefit.

Whatever decision you end up making when it comes to buying a home, the important thing is to do what is best for both your personal and financial situation. Since buying a home will probably be the largest, most emotional financial decision you ever make, you should spend time to get it right.

No matter where you are in your renting vs. buying journey, you should know the best way to save up for a down payment. This is where we turn our attention in the next chapter.

8. HOW TO SAVE FOR A DOWN PAYMENT (AND OTHER BIG PURCHASES)

Why your time horizon is so important

YOU'VE DECIDED TO take a big leap.

You want to buy your first home. Or maybe you want to get married, or maybe you just desire a new car. Whatever you have your heart set on, it's time to save up.

But, what's the best way to do that? Should you let your money sit in cash, or should you invest it while you wait?

I asked a few financial advisors that I have worked with over the years and they all responded in the same way—cash, cash,

cash. When it comes to saving for a down payment (or other big ticket item), cash is the safest way to get there. Period. Full stop.

I already know what you're thinking. *What about inflation?* Yes, inflation is going to cost you a couple of percentage points a year while you save. However, given that you are only saving for a short period of time (a few years), the impact will be small.

For example, if you needed to save up $24,000 for a down payment on a house and you could afford to save $1,000 a month, it would take you 24 months (two years) to get there without inflation.

However, with 2% annual inflation, it's going take you an extra month of saving $1,000 to reach your goal. That means that you would have to save $25,000 nominal dollars to get $24,000 of real purchasing power in two years' time thanks to inflation.

Yes, this isn't ideal, but it's a small price to pay for the guarantee that you will have your money when you need it. In the grand scheme of things, the extra month isn't a significant cost. This is why cash is the most sure-fire, lowest risk way to save for a big upcoming purchase.

But what if you wanted to fight inflation while you were saving? Or what if you needed to save for a period longer than two years? Is cash still the best option?

To answer this let's look at how saving in cash compares to saving in bonds throughout history.

Does Saving in Bonds Beat Cash?

To test whether investing in bonds beats holding cash, we can run the same exercise of saving $1,000 a month, but this time we will invest that money in U.S. Treasury bonds. We do this via an exchange-traded fund (ETF) or index fund. By buying U.S. Treasury bonds we can earn some return on our money while also holding a low-risk asset.

What's not to like?

Well, low risk isn't the same as no risk. As the chart below illustrates, intermediate-term U.S. Treasury bonds regularly decline by 3% or more in value.

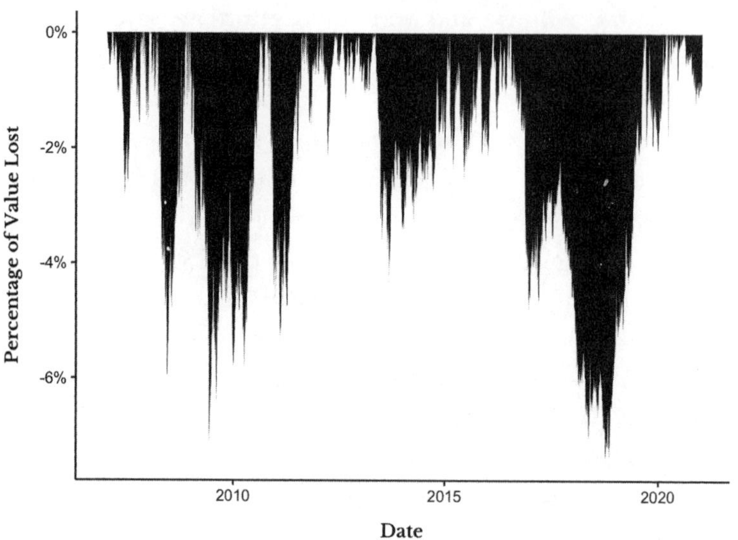

These normal fluctuations in bond prices illustrate why investing your savings into bonds could push your goal *further into the future* compared to saving in cash.

Going back to our example of saving $1,000 a month until you reach $24,000, a 3% drop in bond prices near the finish line would reduce your portfolio value by nearly $750 (~3% of $24,000). This decline in value would be worse than a similar drop earlier in time because you have more money invested and, thus, more to lose.

To counteract this decline, you would have to save an extra $1,000 (i.e., save for one additional month) to reach your $24,000 goal. Even with bonds, it can take more than the expected 24 months to reach your saving goals.

In fact, if we re-run this saving scenario across every period going back to 1926, this is exactly what we find. On average it takes 25 months to save $24,000 when investing $1,000 a month in U.S. Treasury bonds (after adjusting for inflation).

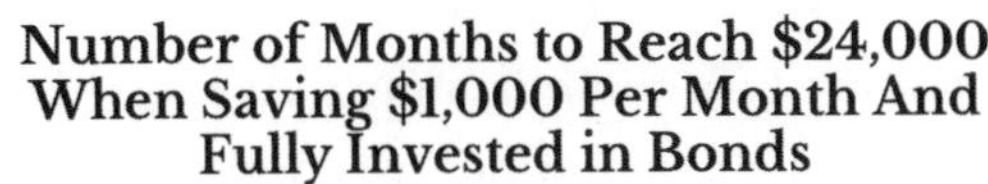

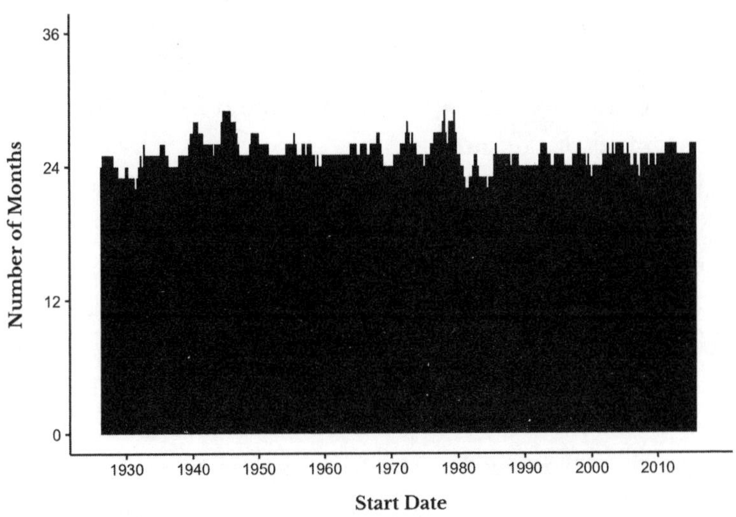

As you can see, when we invest in bonds sometimes it takes us more than 25 months to reach our goal and sometimes it takes less.

Nevertheless, investing in bonds still takes less time to reach our goal than saving in cash. If we re-run the exercise above by saving in cash going back to 1926, we find that it actually takes 26 months on average to reach our $24,000 savings goal after adjusting for inflation.

Why is this longer than the 25 months I mentioned earlier?

Because inflation has varied over time! If inflation was a constant 2%, then cash would always take 25 months to reach the $24,000 goal.

However, higher inflation means that it will take you more time to reach your savings goal. In fact, in some periods it would have taken you almost 30 months of saving $1,000 in cash to reach your $24,000 goal.

Though bonds typically beat cash when saving for about two years, they don't beat them by much. As I stated above, it takes 25 months to save $24,000 when in bonds and 26 months when saving in cash.

Having to save for one extra month is a small inconvenience compared to worrying about whether bond prices might tumble when you need your money.

In fact, about 30% of the time since 1926 you would have been the same, or better off, holding cash versus investing in bonds to reach your $24,000 goal.

This suggests that when saving for less than two years, cash is probably the optimal way to go since there is less risk around what might happen with your money. The intuition of the financial advisors I spoke to was accurate in this regard.

But what if you need to save for a big purchase that will take more than two years to reach? Should you change your strategy?

What if You Need to Save Beyond Two Years?

When saving beyond a two-year time horizon, holding your money in cash can be much riskier than it initially seems.

For example, if you wanted to save $60,000 by saving $1,000 a month in cash, we would expect it to take 60 months (five years) in a world with no inflation.

However, when you actually perform this exercise going back to 1926, 50% of the time it would take you 61–66 months (one month to six months longer than you expected) to reach your goal and 15% of the time it would take you 72 months or more (12 months longer than you had hoped).

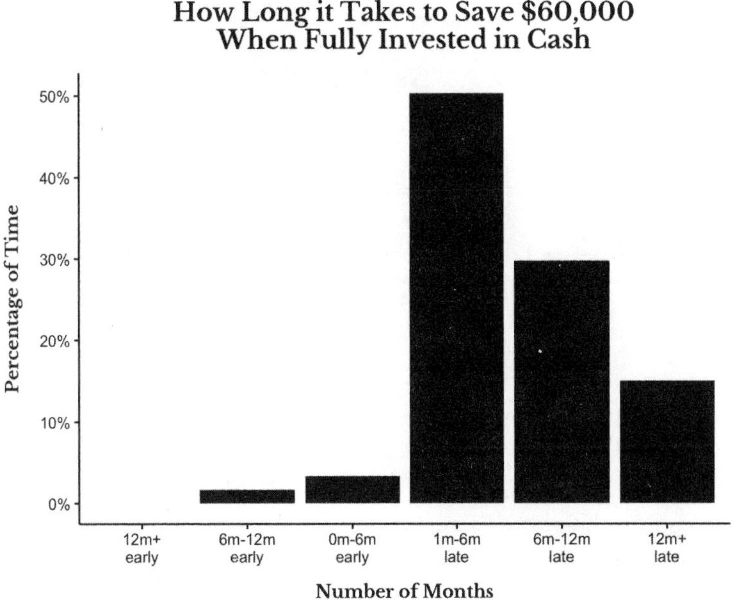

On average, holding cash takes 67 months to reach the $60,000 goal. Why? Because the longer time horizon increases the impact of inflation on your purchasing power.

Compare this to investing in bonds—where it only takes 60 months, on average, to reach your $60,000 goal.

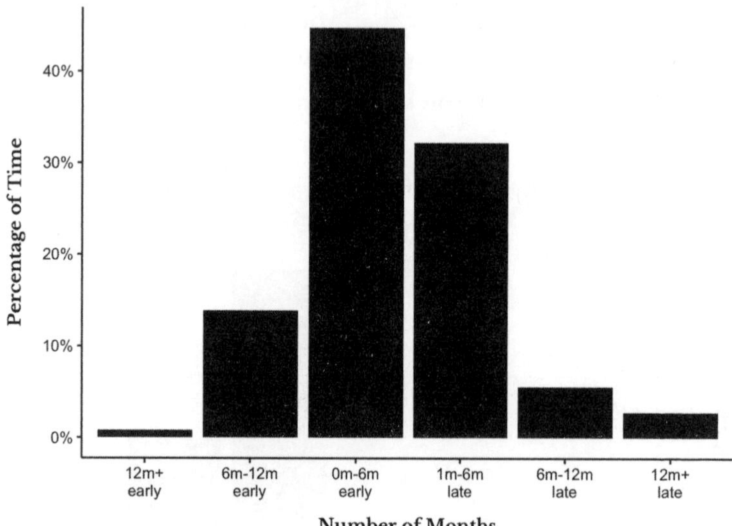

Since bonds provide some return on your money, they offset the impact of inflation and help to preserve your purchasing power.

More importantly, compared to when we were trying to save up $24,000 over 24 months, trying to save up $60,000 over 60 months is much riskier for cash.

It's no longer the case that one or two months of extra saving can offset the impact of inflation. Now, on average, it requires of seven months' additional cash savings to get there.

Yes, there are some scenarios where you can still reach your $60,000 goal in 60 months by holding only cash, but it's not likely. Because of the longer time horizon, the risk of holding cash is now bigger than the risk of holding bonds.

You can see this more clearly by looking at how many *additional months* cash requires to reach the same $60,000 savings goal as bonds, as shown in the following chart.

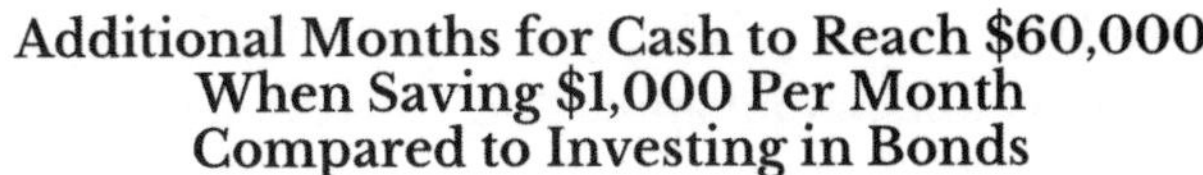

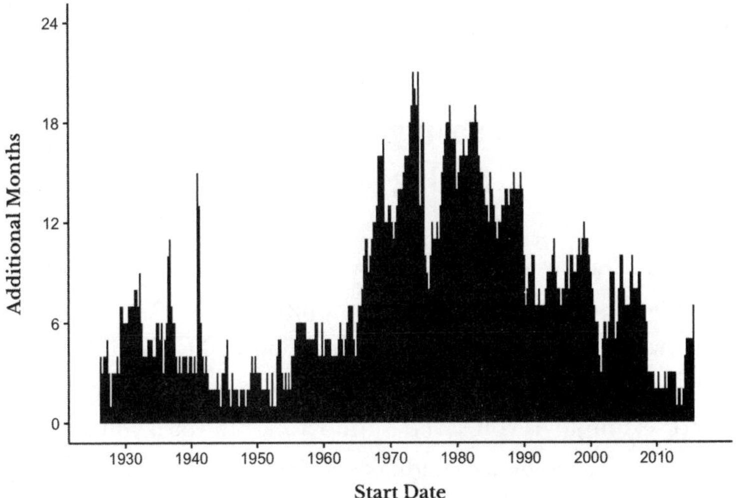

As you can see, in all periods tested, cash underperformed bonds when saving over such a long time horizon.

Does this mean that there is an optimal point at which you should stop saving cash and start saving in bonds? Not exactly, but we can come up with a good guess.

For example, given that a two-year savings time horizon slightly favors cash and a five-year savings time horizon clearly favors bonds, the "switching point" will be somewhere in between. After reviewing the data, I have found that this point seems to be around the three-year mark.

If you need to save for something that will take less than three years, use cash. If you are saving for something that will take longer than three years, put your savings in bonds.

If you had done this throughout history, you would have reached your 36-month savings goal in about 37 months with bonds and 39 months with cash. This is a good rule of thumb that is backed by historical evidence and has worked through periods of high inflation, low inflation, and everything in between.

This now begs the question: Can we do even better than bonds by investing in stocks?

Does Saving in Stocks Beat Saving in Bonds?

Now, let's look at saving $1,000 a month and investing it in the S&P 500 instead of U.S. Treasury bonds.

How does this strategy fare against bonds? Most of the time it does better, but sometimes it does much, much worse.

For example, if you saved $1,000 a month until you reached $60,000, on average it would take you 60 months if you invested that money in bonds, but only 54 months if you had invested that money in stocks.

The following chart shows the number of months it would take to reach your $60,000 goal throughout history while investing in stocks. For example, if you started investing $1,000 a month into U.S. stocks in 1926, you would have reached $60,000 goal in about 37 months.

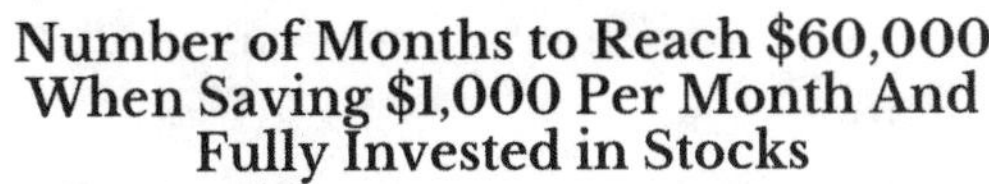

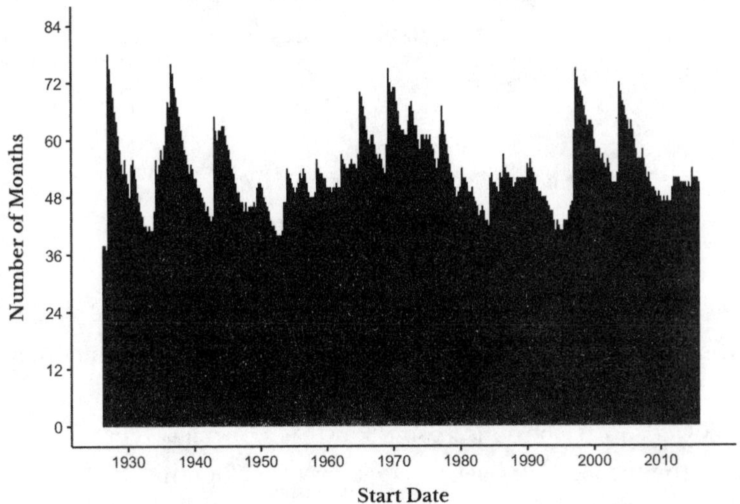

However, as you can see in the chart, sometimes it would have taken you much longer to reach your goal. These are the peaks we can see on the chart—some stretching beyond 72 months.

Why is this?

Because investing in stocks during major crashes (e.g., 1929, 1937, 1974, 2000, and 2008) would have meant you needed to save and invest for an additional year (or longer) to reach your savings goal, when compared to investing in bonds.

More importantly, this analysis assumes that you would have been able to invest $1,000 every month *regardless* of the underlying economic conditions. But this won't always be the case.

After a major market crash you could lose your job or have other financial needs that prevent you from saving money. This is the risk of using stocks to save up for a larger purchase.

Nevertheless, how you decide to invest your savings for a big purchase doesn't have to be an all-or-nothing decision. You don't have to choose between a portfolio of 100% stocks and a portfolio of 100% bonds.

In fact, when saving for a big purchase that is five years away (or more), you can use a balanced portfolio that better fits your timeline and risk profile.

Why Time Horizon is the Most Important Factor

Based on the evidence above, it's clear that the length of time over which you have to save for a big purchase should help determine how you save for it.

Over shorter periods, cash is king. As a purchase goes further into the future, you have to consider other options. Unless you are willing to pay inflation's annual toll, you will need to own bonds, and possibly stocks, to allow your money to maintain its purchasing power over time.

Lastly, this analysis assumed that you would save a constant amount over time until you reach a goal. However, as I have mentioned in prior chapters, our finances are rarely so stable.

If you happen to reach your goal *earlier* than anticipated, then congratulations! You can purchase your big-ticket item immediately.

However, if you need to wait to make the purchase (e.g., a wedding with a fixed future date), then you will need to invest that money in some way to preserve its purchasing power. Unfortunately, that means either forgoing cash in favor of higher-growth options, or saving more cash than you need in anticipation of inflation.

Either way, some areas of personal finance can be more art than science. This is why I recommend that you adapt your strategy based on what investment options you have available to you at the time.

Now that we have looked at how to save for a down payment, we can move on to answering the biggest saving question of them all—when can you retire?

9.
WHEN CAN YOU RETIRE?

And why money isn't the most important factor

IMAGINE YOU HAD a crystal ball that could tell you your financial future. A magical orb that knew all your spending and investment returns over the next several decades. With such a device, we could perfectly plan out when you could retire to match your spending needs with your retirement income over time.

Unfortunately, no such object exists. While we might be able to estimate your future spending based on your expected lifestyle in retirement, we have no idea what investment returns you will get nor how long you will live.

This is why the Nobel Laureate William Sharpe called retirement the "nastiest, hardest problem in finance." If it were easy, there wouldn't be an entire industry dedicated to helping people navigate this period of their lives.

Despite the difficulty of the problem, there are some simple rules you can use to determine when you can retire. One of the simplest is called *The 4% Rule.*

The 4% Rule

William Bengen was trying to figure out how much money retirees could withdraw from their portfolios each year without running out of money. In 1994 he published research that would revolutionize the financial planning world.

Bengen found that retirees throughout history could have withdrawn 4% of a 50/50 (stock/bond) portfolio annually for at least 30 years without running out of money. This was true despite the fact that the withdrawal amount grew by 3% each year to keep up with inflation.[49]

Therefore, if someone had a $1 million investment portfolio, they would have been able to withdraw $40,000 in their first year, $41,200 in their second year, and so forth for *at least* 30 years before running out of money. In fact, running out of money while using the 4% rule has been historically unlikely. When expert financial planner Michael Kitces did an analysis of the 4% rule going back to 1870, he found that it, "quintupled wealth more often than depleting principal after 30 years."[50]

But despite its overwhelming success, the 4% rule seems to be the limit when it comes to annual withdrawal rates. When Bengen tested a 5% withdrawal rate, he found that it was too high to consistently work throughout history. In some periods, the 5% withdrawal rate only gave retirees 20 years of income before running out of money. Since this result wasn't acceptable, he suggested 4% as the highest *safe* withdrawal rate going forward, and it stuck.

The beauty of Bengen's 4% rule was that it provided a simple solution to an otherwise complex problem. Figuring out how much you could spend during your first year of retirement was no longer a stressful decision, but an elementary calculation.

More importantly, the rule could be used to figure out how much you would need to save for retirement in the first place.

Given we know that you can spend 4% of your total retirement savings in your first year, then we know that:

- 4% × Total Savings = Annual Spending
  Using a fraction instead of a percentage we get:
- 1/25 × Total Savings = Annual Spending
  Multiply both sides by 25 to solve for Total Savings, we get:
- Total Savings = 25 × Annual Spending

Tada!

To follow the 4% rule, you would need to save 25 times your *expected* spending in your first year of retirement. When you've reached this total amount of savings, you can retire. This is why I used this guideline in chapter 5 when discussing how getting a raise can affect your retirement savings. It was the 4% rule in disguise all along.

Fortunately, you will probably need to save far less than 25 times your annual expenses to meet your retirement needs. Assuming you will get some sort of guaranteed income during retirement (for example from Social Security), then you only need to save 25 times your expected spending *above this future income.*

For example, if you plan to spend $4,000 a month in retirement and expect to receive $2,000 a month in Social Security benefits, then you only need to save enough to cover the excess $2,000 a month, or $24,000 a year.

We will call this your Annual Excess Spending.

Therefore, the equation to determine how much you need to save is:

- Total Savings = 25 × Annual Excess Spending

Using this rule means that you would need to save $600,000 in order to retire ($24,000 × 25). In your first year of retirement you would withdraw the $24,000. In your second year you would increase your withdrawal amount by 3% to $24,720, and so forth.

Despite the simplicity of Bengen's 4% rule, it does have its naysayers.

For example, one common argument against is that it was created in a time when yields on bonds and dividend yields on stocks were much higher than they are today. As a result, some financial professionals have suggested that the 4% rule doesn't hold anymore.

Since yield is just the income you receive from a bond or stock over a given period of time, if yields drop so does your income. So if you paid $1,000 for a bond with a 10% yield, you would receive $100 in income each year from it. However, if bonds are only paying a 1% yield, then the most income you could generate from a $1,000 investment is only $10 a year. The same logic holds for dividend yields on stocks as well.

While yields have fallen over time, Bengen argues that the 4% rule still holds. In an October 2020 episode of the Financial Advisor Success Podcast, he argued that the safe withdrawal rate has likely *increased* from 4% to 5% because inflation is lower today than it was in the past. As he stated:

> "When you have a low inflation environment, your withdrawals are also going up much more slowly. So, there's an offset to the lower returns that you can't ignore."[51]

If Bengen's logic holds, then the 4% rule may still be the simplest way to answer the question, "When can you retire?"

However, as much as I like the 4% rule, it assumes that spending for retirees stays constant over time. When we look at the data, it suggests otherwise—spending declines as people get older.

Why Spending Declines in Retirement

When J.P. Morgan Asset Management analyzed the financial behavior of over 600,000 U.S. households, they found that spending was highest among households aged 45–49 and dropped in each successive age group. This was especially true among households in retirement age.

For example, among mass affluent households (those with $1 million to $2 million in investable wealth), they found that average annual spending was $83,919 for those aged 65–69 and $71,144 for those aged 75–79—a 15% decline in spending from the younger age group to the older.[52]

They came to a similar conclusion when analyzing data from the Consumer Expenditure Survey. Among U.S. households aged 65–74, average annual spending was $44,897, yet for households over 75 it was only $33,740—the older age group were spending 25% less.

Additionally, most of this decrease in spending occurred in the categories of apparel and services, mortgage payments, and transportation. This makes logical sense as older households are more likely to have paid off existing mortgages and less likely to purchase new clothing or vehicles.

More importantly though, this decline in spending also shows up *within the same group* of households over time as well. It's not just that today's 75-year-old households spend less than today's 65–74-year-old households. Those 75-year-old households also spend less today than they did when they themselves were aged 65–74 as well.

Researchers at the Center for Retirement Research

demonstrated this after examining the spending behavior of retired households over time. They found that spending in retirement typically declined by about 1% per year.[53]

Assuming this estimation is accurate, it suggests that a household spending $40,000 a year in their first year of retirement would spend about $36,000 a year by their 10th year of retirement and only $32,000 a year during their 20th year of retirement.

This is why the 4% rule is conservative when it comes to retirement spending. The rule assumes that your spending will *increase* by 3% each year, even though empirical evidence suggests that it is more likely to *decrease* by 1% each year. Of course, this conservatism is what makes the rule more attractive to a typical retiree.

However, as much as I like the simplicity of the 4% rule, some people won't feel comfortable spending down their assets each year. If this sounds like you, or if you plan on being retired for much more than 30 years, then you may want to consider *the Crossover Point Rule.*

The Crossover Point Rule

Another way to determine "When can you retire?" is to find the point when your monthly investment income exceeds your monthly expenses.

In the book *Your Money or Your Life* by Vicki Robin and Joe Dominguez, this is called *the Crossover Point.*[54]

It's called the Crossover Point because this is the point when your monthly income crosses over your monthly expenses to grant you financial freedom. This is important because the Crossover Point Rule can be used as a proxy for financial independence at any age.

For example, if your monthly expenses are $4,000, once your investments can pay you more than $4,000 a month, then you have reached your Crossover Point.

How do you find the amount of money needed to exceed your Crossover Point? We will call this amount your *crossover assets.*

Let's start with this formula:

Monthly Investment Income = Crossover Assets × Monthly Investment Return

We know this formula is true because your Investable Assets multiplied by your Monthly Investment Return will be equal to your Monthly Investment Income.

We also know that at your crossover point your monthly investment income is equal to your monthly expenses. Therefore, we can rewrite this formula as:

Monthly Expenses = Crossover Assets × Monthly Investment Return

Dividing both sides by the Monthly Investment Return we can solve for Crossover Assets:

Crossover Assets = Monthly Expenses/Monthly Investment Return

In the example above, your Monthly Expenses were $4,000. Therefore, all you need to do to calculate your Crossover Assets is divide this number by your expected Monthly Investment Return.

So, if you expect your investments to earn you 3% per year, then you can approximate your monthly return by dividing this number by 12. Note that this method is only an approximation. To get the exact percentage, use this formula:

Monthly return = (1 + Annual return)^(1/12) – 1

In this case, 3%/12 = 0.25% (or 0.0025).

If you divide your monthly expenses by this monthly return ($4,000/0.0025), you will get $1.6 million. This is the amount of investable assets you would need to reach your Crossover Point.

In other words, $1.6 million earning you 0.25% a month (~3% a year) would generate $4,000 in monthly income.

How does this compare to the 4% rule?

Given that the 4% rule requires 25 times your annual spending in order to retire, this means that you would need $1.2 million (25 x $48,000), which is a bit less than what is required for the Crossover Point ($1.6 million). However, this is only because we assumed a 3% annual return on your assets when using the Crossover Point rule.

If you were able to earn 4% a year on your investments, then both rules would recommend the same amount—$1.2 million.

Nevertheless, the Crossover Point is just another attempt to solve a complex problem (retirement) with simple math. Yet despite the rules, formulas, and guidelines presented thus far, your biggest concern during retirement is unlikely to be money anyways.

The Bigger Retirement Concern

So far in answering the question, "When can you retire?" we have focused on the *financial* aspects of retirement. However, your finances may be the least of your worries when you finally decide to quit your 9 to 5.

As Ernie Zelinski stated in *How to Retire Happy, Wild, and Free*:

> "Contrary to popular wisdom, many elements—not just having a million or two in the bank—contribute to happiness and satisfaction for today's retirees. Indeed, physical well-being, mental well-being, and solid social support play bigger roles than financial status for most retirees."[55]

Zelinski's book suggests that it is not a financial crisis you need to worry about in retirement, but an *existential* one. I have heard similar messages from others who reached financial independence early and hated it.

For example, consider what Kevin O'Leary, a.k.a. Mr. Wonderful from Shark Tank, said about retirement after selling his first company at age 36:

> "I retired for three years. I was bored out of my mind. Working is not just about money. People don't understand this very often until they stop working.
>
> Work defines who you are. It provides a place where you are social with people. It gives you interaction with people all day long in an interesting way. It even helps you live longer and is very, very good for brain health... So when am I retiring? Never. Never.
>
> I don't know where I'm going after I'm dead, but I'll be working when I get there too."[56]

All jokes aside, O'Leary brings up an important point about the value of work and how much it contributes to someone's identity. Take that work away and some people may find it difficult to find meaning elsewhere in their lives.

Writer Julian Shapiro summarized this beautifully when discussing how his friends were affected by earning large amounts of money:

> "In observing friends who've sold startups and made millions: After one year, they're back to toying with their old side projects. They used their money to buy a nice home and eat well. That's it. They're otherwise back to who they were."[57]

Do you think Zelinski, O'Leary, or Shapiro are lying? They aren't. Deciding to retire is far more than just a financial decision, it is a *lifestyle* decision too. So, in order to know *when* you can retire, you need to figure out *what* you will retire to.

How will you spend your time?

What social groups will you interact with?

What will be your ultimate purpose?

Once you have good answers to these questions *then* you can retire. Otherwise, you may be setting yourself up for a future of disappointment and failure. Because as much as I want you to succeed financially, that won't matter if you don't succeed mentally, emotionally, and physically as well.

This is one of the reasons why I am not a big fan of the FIRE (financial independence retire early) movement. Though some people can leave the rat race at 35 and enjoy their lives, others find it much more difficult (and not for financial reasons).

For example, after having a discussion about the FIRE movement online, a man named Terrence (not his real name) reached out to me on Twitter to describe his experience as a FIRE nomad. Terrence had retired two years earlier and was now traveling the world and living out of Airbnbs for one to three months at a time.

Though his lifestyle would be considered glamorous to many, Terrence described his life as a "lonely existence" that ultimately wouldn't work for most people. He concluded:

> "Embracing a nomadic FIRE lifestyle means accepting that you are no longer relevant or important and in some ways now operate in the ether between existence and non-existence."[58]

It can be scary stuff. Though Terrence's experience is not the norm in the FIRE community, it showcases some of the possible downsides of an early retirement.

I share Terrence's story because it illustrates an important truth. Though money can solve many of your problems, it won't solve all of your problems. Money is merely a tool to help you get what you want out of life. Unfortunately, figuring out what you want out of life is the hard part.

Now that we have discussed retirement, the biggest savings goal of all, let's turn our attention to the second part of this book—investing. We begin with why you should even invest in the first place.

II.

INVESTING

10. WHY SHOULD YOU INVEST?

Three reasons why growing your money is more important than ever before

THE CONCEPT OF retirement didn't exist until the late 19th century. Before then, most people worked until the day they died. No golden years. No new hobbies. No long walks on the beach.

But in 1889 the Chancellor of Germany, Otto von Bismarck, changed that by designing the world's first government-sponsored retirement program. At the time, those over age 70 became eligible to receive government income.

When asked why he created such a program Bismarck replied, "those who are disabled from work by age and invalidity have a well-grounded claim to care from the state."[59] Though the retirement age in Germany was initially set at 70, it was lowered to 65 in 1916.

Bismarck's revolutionary idea would eventually be the inspiration for government-sponsored retirement programs across the globe, including in the United States.

Why did such an idea take the world by storm? Because people started to live longer.

In 1851 only about 25% of people in England and Wales survived to age 70. By 1891, that number had reached 40% and today over 90% of people make it to age 70. Similar increases were seen in the U.S. and other developed countries over the same time period.[60]

This large increase in global lifespans was the catalyst for our current idea of retirement. And with the creation of retirement came increased demand for investing and preserving wealth.

Before this time, there was no need for investing simply because there was no individual future to invest for. But, advances in health and medicine over the last 150 years changed all of this.

Now we have a reason to invest. We have a *why* that didn't used to exist. But it's not the only reason to invest, just one of the most important ones.

In this chapter we will cover the three primary reasons *why* you should invest:

1. To save for your future self.
2. To preserve your money against inflation.
3. To replace your human capital with financial capital.

We will review each of these ideas in turn and discuss why they are important for your personal finances.

1. Saving for Your Future Self

As we just discussed, saving for your future, *older* self is one of the main reasons why you should invest. Since one day you will either be unwilling or unable to work, investing allows you to have a pool of resources you can draw upon in old age.

Of course, it can be hard to imagine an older version of yourself, because that person can feel like a stranger. Will they be like you or will they be vastly different? What experiences might shape or mold them? Would you even get along with them?

Despite how different your future self might be from your present self, research has shown that thinking about your future self is one of the best ways to improve your investment behavior.

For example, one experiment had a group of people look at "age-progressed renderings"—digitally aged photos—of themselves to see whether it had any impact on how they allocated money to retirement. It did!

Individuals who saw the older versions of themselves allocated about 2% more of their pay (on average) to retirement than people who didn't see such photos.[61] This suggests that seeing a *realistic* older version of yourself may be helpful in encouraging long-term investing behavior.

Other researchers came to similar conclusions when examining *which motives* had the biggest impact on saving behavior. They found that, besides saving for an emergency, those who cited retirement as a savings motive regularly saved more than those who didn't.[62]

This means that other financial goals like saving for your children, saving for a vacation, or saving for a home were *not* associated with improved savings behaviors. However, saving for retirement was. The researchers found this to be true even when controlling for the standard socioeconomic indicators such as income.

As I highlighted in chapter 3, income is one of the biggest determinants of savings rate. However, this finding suggests that, even when we control for income, those who use retirement as a savings motive are *more likely* to save regularly than those who don't.

Therefore, if you want to save and invest more, be selfish (especially towards your *future* self). But, your future self isn't the only reason to invest your money. You should also invest because of the financial forces that are working against you every day.

2. Preserving Wealth Against Inflation

As Henny Youngman once said, "Americans are getting stronger. Twenty years ago, it took two people to carry $10 worth of groceries. Today, a five-year old could do it."

Unfortunately, Youngman wasn't talking about the increasing strength of American youth, but about the declining value of the U.S. dollar. Youngman's joke highlights why inflation, or the general increase in prices over time, is an unavoidable reality.

You can think of inflation as an invisible tax that is paid by all the holders of a given currency. The holders pay this tax year in and year out without even realizing it. Their grocery bill slowly climbs, maintaining their property and vehicles gets more expensive, and the cost of their child's education increases each year. Meanwhile, has their pay gone up to offset these increased costs? Maybe it has. Maybe it hasn't.

Either way, the scourge of inflation continues unabated. And while the effects of inflation are usually small in the short run, over longer periods of time they can be quite significant.

As the following chart illustrates, with 2% annual inflation a currency's purchasing power will be cut in half within the span of 35 years. And with an inflation rate of 5% annually, purchasing power is halved every 14 years.

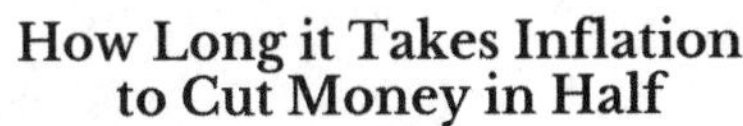

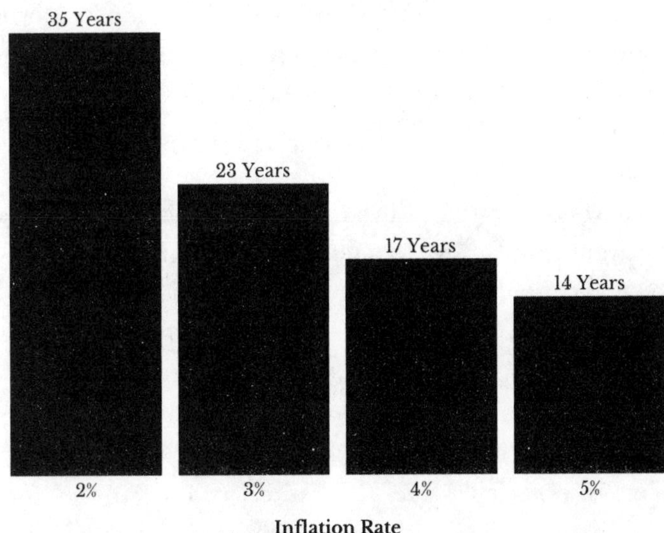

This implies that the prices of everyday goods should *double* every two to three decades, under modest levels of inflation, and far more quickly if the inflation rate is higher.

A more extreme example of inflation (hyperinflation) came from Germany's Weimar Republic following the end of WWI. The inflation rate got so high during certain periods that prices would often change throughout the day.

As Adam Fergusson described in *When Money Dies*:

> "There were stories… of restaurant meals which cost more when the bills came then when they were ordered. A 5,000-mark cup of coffee would cost 8,000 marks by the time it was drunk."

While these kinds of situations are rare, they illustrate the damaging effects of inflation when taken to an extreme.

However, there is an effective way to fight back—investing. By owning assets that preserve or grow their purchasing power over time, you can successfully counteract the effects of inflation.

For example, from January 1926 to the end of 2020, $1 would have needed to grow to $15 to keep up with inflation. Would investing in U.S. Treasury bonds or U.S. stocks keep up over this time period?

Easily.

If you had invested $1 in long-term U.S. Treasury bonds in 1926, it would have grown to $200 (13 times greater than inflation) by the end of 2020. And if you had invested $1 in a broad basket of U.S. stocks in 1926, it would have grown to $10,937 (729 times greater than inflation) over the same time period!

This illustrates the power of investing to offset the effects of inflation to preserve and grow your wealth.

This is especially true for retirees, who will be forced to pay higher prices without the benefit of earning higher wages. Since retirees don't work, their only weapon against inflation is asset appreciation. Keep this in mind, especially as retirement approaches.

In full, while there are some good reasons to hold cash (e.g., emergencies, short-term savings, etc.), in the long run holding cash is almost always a bad bet because of inflation's annual toll. Therefore, if you want to minimize the impact of this toll, invest your non-emergency cash today.

If fighting against inflation isn't enough to get you to invest, then maybe fighting against time will be.

3. Replacing Your Human Capital with Financial Capital

The last reason why you should invest your money is to replace your human capital with financial capital.

In chapter 3 we defined human capital as the value of your skills, knowledge, and time. While your skills and knowledge can increase throughout your life, you will never get more time.

As a result, investing is the only way in which you can fight back against the march of time and turn your *diminishing* human capital into *productive* financial capital. Financial capital that will pay you long into the future.

What is Your Financial Capital Worth Today?

But before we get into that, we first must figure out how much your human capital is worth today. We can do this by approximating the *present value* of your estimated future earnings.

Present value is the amount of money that a future payment stream is worth today. For example, if a bank promises to pay you 1% a year on your money, then you could give them $100 today and you would get back $101 a year from now. Applying this logic in reverse, $101 one year from now has a *present value* of $100 today.

In this example, the $101 in the future is discounted to the present using a 1% interest rate, commonly called the *discount rate*. When valuing lost income, most personal injury lawyers utilize a discount rate of 1%–3%.

Therefore, if we know how much you will earn into the future and we have a discount rate, we can calculate how much all of those earnings are worth today.

For example, if you expect to earn $50,000 a year for the next 40 years, your total future earnings would be $2 million. However, assuming a 3% discount rate, those future earnings have a present value of about $1.2 million today.

This implies that your human capital is worth about $1.2 million. Assuming these estimates are accurate, then you should be willing to trade your ability to work for $1.2 million. Why? Because you could use that $1.2 million to replicate your future earnings.

In other words, if you invested that $1.2 million today while it earned 3% per year, you would be able to withdraw $50,000 a year over the next 40 years before running out of money.

As you can see, this $50,000 annual payment stream is *identical* to the earnings you would have received over the next 40 years! This is why human capital and financial capital can be thought of as interchangeable.

This is an important point because your human capital is a dwindling asset. Each year you work reduces the present value of your human capital because you have one less year of future earnings.

As a result, the only way to guarantee that you will have some income in the future (outside of government-sponsored income) is to build up financial capital.

Build up Financial Capital to Replace Human Capital

Visually, you can imagine the present value of your human capital decreasing each year as your financial capital increases to offset it. In the following chart I assume that you earn $50,000 a year for 40 years, save 15% of your income, and earn a 6% annual return.

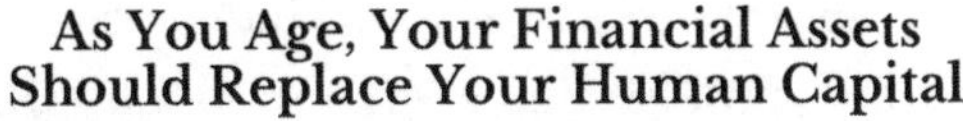

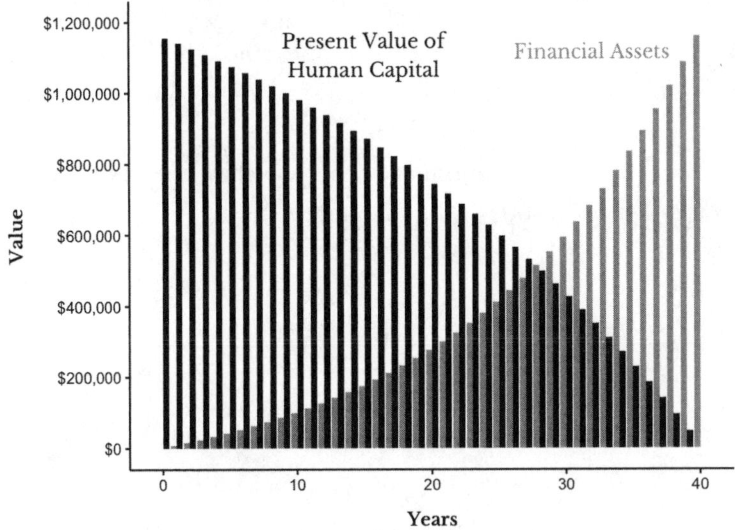

This is what should happen as you save and invest over your lifetime. Each year, a portion of the money you get while working should be converted into financial capital. When you start looking at money in this way, you will realize that it can be used both to consume goods and *to produce* more money for you as well.

In essence, by investing your money you are rebuilding yourself as a financial asset equivalent that can provide you with income once you are no longer employed. So, after you stop working your 9 to 5, your money can keep working for you.

Of all the reasons why someone should invest, this might be the most compelling and also the most ignored.

This concept helps explain why some professional athletes can make millions of dollars a year and still end up bankrupt. They didn't convert their human capital to financial capital quickly enough to sustain their lifestyle once they left professional sports.

When you make the bulk of your lifetime earnings in four to six years, saving and investing is even more important than it is for the typical worker.

Regardless of how you earn money though, realizing that your abilities will eventually fade away can be one of the best motivators for investing.

Now that we have discussed why you should invest, we will now look at *what* you should invest in.

11. WHAT SHOULD YOU INVEST IN?

There is no one true path to wealth

THOUGH YOU HAVE probably never heard of Wally Jay, he is considered one of the greatest judo instructors of all time. Despite never once competing in judo (only in jiujitsu), Jay consistently produced champions in judo and other martial arts.

One of Jay's key insights was that not everyone learned like he did:

> "The biggest mistake is for an instructor to teach exactly the way he was taught. Once a teacher said to me, 'All of my boys fight like me.' Then when we got on the mat, not one of his students could beat one of mine. Not one. So I told him that he had to individualize his instruction."[63]

Jay's realization—what works for some people won't necessarily work for others—is as true in judo as it is in investing.

However, investment advice is rarely presented this way. Instead you typically get a supposed guru who claims to know the one true path to wealth. But, in reality, there are many such paths. There are many ways to win.

As a result, the proper approach to building wealth is to explore *all* of these paths in order to find what will best fit your needs. This is why I say that if you want to get rich, then you need to continually buy a diverse set of income-producing assets. You'll remember this from the book's introduction. It's the core ethos of Just Keep Buying.

The hard part is deciding *what kind* of income-producing assets to own. Most investors rarely venture past stocks and bonds when creating an investment portfolio. And I don't blame them. These two asset classes are great candidates for building wealth.

However, stocks and bonds are just the tip of the investment iceberg. If you are really serious about growing your wealth, you should consider everything that the investing world has to offer.

To this end, I have compiled a list of the best income-producing assets that you can use to grow your wealth. For each asset class discussed, I will define what it is, examine the pros and cons of investing in it, and finally tell you how you can actually invest in it as well.

The list that follows isn't a recommendation, but a *starting point* for further research. Because I don't know your current circumstances, I can't say which, if any, of the following assets would be a good fit for you.

In fact, I have only ever owned four of the asset classes listed below because some of them don't make sense for me. I advise that you evaluate each asset class fully before adding or removing anything from your portfolio.

With that being said, let's begin with my personal favorite.

Stocks

If I had to pick one asset class to rule them all, stocks would definitely be it. Stocks, which represent ownership (i.e., equity) in a business, are great because they are one of the most reliable ways to create wealth over the long run.

Why You Should/Shouldn't Invest in Stocks

As Jeremy Seigel stated in *Stocks for the Long Run*, "The real return on [U.S.] equities has averaged 6.8 percent per year over the last 204 years."[64]

Of course, the U.S. has been one of the best performing equity markets over the past few centuries. However, the data suggests that many other global equity markets have provided positive inflation-adjusted returns (aka real returns) over time as well.

For example, when Elroy Dimson, Paul Marsh, and Mike Staunton analyzed the equity returns of 16 different countries from 1900–2006, they found that all of them had long-term positive real returns. The lowest of the group was Belgium with 2.7% annualized real returns while the highest was Sweden with almost an 8% annualized real return over this time period.

Where did the U.S. fall in this group?

The top 25% (75th percentile). While returns in the U.S. were above the world average, they still trailed behind those of South Africa, Australia, and Sweden.[65] This illustrates that though U.S. equity returns are exceptional, they aren't a complete outlier on the global stage.

More importantly, the analysis conducted by Dimson, Marsh, and Staunton was on the 20th century, one of the most destructive in human history. Despite having two World Wars and the Great Depression, global equities (as a whole) provided positive long-term real returns.

Barton Biggs, the author of *Wealth, War, & Wisdom,* came to a similar conclusion when examining which asset classes were most likely to preserve wealth over the centuries. He stated, "considering their liquidity, you have to conclude equities are the best place to be with the bulk of your wealth."[66]

Of course, the upward trend of global stocks that occurred in the 20th century may not continue into the future, but I bet it will.

One of the other benefits of owning stocks is that they require no ongoing maintenance. You own the business and reap the rewards while someone else (the management) runs the business for you.

Despite all the praise that I have just given to stocks, they are not for the faint of heart. In fact, you should expect to see a 50%+ price decline a couple times a century, a 30% decline once every four to five years, and a 10% price decline *at least* every other year.

It is this highly volatile nature of stocks that makes them difficult to hold during turbulent times. Seeing a decade's worth of growth disappear in a matter of days can be gut-wrenching even for the most seasoned investors.

The best way to combat such emotional volatility is to focus on the long term. While this does not guarantee returns, the evidence of history suggests that, with enough time, stocks tend to make up for their periodic losses. Time is an equity investor's friend.

How Do You Buy Stocks?

You can purchase individual stocks, or an index fund or exchange-traded fund (ETF) that will get you broader stock exposure. For example, an S&P 500 index fund will get you U.S. equity exposure while a Total World Stock Index Fund will get you worldwide equity exposure.

I prefer owning index funds and ETFs over individual stocks for a host of reasons (many of which will be discussed in the following chapter), but mainly because index funds are an easy way to get cheap diversification.

Even if you decide to only own stocks through index funds, opinions differ on *which* kinds of stocks you should own. Some argue that you should focus on size (smaller stocks), some argue that you should focus on valuations (value stocks), and some argue that you should focus on price trends (momentum stocks).

There are even others that suggest that owning stocks that pay frequent dividends is the sure-fire way to wealth. As a reminder, dividends are just profits from a business that are paid out to its shareholders (i.e., you). So, if you own 5% of a company's shares and it pays out a total of $1 million in dividends, you would receive $50,000. Pretty nice, huh?

Regardless of what stock strategy you choose, having some exposure to this asset class is what matters. Personally, I own U.S. stocks, developed market stocks, and emerging market stocks across three different equity ETFs. I also have some additional exposure to small value stocks as well.

Is this the optimal way to invest in stocks? Who knows? But it works for me and it should do well over the long run.

Stocks Summary

- Average compounded annual return: 8%–10%.
- **Pros**: High historic returns. Easy to own and trade. Low maintenance (someone else runs the business).
- **Cons**: High volatility. Valuations can change quickly based on sentiment rather than fundamentals.

Bonds

Now that we have discussed the high-flying world of stocks, let's discuss the much calmer world of bonds.

Bonds are loans made from investors to borrowers, to be paid back over a certain period of time. This period of time is called the term, tenor, or maturity. Many bonds require periodic payments (known as coupons) to be paid to the investor over the term of the loan before the full principal balance is paid back at end of the term. The annual coupon payments divided by the price of the bond is its yield. So if you bought a bond for $1,000 and it paid you $100 a year, it would have a 10% yield [$100/$1,000].

The borrower can either be an individual, a business, or a government. Most of the time when investors discuss bonds they are referring to U.S. Treasury bonds—these are bonds where the U.S. government is the borrower.

U.S. Treasury bonds come in various maturities and have different names based on the length of those maturities:

- Treasury *bills* mature in 1–12 months.
- Treasury *notes* mature in 2–10 years.
- Treasury *bonds* mature in 10–30 years.

You can find the interest rates paid on U.S. Treasury bonds for each of these maturities online at treasury.gov.[67]

In addition to U.S. Treasury bonds, you can also purchase foreign government bonds, corporate bonds (loans to businesses), and municipal bonds (loans to local/state governments). Though these kinds of bonds generally pay more interest than U.S. Treasury bonds, they also tend to be riskier.

Why are they riskier than U.S. Treasury bonds? Because the U.S. Treasury is the most creditworthy borrower on the planet.

Since the U.S. government can just print any dollars they owe at will, anyone who lends to them is virtually guaranteed to get their money back. This is not necessarily true when it comes to foreign governments, local governments, or corporations, all of which may default on their obligations.

This is why I tend to only invest in U.S. Treasury bonds and some tax-free municipal bonds in my state of residence. If I wanted to take more risk, I wouldn't take it in the bond portion of my portfolio by buying riskier bonds. Bonds should act as a diversifying asset, not a risk asset.

I understand that there is a case to be made for owning higher-yielding, riskier bonds, especially considering how low yields on U.S. Treasuries have been since 2008. However, yield isn't the only thing that matters—bonds have other properties that are useful for investors.

Why You Should/Shouldn't Invest in Bonds

I recommend bonds because of these characteristics:

1. Bonds tend to rise when stocks (and other risky assets) fall.
2. Bonds have a more consistent income stream than other assets.

3. Bonds can provide liquidity to rebalance your portfolio or cover liabilities.

During market sell-offs, bonds are one of the only assets that tend to rise while everything else is falling. This happens as investors sell their riskier assets to buy bonds in what is commonly known as a "flight to safety." Because of this tendency, bonds can act as a behavioral crutch within your portfolio during the worst of times.

Similarly, bonds also tend to provide more consistent income over time due to their stability. Since the U.S. government can print money (and pay back bondholders) at will, you don't have to worry about your income changing after you buy a bond.

Lastly, because bonds are more stable during market crashes, they also tend to be good at providing liquidity in case you need extra cash to rebalance your portfolio or cover your liabilities. For example, if you lose your job because of a financial panic, you will be pleased to know that you should be able to rely on the bond portion of your portfolio to get you through these tough times; in other words, you can sell some bonds to generate cash.

You can visualize how much bonds help to stabilize a portfolio by examining what happened to various portfolios during the Covid-19 related crash in early 2020. As the following chart illustrates, portfolios with more bonds (U.S. Treasuries) declined less than those with fewer bonds.

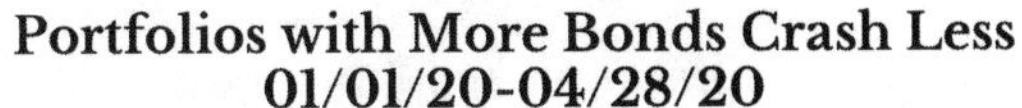

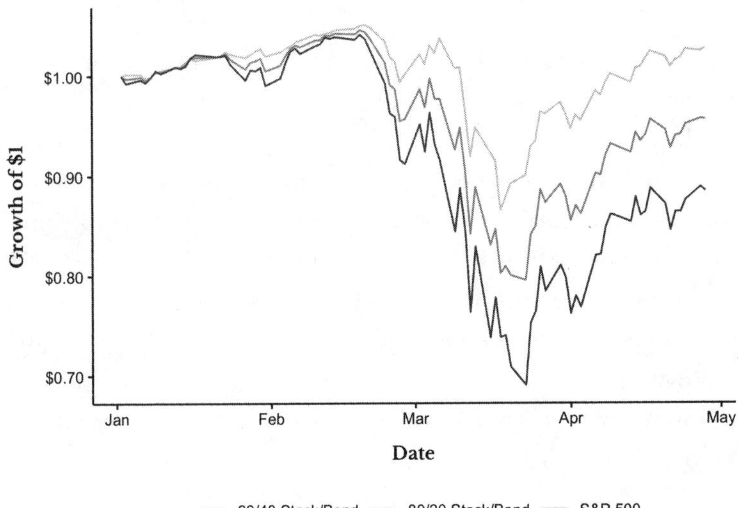

In this instance, the 60/40 and 80/20 portfolios both declined less than the S&P 500 only portfolio during March 2020.

More importantly, those investors that had bond exposure and rebalanced during the crash saw an even bigger benefit during the recovery that followed. For example, I was lucky enough to rebalance my portfolio—I sold some bonds and bought stocks—on March 23, 2020, the exact day the market bottomed. Yes, this timing was complete luck, but the fact that I owned bonds and was able to sell some of them to rebalance into stocks was not luck.

The one major downside to owning bonds is that their returns tend to be much lower than stocks and most other risk assets. This is especially true when yields are low, as they were from 2008–2020. In this kind of environment bond returns may be near zero or negative going forward after taking into account inflation.

How Can You Buy Bonds?

You can choose to buy individual bonds directly, but I recommend buying them through bond index funds or ETFs because it's much easier.

Though there has been a debate in the past about whether there is a material difference in performance between individual bonds and bond funds, there isn't. Cliff Asness, founder of AQR Capital Management, thoroughly debunked this notion in the *Financial Analysts Journal* in 2014.[68]

Regardless of how you buy your bonds, they can play an important role in your portfolio beyond providing growth. As the old saying goes:

> "We buy stocks so we can eat well, but we buy bonds so we can sleep well."

Bonds Summary

- Average compounded annual return: 2%–4% (can approach 0% in a low-rate environment).
- **Pros**: Lower volatility. Good for rebalancing. Safety of principal.
- **Cons**: Low returns, especially after inflation. Not great for income in a low-yield environment.

Investment Property

Outside of the realm of stocks and bonds, one of the next most popular income-producing assets is an investment in property.

Owning an investment property can be great because you can use it yourself, and it can also earn you extra income if you rent it out to others when you are not using it.

Why You Should/Shouldn't Buy Investment Property

If you manage your property correctly, you will have other people (rent-paying guests) helping you to pay off the mortgage while you enjoy the long-term price appreciation on the property. Additionally, if you were able to borrow money when acquiring the property, your return can be a bit magnified due to the leverage. When borrowing to buy investment property, leverage boosts your exposure to the price changes of your property.

For example, if you put down $100,000 for a $500,000 property, that means that you would have borrowed the remaining $400,000. Now let's assume that the property increases in value to $600,000 after a year. If you sell the property and pay off the loan you will have about $200,000 left instead of your original $100,000. Because of the leverage, the 20% increase in the price of the home allows you to earn a 100% return ($100,000 became $200,000).

If this sounds too good to be true, it's because it is. You have to remember that leverage can also work against you if prices fall. For example, if the price of your home fell from $500,000 to $400,000 and you sold the house, your equity would be completely wiped out. A 20% decline in the value of the property led to a 100% decline in your investment.

Since major price crashes in real estate tend to be rare, leverage usually provides a positive financial benefit to real estate investors.

Despite the many financial upsides to owning an investment property, it also requires far more work than many other assets that you can set and forget.

A property investment requires the ability to deal with people (the renters), list the property on a rental site and make it look appealing to prospective guests, provide ongoing maintenance, and much more. While doing all of this, you also have to deal with the added stress of having another liability on your balance sheet.

When this goes right, owning an investment property can be wonderful, especially when you have borrowed most of the money to finance the purchase. However, when things go wrong, like they did in 2020 with pandemic-induced travel restrictions, they can go really wrong. As many Airbnb entrepreneurs learned the hard way, investment properties aren't always so easy.

While the returns on investment properties can be much higher than stocks or bonds, these returns also require far more work to earn them.

Lastly, buying individual investment properties is similar to buying individual stocks in that they aren't diversified. When you buy an investment property you take on all the specific risks to that property. The real estate market can be booming yet you could get a bad result if your property has too many underlying issues and costs.

Given that most investors are not likely to own enough investment properties to be diversified, single property risk is an issue.

Nevertheless, if you are someone that wants to have more control over their investments and like the tangibility of real estate, then you should consider an investment in property as a part of your portfolio.

How Do You Buy Investment Properties?

The best way to buy investment properties is through a real estate agent or by negotiating directly with the sellers themselves. The process can be rather involved, so I recommend doing thorough research before going down this route.

Investment Property Summary

- Average compounded annual return: 12%–15% (dependent on local rental conditions).
- **Pros**: Higher returns than other more traditional asset classes, especially when using leverage.
- **Cons**: Managing the property and tenants can be a headache. Hard to diversify.

Real Estate Investment Trusts (REITs)

If you like the idea of owning real estate, but hate the idea of managing it yourself, then the real estate investment trust (REIT) might be right for you. A REIT is a business that owns and manages real estate properties and pays out the income from those properties to its owners.

In fact, REITs are legally required to pay out a minimum of 90% of their taxable income as dividends to their shareholders. This requirement makes REITs one of the most reliable income-producing assets.

However, not all REITs are the same. There are residential REITs that can own apartment buildings, student housing, manufactured homes, and single-family homes; and commercial

REITs that can own office buildings, warehouses, retail spaces, and other commercial properties.

In addition, REITs can be offered as publicly traded, private, or publicly non-traded.

- **Publicly traded REITs**: Trade on a stock exchange like any other public company and are available to all investors.
  1. Anyone who owns a broad stock index fund already has some exposure to publicly traded REITs, so buying additional REITs is only necessary if you want to increase your exposure to real estate.
  2. Instead of buying individual publicly traded REITs, there are publicly traded REIT index funds – which invest across a basket of REITs – that you can buy instead.
- **Private REITs**: Not traded on a stock exchange and only available to accredited investors (people with a net worth >$1 million or annual income >$200,000 for the last three years).
  1. Requires a broker, which may result in high fees.
  2. Less regulatory oversight.
  3. Less liquid due to longer required holding period.
  4. May generate higher returns than public market offerings.
- **Publicly non-traded REITs**: Not traded on a stock exchange, but available to all public investors through crowdsourcing.
  1. More regulatory oversight than private REITs.
  2. Minimum investment requirements.
  3. Less liquid due to longer required holding period.
  4. May generate higher returns than public market offerings.

Though I have only ever invested in publicly traded REIT ETFs, real estate crowdsourcing firms are a non-traded alternative that could offer higher long-term returns.

Why You Should/Shouldn't Invest in REITs

No matter how you decide to invest in REITs, they generally have stock-like returns (or better) with a somewhat low correlation (0.5–0.7) to stocks during good times. This means that REITs can do well when stocks aren't doing well.

However, like most other risky assets, publicly traded REITs tend to sell off during stock market crashes. Therefore, don't expect diversification benefits from REITs on the downside.

How Do You Invest in REITs?

As mentioned above, you can either invest in publicly traded REITs available through any brokerage platform, or go to a crowdsourced site to buy publicly non-traded or private REITs. I personally lean towards publicly traded REITs simply because they are more liquid (i.e., easier to buy/sell), but there can be benefits to looking at publicly non-traded or private options where you get to pick which specific properties you invest in.

REITs Summary

- Average compounded annual return: 10%–12%.
- **Pros**: Real estate exposure that you don't have to manage. Less correlated with stocks during good times.
- **Cons**: Volatility greater than or equal to stocks. Less liquidity for non-traded REITs. Highly correlated with stocks and other risk assets during stock market crashes.

Farmland

Outside of real estate, farmland is another great income-producing asset that has been a major source of wealth throughout history.

Why You Should/Shouldn't Invest in Farmland

Today, one of the best reasons to invest in farmland is its low correlation with stock and bond returns. After all, farm income tends to be uncorrelated with what is happening in financial markets.

In addition, farmland has lower volatility than stocks because the value of land doesn't change much over time. Since the productivity of land is more stable than the productivity of businesses from year to year, you can see why farmland has lower overall volatility when compared to stocks.

In addition, farmland also provides inflation protection because it tends to rise in value alongside broader price trends. Because of its specific risk profile (i.e., low volatility with decent returns), farmland is unlikely to go to zero, unlike an individual stock or bond. Of course, the effects of climate change may alter this in the future.

What kind of returns can you expect from farmland? According to Jay Girotto in an interview with Ted Seides, farmland is modeled to return in the "high single digits" with roughly half of the return coming from farm yields and half coming from land appreciation.[69]

How Do You Invest in Farmland?

While buying individual farmland is no small undertaking, the most common way for investors to own farmland is through a publicly traded REIT or a crowdsourced solution. The crowdsourced solution can be nice because you have more control over which farmland properties you specifically invest in.

The downside of crowdsourced solutions is that they are only typically available to accredited investors (people with a net worth >$1 million or annual income >$200,000 for the last three years). In addition, the fees for these crowdsourced platforms can be higher than with other public investments.

I don't think these fees are predatory given the amount of work that goes into structuring these deals, but if you hate the idea of fees, this is something to keep in mind.

Farmland Summary

- Average compounded annual return: 7%–9%.
- **Pros**: Lower correlation with stocks and other financial assets. Good inflation hedge. Lower downside potential (land less likely to "go to zero" than other assets).
- **Cons**: Less liquidity (harder to buy and sell). Higher fees. Requires "accredited investor" status to participate in crowdsourced solution.

Small Businesses/Franchise/ Angel Investing

If farmland isn't for you, maybe you should consider owning a small business or part of a small business. This is where angel investing and small business investing come in.

However, before you embark on this journey you have to decide whether you will operate the business or just provide investment capital and expertise.

Owner + Operator

If you want to be an owner + operator of a small business or franchise, just remember that as much work as you think it will take, it will likely take more.

Brent Beshore, an expert on small business investing, once tweeted that the operator's manual to run a Subway restaurant is 800 pages long. Imagine trying to run a $50m manufacturer.[70]

I don't mention Brent's comments to discourage you from starting a small business, only to provide a realistic expectation for how much work they require. Owning and operating a small business can generate much higher returns than many of the other income-producing assets on this list, but you have to work for them.

Owner Only

Assuming you don't want to go down the operator route, being an angel investor or passive owner of a small business can earn you very outsized returns. In fact, according to multiple studies, the expected annual return on angel investments is in the 20%–25% range.[71]

However, these returns aren't without a very large skew. An Angel Capital Association study found that just one in nine angel investments (11%) yielded a positive return.[72] This goes to show that though some small businesses may become the next Apple, most never make it too far out of the garage.

As Sam Altman, famed investor and President of YCombinator, once wrote:

> "It's common to make more money from your single best angel investment than all the rest put together. The consequence of this is that the real risk is missing out on that outstanding investment, and not failing to get your money back (or, as some people ask for, a guaranteed 2x) on all of your other companies."[73]

This is why small business investing can be so tough, yet also so rewarding.

However, before you decide to go all-in, you should know that small business investing can be a huge time commitment. This is why Tucker Max gave up on angel investing and why he thinks most people shouldn't even start. Max's argument is quite clear—if you want access to the best angel investments with big, outsized returns, then you have to be deeply embedded in that community.[74]

Research on this topic supports Max's claim, finding that time spent on due diligence, experience, and participation were all positively correlated with an angel investor's long-term returns.[75]

How Do You Invest in Small Businesses?

You can't do angel/small business investing as a side hustle and expect big results. While some crowdsourcing platforms allow retail investors to invest in small businesses (with other opportunities for accredited investors), it is highly unlikely they are going to have early access to the next big thing.

I don't say this to discourage you, but to reiterate that the most successful small business investors commit more than just capital to this pursuit. If you want to be a small business investor, keep in mind that a larger lifestyle change may be warranted in order to see significant results.

Small Business Summary

- Average compounded annual return: 20%–25%, but expect lots of losers.
- **Pros**: Can have extremely outsized returns. The more involved you are, the more future opportunities you will see.
- **Cons**: Huge time commitment. Lots of failures can be discouraging.

Royalties

If you aren't a fan of small business, maybe you need to invest in something with a bit more… culture. This is where royalties come in. Royalties are payments made for the ongoing use of a particular asset, usually a copyrighted work. There are websites where you can buy and sell the royalties to music, film, and trademarks and earn income from their use.

Why You Should/Shouldn't Invest in Royalties

Royalties can be a good investment because they generate steady income that is uncorrelated with financial markets.

For example, Jay-Z and Alicia Keys' "Empire State of Mind" earned $32,733 in royalties over a 12-month period. On RoyaltyExchange.com, 10 years' worth of this song's royalties were sold for $190,500.

If we assume that the annual royalties ($32,733) remain unchanged going forward, then the owner of those royalties will earn 11.2% per year on their $190,500 purchase over the next decade.

Of course, no one knows whether the royalties for this song will increase, stay the same, or decrease over the next 10 years. That is a matter of musical tastes and how they will change year to year.

This is one of the risks (and benefits) of royalty investing. Culture changes and things that were once in fashion can go out of fashion and vice versa.

However, RoyaltyExchange has a metric called Dollar Age that they use to try and quantify how long something might stay in fashion.

For example, if two different songs both earned $10,000 in royalties last year, but one of the songs was released in 1950 and the other was released in 2019, then the song released in 1950 has the higher (older) Dollar Age and will probably be a better long-term investment.

Why?

The song from 1950 has 70 years of demonstrated earnings compared to only one year of demonstrated earnings for the song from 2019. Though the song from 2019 may be a passing fad, the song from 1950 is an undeniable classic.

This concept, more formally known as the Lindy Effect, states that something's popularity in the future is proportional to how long it has been around in the past.

The Lindy Effect explains why people in the year 2220 are more likely to listen to Mozart than to Metallica. Though Metallica probably has more worldwide listeners today than Mozart, I am not sure this will be true in two centuries.

Lastly, the other downside to investing in royalties is the potentially high fees charged to sellers. Typically sellers have to pay a percentage of the final sale price after an auction closes and this percentage fee can be a sizeable chunk. So, unless you plan on investing only in royalties (and doing it at scale), then royalty investing might not be right for you.

How Do You Invest in Royalties?

The most common way for your typical investor to purchase royalties is to use an online platform that matches buyers and sellers. Though you can also buy royalties through private deals, online is probably the easier way to go.

Royalties Summary

- Average compounded annual return: 5%–20%[76]
- **Pros**: Uncorrelated to traditional financial assets. Generally steady income.
- **Cons**: High seller fees. Tastes can change unexpectedly and impact income.

Your Own Products

Last, but not least, one of the best income-producing assets you can invest in is your own products. Unlike all of the other assets on this list, creating products (digital or otherwise) allows for far more control than most other asset classes.

Since you are the 100% owner of your products, you can set the price, and, thus, determine their returns (at least in theory). Products include things like books, information guides, online courses, and many others.

Why You Should/Shouldn't Invest in Your Own Products

I know quite a few people who have managed to earn five to six figures from selling their products online. More importantly, if you already have an audience via social media, an email list, or website, selling products is one way to monetize that audience.

And even if you don't have one of these distribution channels, it's never been easier to sell products online thanks to platforms like Shopify and Gumroad, and online payment processors.

The hard part about products as investments is that they require lots of work upfront with no guarantee of a payout. There is a long road to monetization.

However, once you get one successful product under your belt, it is much easier to expand your branding and sell other things as well.

For example, I have seen my income on my blog, OfDollarsAndData.com, grow beyond small affiliate partnerships to include ad sales along with more freelancing opportunities. It took years of blogging before I started earning any significant amount of money, but now new opportunities are always popping up.

How to Invest in Your Own Products

If you want to invest in your own products, you have to build them. Whether that means starting a website for a blog or creating your own Shopify store, creating a product takes lots of time and effort.

Your Own Product(s) Summary

- Average compounded annual return: Highly variable. Distribution is fat-tailed (i.e., most products return little, but some go big).
- **Pros**: Full ownership. Personal satisfaction. Can create a valuable brand.
- **Cons**: Very labor intensive. No guarantee of payoff.

What About Gold, Crypto, Art, Etc?

A handful of asset classes did not make the above list for the simple reason that they don't produce income. Gold, cryptocurrency, commodities, art, and wine have no reliable income stream associated with their ownership, so I have not included them in my list of income-producing assets.

Of course, this does not mean that you can't make money with these assets. What it does mean is that their valuations are based *solely* on perception—what someone else is willing to pay for them. Without underlying cash flows, perception is everything.

It's different for income-producing assets, though. While perception does play a role in how these assets are priced, cash flows should anchor their valuations, at least in theory.

For this reason, the bulk of my investments (90%) are in income-producing assets, with the remaining 10% spread out among non-income-producing assets such as art and various cryptocurrencies.

Final Summary

Here is a summary table of the information covered in this chapter, for better comparison purposes.

Asset Class	Annual Compounded Return	Pros	Cons
Stocks	8%-10%	High historic returns. Easy to own and trade. Low maintenance.	High volatility. Valuations can change quickly.
Bonds	2%-4%	Low volatility. Good for rebalancing. Safety of principal.	Low returns, especially after inflation. Low income in low-yield environment.
Investment Property	12%-15%	Higher returns (especially when you include leverage).	Managing the property can be a headache. Hard to diversify.
REITs	10%-12%	Real estate exposure that you don't have to manage.	Volatility greater than or equal to stocks. Crashes when other risk assets do.
Farmland	7%-9%	Lower correlation with traditional financial assets. Good inflation hedge.	Less liquid + higher fees. Requires "accredited" status to participate.
Small Businesses	20%-25%	Extremely outsized returns. More involvement creates more opportunity.	Huge time commitment. Lots of failures can be discouraging.

Asset Class	Annual Compounded Return	Pros	Cons
Royalties	5%-20%	Uncorrelated with traditional financial assets. Generally steady income.	High seller fees. Tastes can change suddenly and impact income.
Your Own Product(s)	Variable	Full ownership. Personal satisfaction. Can create a valuable brand.	Very labor intensive. No guarantee of payoff.

No matter what mix of income-producing assets you end up choosing, the optimal asset allocation is the one that will work best for *you* and your situation. Remember that two people can have very different investment strategies and they can both be right.

Now that we have talked about what you should invest in, we will spend some time discussing why you shouldn't invest in individual stocks.

12. WHY YOU SHOULDN'T BUY INDIVIDUAL STOCKS

Why underperforming is the least of your worries

IT WAS 8 AM on Monday January 25, 2021 when I got the text from my friend Darren (not his real name).

"Nick tell me why I shouldn't put 50–100k in GME at 930."

He was referring to GameStop (GME), the stock that would soon become an international sensation after a group of online traders caused its price to go up 5x in less than a week. Unfortunately, neither of us knew that at the time.

What Darren did know was that I would *never* recommend buying an individual stock. He didn't care though, he just wanted some sort of affirmation. I jokingly replied, "Darren, it could turn into the best thing that's ever happened to you."

That was all it took. Over the course of the next hour the conversation in our group chat descended into the merits of GME and whether the wallstreetbets Reddit forum was right about its imminent price increase.

As soon as the market opened, it was clear that wallstreetbets had called it perfectly. GME started the day at $96, up from its previous close of $65, and didn't stop there.

By 10:22 AM, Darren couldn't stand to be on the sidelines any longer. He texted the group, "I'm in" after buying GME at $111 a share. His total investment amounted to over $30,000, meaning that every $1 move in GME's share price was worth $300 to Darren. If the GME share price went up $1, Darren would make $300; if the GME share price went down $1, Darren would lose $300.

Within 15 minutes GME climbed to $140 a share and Darren was up over $9,000. Text messages flooded the group chat praising Darren for his newly acquired riches while also speculating on where he would soon retire.

But, as quickly as GME rose, it fell. Within an hour the price was below $111 and Darren's texts showed increasing levels of worry. He put in a limit order to sell at $111 in hopes of getting his investment back, but it was too late. The freefall had already begun.

With each $1 drop in GME's share price Darren's pain was magnified 300-fold. There goes another $300, then another $300, then another. The losses didn't let up. At 12:27 PM Darren finally capitulated. "I'm out at 70" he texted the group.

Darren had lost $12,000 in two hours.

It's not as bad as it sounds, though. Darren's loss only represented a small percentage of his net worth. Despite his emotional distress, he had just received the financial equivalent of a papercut, not an amputation.

And while I won't commend Darren for what he did, I will praise him for *how* he did it. Because Darren only bet what he was willing to lose, and he made sure that any such loss wouldn't affect his financial future. If you ever decide to buy individual stocks, I can only hope that you do the same.

Nevertheless, Darren's story is a microcosm of what it's like to be a stock picker. The mental turmoil. The fear of missing out. The elation, triumph, pain, and regret. It was all perfectly packaged into a single two-hour window.

Battling emotions is just the tip of the stock picking iceberg. I know because I used to pick stocks years ago as well. In addition to the emotional difficulties, you also have to deal with periods of underperformance and the possibility that you don't actually have any stock picking skill.

As a result, I've since given up picking individual stocks and I recommend that you do the same. But, my reasoning for why you shouldn't pick individual stocks has evolved over time.

Originally, I gave up on buying individual stocks because of what I will call *the financial* argument. It's a good argument and one you may have heard before, but it pales in comparison to the *existential* argument against stock picking.

Let me explain.

The Financial Argument Against Stock Picking

The traditional argument against stock picking (the *financial* argument) is one that has been around for decades. It goes as follows: since most people (even the professionals) can't beat a broad index of companies, you shouldn't bother trying.

The data backing this argument is undeniable. You can look through the SPIVA report for every equity market on earth and you will see (more or less) the same thing—over a five-year period 75% of funds don't beat their benchmark.[77] And remember, this 75% consists of professional money managers working full-time with teams of analysts. If they can't outperform with all these resources, what chance do you have?

More importantly, research has shown that only a small percentage of individual stocks do well in the long run. As Hendrik Bessembinder found in his paper "Do Stock Outperform Treasury Bills?": "the best-performing 4% of listed companies explain the net gain for the entire U.S. stock market since 1926."[78]

That's it. Just 4% of stocks from 1926–2016 created all the excess return for stocks above U.S. Treasury bills. In fact, "just five firms (ExxonMobil, Apple, Microsoft, General Electric, and IBM) account for 10% of the total wealth creation."

Can you be sure you can find one of these 4% of stocks and not pick one of the 96%?

But even these titans of industry will one day lose their edge. As Geoffrey West calculated, "Of the 28,853 companies that traded on U.S. markets since 1950, 22,469 (78 percent) died by 2009." In fact, "half of all companies in any given cohort of U.S. publicly traded companies disappear within 10 years."[79]

While West's statistical analysis illustrates the transitory nature of equity markets, I prefer a much simpler demonstration of this fact. Of the 20 companies in the Dow Jones Industrial Average in March 1920, not a single one was still in the index 100 years later. Nothing lasts forever.

You can see the problem. Beating the performance of a broad basket of stocks (an index) is so hard that most professional investors don't achieve it; the proportion of winning stocks that you're trying to find is very low; and even those winning stocks aren't winners forever.

This is why owning *all* of the stocks—by buying an index fund or ETF—is usually a far better bet than trying to pick big winners among individual stocks. You are likely to end up with more money and experience less stress while doing so.

But let's put that argument aside for now, because the *existential* argument against stock picking is far more convincing.

The Existential Argument Against Stock Picking

The existential argument against stock picking is simple—how do you *know* if you are good at picking individual stocks? In most domains, the amount of time it takes to judge whether someone has skill in that domain is relatively short.

For example, any competent basketball coach could tell you whether someone was skilled at shooting within the course of 10 minutes. Yes, it's possible to get lucky and make a bunch of shots early on, but eventually they will trend towards their actual shooting percentage. The same is true in a technical field like computer programming. Within a short period of time, a good programmer would be able to tell if someone doesn't know what they are talking about.

But, what about stock picking? How long would it take to determine if someone is a good stock picker? An hour? A week? A year?

Try multiple years, and even then you still may not know for sure. The issue is that causality is harder to determine with stock picking than with other domains.

When you shoot a basketball or write a computer program, the result comes *immediately* after the action. The ball goes in the hoop or it doesn't. The program runs correctly or it doesn't. But, with stock picking, you make a decision now and have to wait for it to pay off. The feedback loop can take years.

And the payoff you do eventually get has to be compared to the payoff of buying an index fund like the S&P 500. So, even if you make money on absolute terms, you can still lose money on relative terms.

More importantly, though, the result that you get from that decision may have nothing to do with why you made it in the first place. For example, imagine you had bought GME in late 2020 because you believed the price would increase as a result of the company improving its operations. Well, 2021 comes along and the price of GameStop surges due to the retail investor frenzy highlighted at the beginning of this chapter. Though you got a positive result, it had *nothing* to do with your original thesis.

Now imagine how often this happens to stock pickers—where the linkage between the decision and the result is far less obvious. Did the stock go up because of some change you anticipated or was it another change altogether? What about when market sentiment shifts against you? Do you double down and buy more, or do you reconsider?

These are just a few of the questions you have to ask yourself with every investment decision you make as a stock picker. It can be a never-ending state of existential dread. You may convince yourself that you know what's going on, but do you *really* know?

For some people, the answer is clearly, "Yes." For example, in "Can Mutual Fund 'Stars' Really Pick Stocks?" researchers found that "the large, positive alphas of the top ten percent of funds, net of costs, are extremely unlikely to be a result of sampling variability (luck)."[80] In other words, 10% of people who pick stocks professionally do actually have skill that persists over time. However, this also suggests that 90% probably don't.

For argument's sake, let's assume that the top 10% of stock pickers and the bottom 10% of stock pickers can easily identify their skill (or lack thereof). This means that, if we choose a stock picker at random, there is a 20% chance we could identify their skill level and an 80% chance that we couldn't! This implies that four out of five stock pickers would find it difficult to prove that they are good at stock picking.

This is the existential crisis that I am talking about. Why would you want to play a game (or make a career) out of something that you can't prove that you are good at? If you are doing it for fun, that's fine. Take a small portion of your money like my friend Darren did and have at it. But, for those that aren't doing it for fun, why spend so much time on something where your skill is so hard to measure?

And even if you are someone who can demonstrate their stock picking prowess (i.e., the top 10%), your issues don't stop there. For example, what happens when you inevitably experience a period of underperformance? After all, underperformance isn't a matter of if, but when.

As a study by Baird noted, "at some point in their careers, virtually all top-performing money managers underperform their benchmark and their peers, particularly over time periods of three years or less."[81]

Just imagine how nerve-racking this must be when it finally happens. Yes, you had skill in the past, but what about *now*? Is your underperformance a normal lull that even the best investors experience, or have you lost your touch? Of course, losing your touch in any endeavor isn't easy, but it's so much harder when you don't know for sure if you have actually lost it.

Track Your Performance (Or Just Do it For Fun)

I'm not the only one who has argued against stock picking either. Consider what Bill Bernstein, the famed investment writer, said on the topic:

> "The very best way to learn about the dangers of individual stock investing is to familiarize yourself with the basics of finance and the empirical literature. But if you can't do that, then, sure, what you have to do is put 5% or 10% of your money into individual stocks. And make sure you rigorously calculate your return, your annualized return, and then ask yourself, 'Could I have done better just by buying a total stock market index fund?'"[82]

While you may not want to compare your performance to an index fund, it is something you have to do if you aren't doing it for fun.

Lastly, I have nothing against *stock pickers*, but I do have something against *stock picking*. The difference is crucial.

Skilled stock pickers provide a valuable service to markets by keeping prices reasonably efficient. However, stock picking is an investment philosophy that has gotten far too many retail investors burned in the process. I have seen it happen to friends like Darren. I have seen it happen to family. I just hope it doesn't happen to you too.

I know I won't convince every stock picker to change their ways, and that's a good thing. We need people to keep analyzing companies and deploying their capital accordingly. However, if you are on the fence about it, this is your wake-up call. Don't keep playing a game with so much luck involved. Life already has enough luck as it is.

After considering the possible emotional, financial, and existential costs of buying individual stocks, you can see why I prefer investing in index funds and ETFs. The simplicity of indexing allows me to focus my attention on the things in life that are far more important than my portfolio.

Now that we have discussed what you should invest in (and why it shouldn't be individual stocks), let's explore the topic of *how soon* you should invest your money.

13.
HOW SOON SHOULD YOU INVEST?

And why earlier is better than later

BEFORE AMERICAN PHAROAH won the Triple Crown in 2015, no one expected much from the horse. But Jeff Seder felt differently.

Seder had worked as an analyst at Citigroup before quitting and following his passion to predict the outcome of horse races. Seder wasn't like other equine researchers because he didn't care about the thing that other horse breeders obsessed over—pedigree.

The traditional view among horse breeders was that a horse's mother, father, and general lineage were the primary determinant of its racing success. However, after looking through historical records, Seder realized pedigree wasn't a great predictor. Seder needed to find another predictor and to do that he needed data.

And it was data that he collected. For years Seder measured everything on horses. Nostril size. Excrement weight. Fast-twitch muscle fiber density. And for years he came up empty-handed.

Then, Seder got the idea to measure the size of a horse's internal organs using a portable ultrasound. Bingo. He hit pay dirt.

Seth Stephens-Davidowitz tells of Seder's discovery in *Everybody Lies*:

> "He found that the size of the heart, and particularly the size of the left ventricle, was a massive predictor of a horse's success, the single most important variable."[83]

That was it. Heart size was a better predictor of horse racing ability than anything else. And this is what Seder knew when he convinced his buyer to purchase American Pharoah and disregard the other 151 horses at auction. The rest is history.

Seder's story highlights how deep insight can be gleaned from one useful data point. Hans Rosling echoes this sentiment in *Factfulness* when he discusses the importance of child mortality in understanding a country's development:

> "Do you know I'm obsessed with the number for the child mortality rate?… Because children are very fragile. There are so many things that can kill them. When only 14 children die out of 1,000 in Malaysia, this means that the other 986 survive. Their parents and their society manage to protect them from all the dangers that could have killed them: germs, starvation, violence and so on.
>
> So this number 14 tells us that most families in Malaysia have enough food, their sewage systems don't leak into their drinking water, they have good access to primary health care, and mothers can read and write. It doesn't

just tell us about the health of children. It measures the quality of the whole society."[84]

Rosling's use of childhood mortality and Seder's use of heart size exemplify how complex systems can be more easily understood with a single piece of accurate information.

When it comes to *how soon* you should invest your money, there is also one piece of information that can guide all of your future decisions.

Most Markets Go Up Most of the Time

The one piece of information that can guide your investing decisions is:

Most stock markets go up most of the time.

This is true despite the chaotic and sometimes destructive course of human history. As Warren Buffett so eloquently stated:

> "In the 20th century, the United States endured two world wars and other traumatic and expensive military conflicts; the Depression; a dozen or so recessions and financial panics; oil shocks; a flu epidemic; and the resignation of a disgraced president. Yet the Dow rose from 66 to 11,497."[85]

This logic doesn't apply solely to U.S. markets either. As I illustrated at the beginning of chapter 11, equity markets across the world have exhibited a long-term positive trend.

Given this empirical evidence, it suggests that you should invest your money as soon as possible.

Why is this?

Because most markets going up most of the time means that every day you end up waiting to invest usually means higher prices you will have to pay in the future. So, instead of waiting for the best time to get invested, you should just take the plunge and invest what you can now.

We can illustrate this with a rather absurd thought experiment.

Imagine you have been gifted $1 million and you want to grow it as much as possible over the next 100 years. However, you can only undertake one of two possible investment strategies. You must either:

1. Invest all your cash now, or
2. Invest 1% of your cash each year for the next 100 years.

Which would you prefer?

If we assume that the assets you are investing in will increase in value over time (otherwise why would you be investing?), then it should be clear that buying now will be better than buying over the course of 100 years. Waiting a century to get invested means buying at ever higher prices while your uninvested cash also loses value to inflation.

We can take this same logic and generalize it downward to periods much smaller than 100 years. Because if you wouldn't wait 100 years to get invested, then you shouldn't wait 100 months or 100 weeks either.

It's as the old saying goes:

> "The best time to start was yesterday. The next best time is today."

Of course, this never *feels* like the right decision because you are left wondering whether you could get a better price in the future.

And guess what? That feeling is accurate because it is very likely that a better price will appear at some point in the future.

However, the data suggests that the best thing to do is ignore that feeling altogether.

We now turn to look at why better prices in the future are likely, why you should not wait for these better prices, and why you should invest as soon as you can instead. Investing sooner rather than later is the best strategy for U.S. stocks and also for nearly every other asset class out there.

Why Better Prices in the Future are Likely (And Why You Shouldn't Wait for Them)

If you randomly picked a trading day for the Dow Jones Industrial Average between 1930–2020, there is over a 95% chance that the Dow would close *lower* on *some* trading day in the future.

This means that roughly 1 in 20 trading days (one a month) would provide you with an absolute bargain. The other 19 would give you the feeling of buyer's remorse at *some point* in the future.

This is why it feels like waiting for a lower price is the right thing to do. Technically, there is a 95% chance that you will be right.

In fact, since 1930 the median amount of time you would have to wait to see a lower price after buying the Dow is only two trading days. However, the average is 31 trading days (1.5 months).

The real problem though is that sometimes a lower price never occurs, or you have to wait a very long time before you see this lower price.

For example, on March 9, 2009 the Dow Jones Industrial Average closed at 6,547. This was the exact bottom during the Great Financial Crisis.

Do you know the last time the Dow closed below 6,547 before then?

April 14, 1997—12 years earlier.

This means that if you bought the Dow on April 15, 1997, you would have needed to wait almost 12 years before you saw a lower price. Having the patience to wait this long for a better price is nearly impossible for any investor.

This is why market timing, though appealing in theory, is difficult in practice.

As a result, the best market timing approach is to invest your money as soon as you can. This isn't just an opinion of mine either. It is backed by historical data across multiple asset classes and multiple time periods.

Invest Now or Over Time?

Before we get started on the data, let's define some terms that I will use for the remainder of this chapter:

- **Buy Now**: The act of investing all of your available money *at once.* The amount of money being invested is not important, only that the entire amount is invested immediately.
- **Average-In**: The act of investing all of your available money *over time.* How you decide to invest these funds over time is up to you. However, the typical approach is equal-sized payments over a specific time period (e.g., one payment a month for 12 months).

Visually, we can see the difference between investing $12,000 through Buy Now vs. Average-In over a period of 12 months.

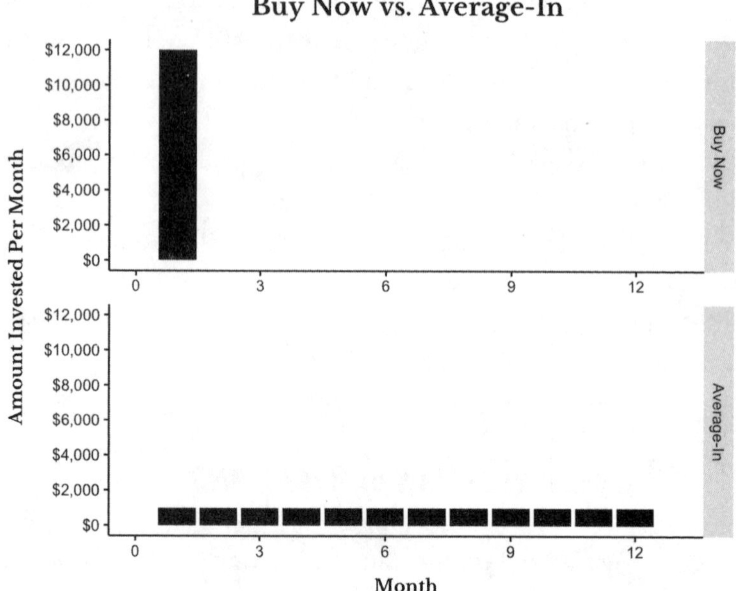

With Buy Now you invest the $12,000 (all of your funds) in the first month, but with Average-In you only invest $1,000 in the first month with the remaining $11,000 being invested in $1,000 payments over the next 11 months.

If you invested into the S&P 500 using these two approaches across history, you would find that the Average-In strategy generally *underperforms* Buy Now most of the time.

To be more precise, Average-In underperforms Buy Now by 4% in each rolling 12-month period, on average, and in 76% of all rolling 12-month periods from 1997–2020.

While 4% might not seem like much in a year, this is only *on average.* If we look at the level of underperformance over time, we would see that it can get far worse.

For example, the next chart illustrates this by plotting the performance premium of the Average-In over Buy Now when investing into the S&P 500 over all rolling 12-month periods since 1997.

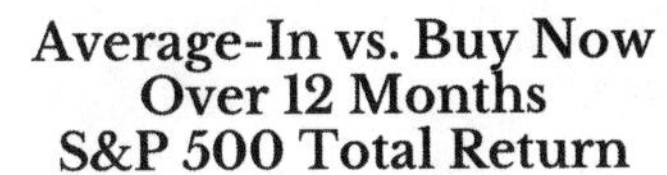

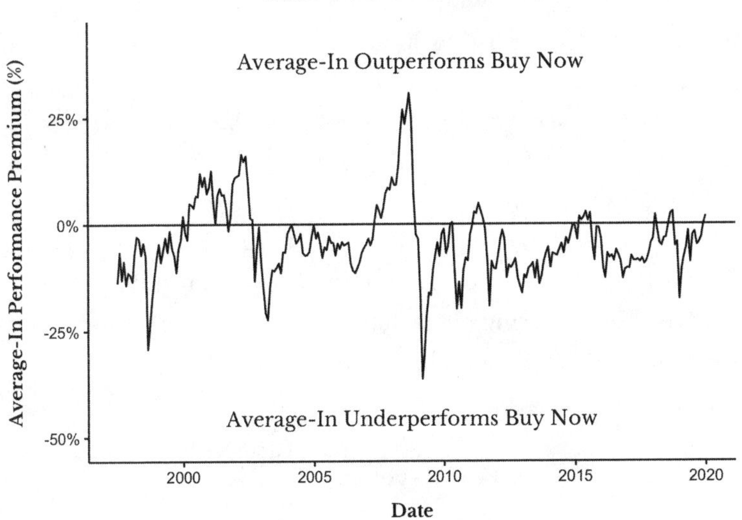

Each point on this line represents the difference in return between the Average-In and Buy Now strategies after 12 months. For example, the highest point on this line occurs in August 2008 where the Average-In strategy outperformed the Buy Now strategy by 30% in 1 year.

Why did Buy Now perform so badly relative to Average-In in August 2008?

Because the U.S. stock market crashed shortly after August 2008. More specifically, if you had invested $12,000 in the S&P 500 at the end of August 2008, by the end of August 2009 you would only have $9,810 (including reinvested dividends) for a total loss of 18.25%.

However, if you had followed the Average-In strategy and

invested $1,000 a month over this same time period, you would have about $13,500 (or a 12.5% *gain*) by the end of August 2009.

This is how we get to the 30% performance premium for the Average-In strategy from August 2008 to August 2009.

The real takeaway from this chart isn't this peak though, but that the line is usually below 0%. Where the line is below 0%, Average-In has underperformed Buy Now, and where it is above 0%, Average-In has outperformed Buy Now.

As you can see, most of the time, Average-In *underperforms* Buy Now. This isn't just recency bias either. If we were to look at U.S. stock returns going back to 1920, we would find that Average-In underperforms Buy Now by 4.5% in each rolling 12-month period, on average, and in 68% of all rolling 12-month periods. The following chart illustrates this longer period in the same way as the previous chart.

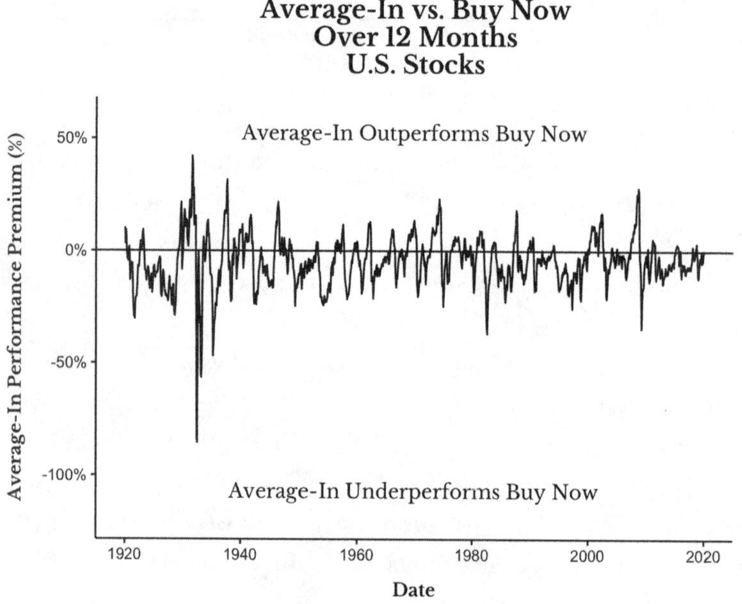

The only times when Average-In outperforms Buy Now are at the peaks before major market crashes (e.g., 1929, 2008, etc.). This is true because Average-In buys into a falling market, and, thus, buys at a lower average price than Buy Now would with a single investment.

And while it can feel like we are always on the cusp of a market crash, the truth is that major crashes have been quite rare. This is why Average-In has underperformed Buy Now throughout most of history.

As we have seen above, Buy Now is better than Average-In when investing in stocks, but what about other assets?

What About Assets Other Than U.S. Stocks?

Rather than filling this book with endless charts illustrating the superiority of Buy Now over Average-In for various asset classes, I have created a summary table instead. The table shows how much the Average-In strategy has *underperformed* Buy Now over all 12-month periods from 1997–2020.

Asset (1997-2020)	Average-In Underperformance Over 12 Months	Percentage of 12-Month Periods Where Average-In Underperforms
Bitcoin (2014-2020)	96%	67%
U.S. Treasury Index	2%	82%
Gold	4%	63%
Developed Market Stocks	3%	62%
Emerging Market Stocks	5%	60%
60/40 U.S. Stock/Bond Portfolio	3%	82%
S&P 500 Total Return	4%	76%
U.S. Stocks (1920-2020)	4%	68%

For example, the table shows us that for an investor Averaging-In to gold in any 12-month period from 1997 to 2020, the average underperformance against Buy Now was 4%, with Average-In underperforming Buy Now 63% of the time.

As you can see, Average-In underperformed Buy Now by 2%-4%, on average, over 12 months for most assets and in 60%–80% of all starting months.

This implies that if you picked a random month to start averaging into an asset, you are very likely to underperform a similar one-time investment into that same asset.

What About Risk?

We have only compared *performance* between the Buy Now and Average-In strategies thus far, but we know that investors also care about the difference in risk between two strategies.

Isn't it riskier to Buy Now than to Average-In? The answer is a resounding "Yes!"

As the next chart illustrates, the standard deviation of the Buy Now strategy is *always higher* than the Average-In strategy when investing in the S&P 500. As a reminder, the standard deviation shows how much a particular data series deviates from its average outcome. Therefore, a higher standard deviation usually corresponds with a riskier investment or investment strategy.

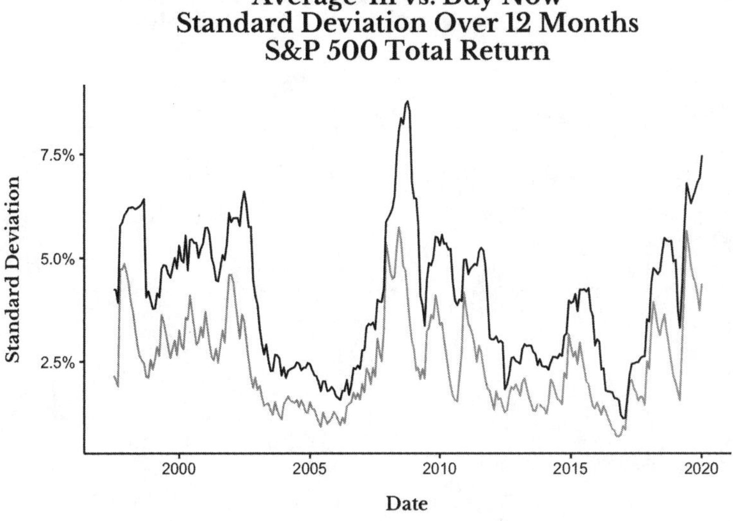

It is true that Buy Now is riskier because Buy Now invests right away and gets full exposure to the underlying asset straightaway, while Average-In is partially in cash throughout the buying period. We know that stocks are a riskier asset than cash, so it follows that the more exposure you have to stocks, the higher the risk.

However, if you are worried about risk, then maybe you should consider following the Buy Now strategy and investing into a *more conservative* portfolio instead.

For example, if originally you were going to Average-In to a

100% U.S. stock portfolio, you could follow the Buy Now strategy into a 60/40 U.S. stock/bond portfolio to have slightly better returns *for the same level of risk.*

As the next chart illustrates, Averaging-In to a 100% U.S. stock portfolio has underperformed Buy Now into a 60/40 U.S. stock bond portfolio most of the time since 1997.

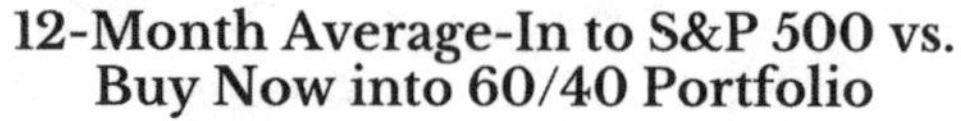

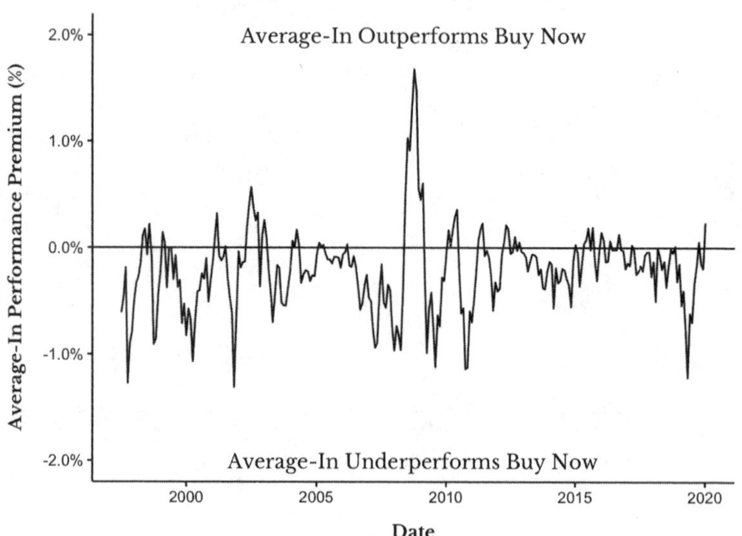

Yes, the underperformance of Average-In is small in this case, but you are getting the small outperformance of Buy Now for the same (or lower) level of risk most of the time. This is what investors want: outperformance, with lower risk. The following chart illustrates the rolling standard deviation of returns for these two strategies over this time period.

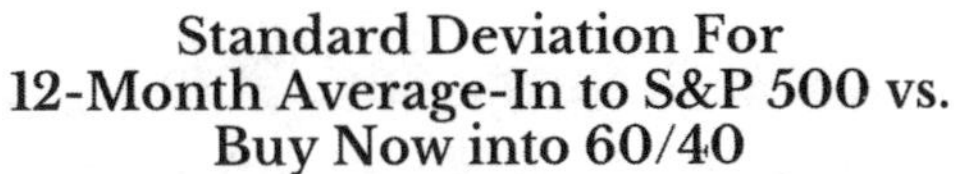

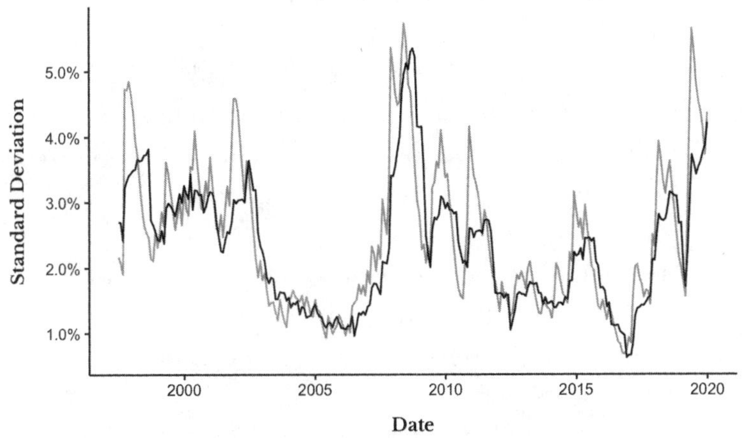

As you can see, most of the time the Buy Now strategy into a 60/40 portfolio has the same or a lower level of risk than Averaging-In to the S&P 500 (100% stocks).

In summary, the Buy Now strategy with a balanced 60/40 portfolio usually beats the Average-In strategy for a portfolio of 100% stocks.

So if you are worried about the risk associated with using the Buy Now strategy to go all-in to a portfolio of stocks, there is a better way. Rather than compromising by Averaging-In to a portfolio of 100% stocks, you should consider using the Buy Now strategy to invest in a less risky portfolio, such as 60% stocks and 40% bonds.

Does Investing Your Side Cash in Treasury Bills Make a Difference?

One of the common criticisms of this analysis is that the Average-In method assumes that all of your money sits in cash while you wait to get allocated. Some have argued that this side cash should be invested in U.S. Treasury bills earning a return while you Average-In.

I agree with this logic in theory, but the problem is that most investors don't follow this advice in practice. Few investors move their money into Treasury bills while they slowly move their money into stocks.

I know this anecdotally because I've spoken with financial advisors who have told me so. They have had countless conversations where prospective clients had been in cash for *years* waiting on the right time to get into the market.

But I also know this from the monthly asset allocation survey conducted by the American Association of Individual Investors (AAII). The AAII survey shows that, since 1989, the average individual investor has had over 20% of their portfolio allocated in cash.[86]

Even though the premise doesn't work because investors don't do this in practice, I've examined the data anyway. The next table shows the average underperformance of Average-In compared to Buy Now *when you invest your side cash in Treasury bills* while Averaging-In to the market.

Asset (1997-2020)	Average-In Underperformance Over 12 Months	Percentage of 12-Month Periods Where Average-In Underperforms
Bitcoin (2014-2020)	96%	65%
U.S. Treasury Index	1%	72%
Gold	3%	60%
Developed Market Stocks	2%	60%
Emerging Market Stocks	4%	57%
60/40 U.S. Stock/Bond Portfolio	2%	77%
S&P 500 Total Return	3%	74%

For example, the table shows us that for an investor Averaging-In to Bitcoin in any 12-month period from 1997 to 2020, while also holding their cash in Treasury bills, the average underperformance against Buy Now was 96% and this strategy of Averaging-In underperformed Buy Now 65% of the time.

The primary difference from our earlier results is that instead of Average-In underperforming by 2%–4% on average, it now only underperforms by about 1%–3% on average and only in 60%–70% of starting months (instead of 70%–80% of starting months). While there has been a reduction in the size of Average-In's underperformance, it still exists even if you invest your side cash into Treasury bills.

Do Valuations Matter?

A common response I hear when recommending Buy Now over Average-In is, "In normal times this makes sense, but not at these extreme valuations!"

So, when valuations are elevated across the market, does this imply we should reconsider the Average-In strategy?

Not really.

For the uninitiated, the valuation ratio I am using is called the cyclically-adjusted price-to-earnings ratio (CAPE). CAPE is a measure of how much you would have to pay to own $1 worth of earnings across U.S. stocks. So a CAPE of 10 implies that you need to pay $10 for $1 of earnings. When the CAPE ratio is higher, stocks are more expensive, and when it is lower they are considered cheaper.

If we break down the performance of Average-In versus Buy Now by the CAPE Percentiles since 1960 we can see that Average-In underperforms Buy Now under all of them.

CAPE Percentiles	Average-In Underperformance Over 12 Months	Percentage of 12-Month Periods Where Average-In Underperforms
CAPE <15 (<25th percentile)	5%	67%
CAPE 15-20 (25-50th percentile)	4%	68%
CAPE 20-25 (50-75th percentile)	3%	71%
CAPE >25 (>75th percentile)	2%	70%

The size of Average-In's underperformance does decrease as CAPE increases, but, unfortunately, as we try to analyze the periods with the highest valuations, we run into sample size problems.

For example, if we only consider when CAPE was greater than 30 (about the level it was at the end of 2019), Average-In *outperformed* Buy Now by 1.2% on average over the next 12 months.

However, the only time when CAPE exceeded 30 prior to the last decade was the DotCom Bubble!

But if you wait to invest because the CAPE ratio is too high, you could miss out on some big gains. For example, CAPE most recently passed 30 in July 2017. If you had moved to cash then, you would have missed a 65% increase in the S&P 500 by the end of 2020 (including dividends).

If you think that the market is overvalued and due for a major pullback, you may need to wait years, if ever, before you are vindicated. Consider this before you use valuation as an excuse to stay in cash.

Final Summary

When deciding between investing all your money now or over time, it is almost always better to invest it now. This is true across all asset classes, time periods, and nearly all valuation regimes. Generally, the longer you wait to deploy your capital, the worse off you will be.

I say generally because the only time when you are better off by averaging-in over time is while the market is crashing. However, it is precisely when the market is crashing that you will be the *least enthusiastic* to invest.

It is difficult to fight off these emotions, which is why many investors won't be able to keep buying as the market falls anyways.

If you are still worried about investing a large sum of money right now, the problem may be that you're considering a portfolio that is too risky for your liking. What's the solution to this? Invest your money now into a more conservative portfolio than you normally would.

If your target allocation is a 80/20 stock/bond portfolio, you might want to consider investing it all into a 60/40 stock/bond portfolio and transitioning it over time. For example, you could invest your portfolio into a 60/40 today with a specific plan to rebalance to a 70/30 a year from now and then to an 80/20 a year after that.

This way you still earn some return on your money without taking as much risk initially.

Now that we have discussed why getting invested now is better than waiting, let's tackle why you should never wait to buy the dip.

14. WHY YOU SHOULDN'T WAIT TO BUY THE DIP

Even God couldn't beat dollar-cost averaging

IF THE LAST chapter didn't convince you to abandon market timing forever, this one surely will. It's a bold claim, but one I am prepared to back up with data.

To start, let's play a game.

Imagine you are dropped somewhere in history between 1920 and 1980 and you have to invest in the U.S. stock market for the next 40 years. You have two investment strategies to choose from:

1. **Dollar-cost averaging (DCA)**: You invest $100 every month for 40 years.

2. **Buy the Dip**: You save $100 each month and only buy when the market is in a dip. A dip is defined as anytime when the market is not at an all-time high. But, I am going to make this second strategy even better. Not only will you buy the dip, but I am going to make you omniscient (i.e., "God") about when you buy. You will know exactly when the market is at the absolute bottom between any two all-time highs. This will ensure that when you do buy the dip, it is always at the lowest possible price.

The only other rule in this game is that you cannot move in and out of stocks. Once you make a purchase, you hold those stocks until the end of the time period.

So, which strategy would you choose: DCA or Buy the Dip?

Logically, it seems like Buy the Dip can't lose. If you know when you are at a bottom, you can always buy at the cheapest price relative to the all-time highs in that period.

However, if you actually run this strategy you will see that Buy the Dip underperforms DCA in more than 70% of the 40-year periods starting from 1920 to 1980. This is true despite the fact that you know *exactly* when the market will hit a bottom.

Even God couldn't beat dollar-cost averaging!

Why is this true? Because buying the dip only works when you know that a severe decline is coming and you can time it perfectly.

The problem is that severe market declines don't happen too often. In U.S. market history severe dips have only taken place in the 1930s, 1970s, and 2000s. That's rare. This means that Buy the Dip only has a small chance of beating DCA.

And the times where Buy the Dip does beat DCA require impeccable, God-like timing. Missing the bottom by just two months lowers the chance of Buy the Dip outperforming from 30% to 3%.

Instead of taking my word for it, let's dig into the details to see why this is true.

Understanding How Buy the Dip Works

To start, let's consider the U.S. stock market from January 1996 to December 2019, a 24-year period, to familiarize ourselves with this strategy.

In the first chart, I have plotted the S&P 500 (with dividends and adjusted for inflation) over this 24-year period. All-time highs are also plotted, as gray dots.

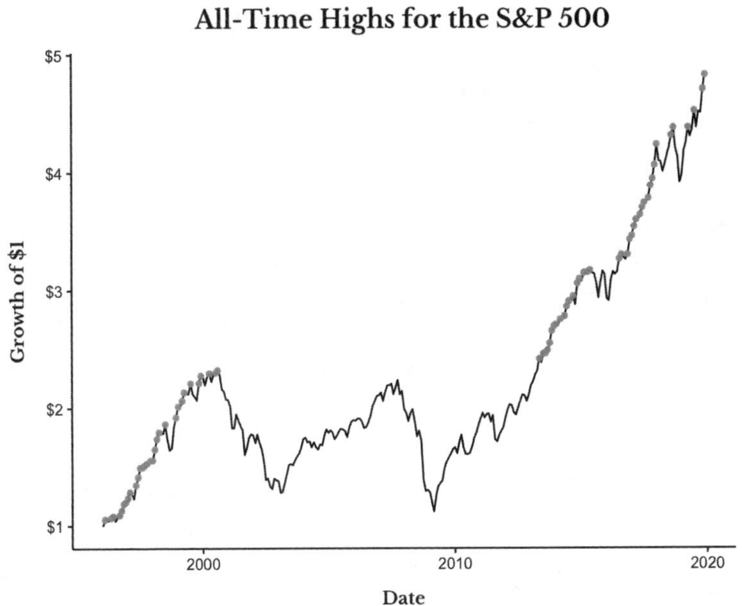

Now, I am going to show the exact same plot as above, but with the addition of a black dot for every dip in the market (defined as the biggest decline between a pair of all-time highs).

These dips are the points at which the Buy the Dip strategy would make purchases.

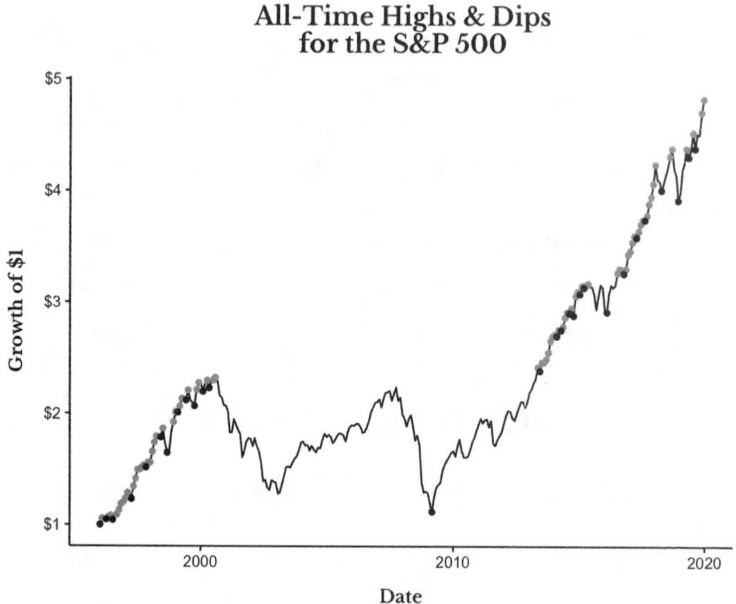

As you can see, the dips (black dots) occur at the lowest point between any two all-time highs (gray dots). The most prominent dip over this time period occurred in March 2009 (the lone black dot before 2010), which was the lowest point after the market high in August 2000.

However, you will also notice that there are many less prominent dips that are nested between all-time highs. These dips cluster during bull markets (in the mid-to-late 1990s, and mid 2010s).

To visualize how the Buy the Dip strategy works, I have plotted the amount the strategy has invested in the market and its cash balance over this time period from 1996 to 2019.

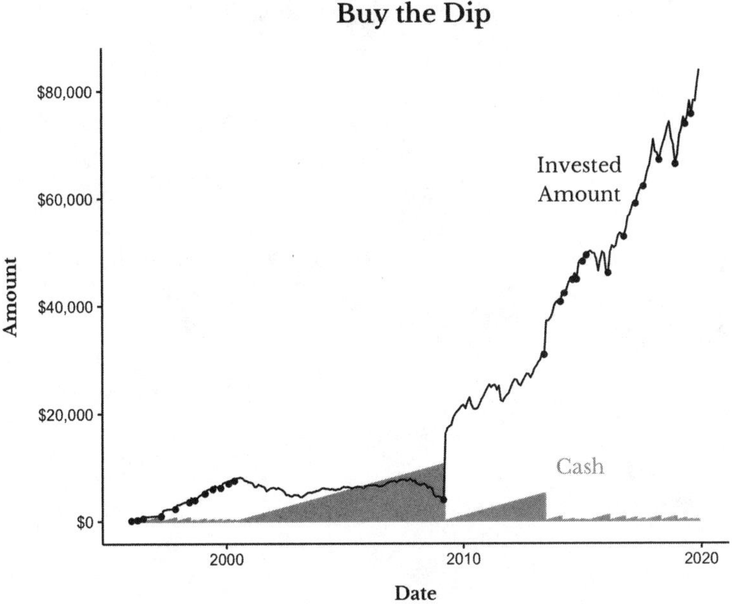

Every time this strategy buys into the market (the black dots), the cash balance (gray shaded area) goes to zero and the invested amount moves upward accordingly. This is most obvious when we look at March 2009 when, after nearly nine years of cash savings, Buy the Dip invests $10,600 into the market.

If we compare the portfolio value of Buy the Dip and DCA, you will see that the Buy the Dip strategy starts outperforming around the March 2009 purchase. This is shown in the next chart. Once again, the black dots represent every time the Buy the Dip strategy makes a purchase.

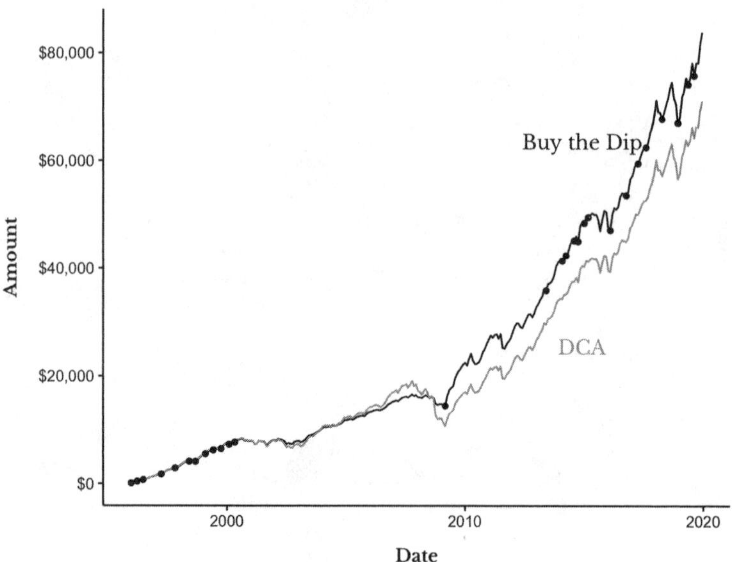

If you want to understand why this one purchase is so important, let's consider how much each individual purchase for the DCA strategy grows to by the end of the time period, along with when the Buy the Dip strategy makes purchases. Each bar in the next chart represents how much a $100 purchase grew to by December 2019.

For example, the $100 purchase in January 1996 grew to over $500. The black dots once again represent when the Buy the Dip strategy makes purchases.

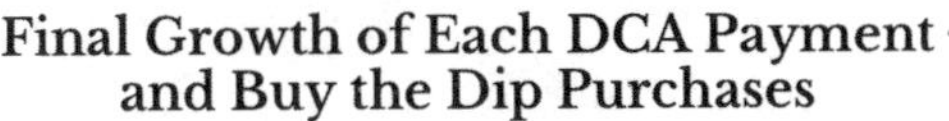

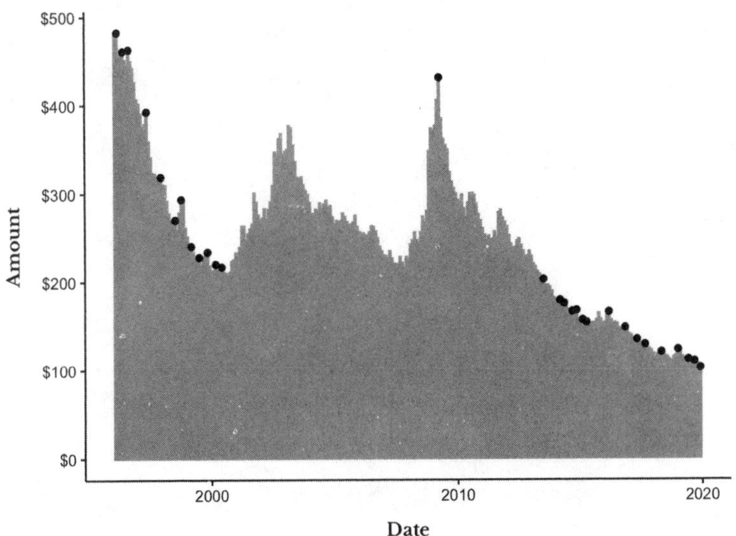

This chart illustrates the power of buying the dip as every $100 invested in March 2009 (that single dot towering near 2010) would grow to nearly $450 by December 2019.

There are two additional things to notice about this plot:

1. The earlier payments, on average, grow to more (compounding works!).
2. There are a handful of months (e.g., February 2003, March 2009) where some payments grow to considerably more than others.

If we put these two points together, this means that Buy the Dip will outperform DCA when *big dips happen earlier* in the time period.

The best example of this is the period 1928–1957, which contains the largest dip in U.S. stock market history (June 1932).

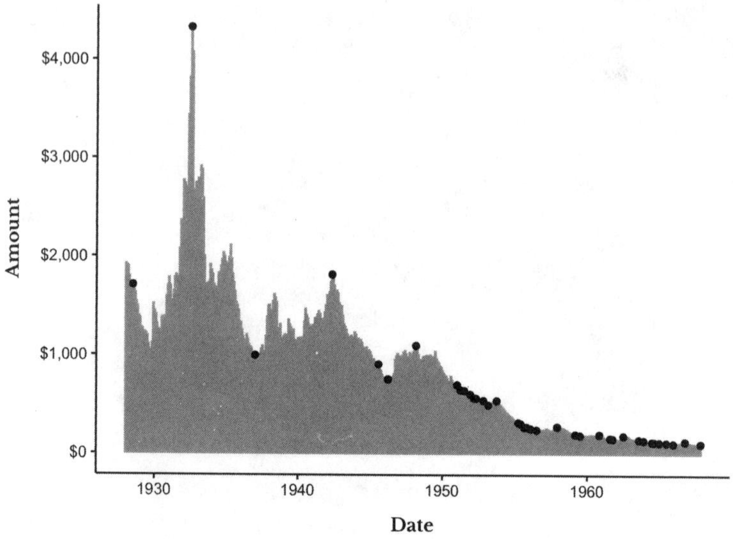

Buy the Dip works incredibly well from 1928–1957 because it buys the biggest dip ever (June 1932) early on. Every $100 you invested at the market bottom in June 1932 would have grown to $4,000 in real terms by 1957! There is no other time period in U.S. market history that even comes close to this.

I know it might sound like I am trying to sell the Buy the Dip strategy, but the 1996–2019 and the 1928–1957 periods just happen to be two periods where there were prolonged, severe bear markets.

If we look over longer time frames, historically, Buy the Dip doesn't outperform most of the time. The next chart shows the amount of outperformance from Buy the Dip (as compared to DCA) over every 40-year period over time. Outperformance is defined as the final Buy the Dip portfolio value divided by the final DCA portfolio value.

When Buy the Dip ends with more money than DCA it is

above the 0% line, and when it ends with less money than DCA it is below the 0% line. To be precise, over 70% of the time, Buy the Dip *underperforms* DCA (i.e., it is below the 0% line).

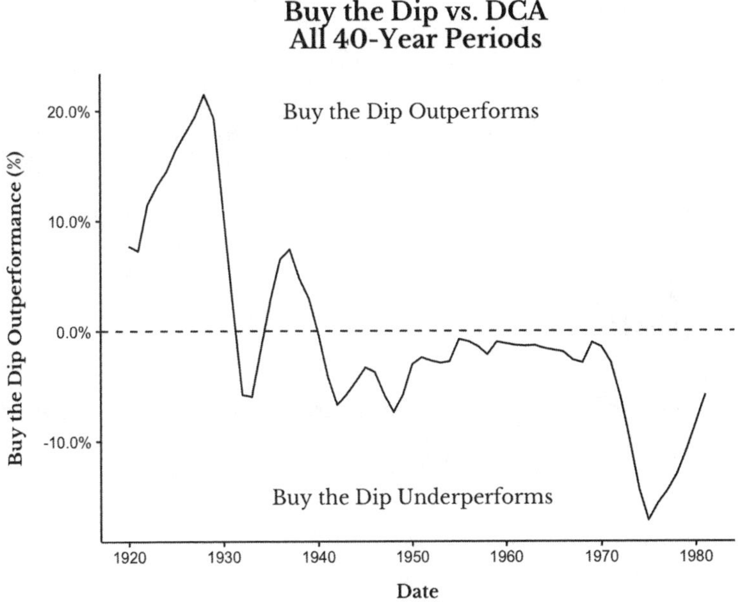

What you will notice is that Buy the Dip does well starting in the 1920s (due to the severe 1930s bear market), with an ending value up to 20% higher than DCA. However, it stops doing as well after the 1930s bear market and does continually worse. Its worst year of performance (relative to DCA) occurs immediately after the 1974 bear market (starting to invest in 1975).

This 1975–2014 period is particularly bad for Buy the Dip because it misses the bottom that occurred in 1974. Starting in 1975, the next all-time high in the market doesn't occur until 1985, meaning there is no dip to buy until after 1985.

Due to this unfortunate timing for Buy the Dip, DCA is easily able to outperform. The following chart shows Buy the Dip vs.

DCA for the 40 years starting in 1975. As usual, the black dots show Buy the Dip purchases.

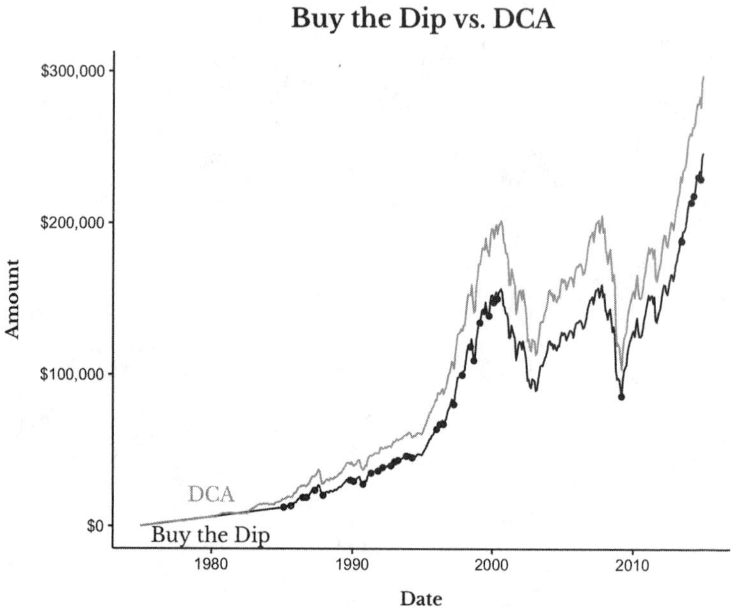

As you can see, DCA grows an early lead over Buy the Dip and never gives it up. Despite the handful of big dips that the Buy the Dip strategy purchases in this time period, because they happen *later* in the time period, there is less time for them to compound.

You can see this more clearly if we look at the purchase growth plot for this period in the next chart.

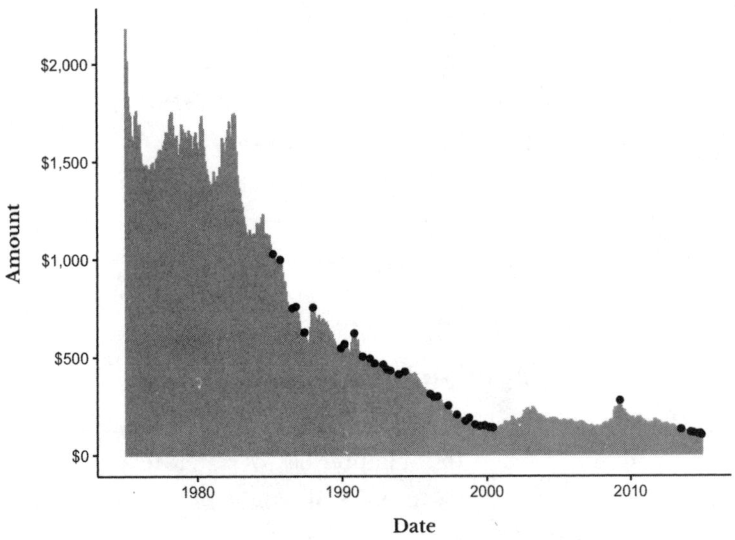

Unlike the 1928–1957 or 1996–2019 simulations, Buy the Dip does not get to buy large dips *early* in the period during the 1975–2014 simulation. It does get to buy the March 2009 dip, but this happens so late in the simulation that it doesn't provide enough benefit to outperform DCA.

This illustrates that even with perfect information, Buy the Dip typically underperforms DCA. Therefore, if you build up cash in hopes of buying at the next bottom, you will likely be worse off than if you had bought as soon as you could.

Why?

Because while you wait for your beloved dip, you may find that it never comes. As a result, you end up missing out on months (or more) of compound growth as the market keeps rising and leaves you behind.

What makes the Buy the Dip strategy even more problematic is that up until now we have assumed that you would know exactly when you were at the market bottom. But, in reality, you will never know this with certainty. You will never have perfect market timing foresight.

I ran a variation of Buy the Dip where the strategy misses the bottom by two months, and guess what? Missing the bottom by just two months leads to underperforming DCA 97% of the time! Even someone who is decent at calling market bottoms and can predict them to within two months of the absolute bottom would still lose in the long run.

Putting It All Together

The main purpose of this chapter is to reiterate that saving up cash to buy the dip is futile. You would be far better off if you Just Keep Buying. And, as we saw in the previous chapter, it's generally better to invest sooner rather than later. Taken together, the conclusion is undeniable:

You should invest as soon and as often as you can.

This is the core ethos of Just Keep Buying and one that transcends both time and space.

For example, if you had picked a random month since 1926 to start buying a broad basket of U.S. stocks and kept buying them for the rest of the following decade, there is a 98% chance that you would have beaten sitting in cash and an 83% chance that you would have beaten 5-Year Treasury notes as well. More importantly, you would have typically earned about 10.5% on your money while doing so.[87]

If you were to run a similar analysis for a group of global stocks since 1970, you would have beaten cash in 85% of 10-year periods and earned about 8% on your money.[88]

In both cases the method for building wealth is the same—Just Keep Buying.

After all, if God can't beat dollar-cost averaging, what chance do you have?

God Still Has the Last Laugh

One of the most important things I learned while crunching all the numbers for this chapter is how dependent our investment lives are on timing luck (formally known as *sequence of return risk,* which will be covered in the next chapter).

For example, the best 40-year period I analyzed in this chapter was from 1922–1961, where your $48,000 (40 years × 12 months × $100) in total DCA purchases grew to over $500,000 (after adjusting for inflation).

Compare this to the worst period 1942–1981, where your $48,000 in total purchases only grew to $153,000. That is a difference of 226%, which is much larger than any divergences we saw between the DCA and Buy the Dip timing strategies!

Unfortunately, this illustrates that your strategy is less important than what the market does. God still has the last laugh.

With that being said, the role of luck in investing is where we turn in our next chapter.

15. WHY INVESTING DEPENDS ON LUCK

And why you shouldn't care

IN THE LATE 1970s the view in the publishing world was that an author should never produce more than one book a year. The thinking was that publishing more than one book a year would dilute the brand name of the author.

This was a bit of a problem for Stephen King, who was writing books at a rate of two per year. Instead of slowing down, King decided to publish his additional works under the pen name of Richard Bachman.

Over the next few years, every book King published sold millions, while Richard Bachman remained relatively unknown. King was a legend. Bachman a nobody.

However, this all changed when a bookstore clerk in Washington, D.C. named Steve Brown noticed the similarity of writing styles between King and Bachman. After being confronted with the evidence, King confessed and agreed to an interview with Brown a few weeks later.

Frans Johnson's book, *The Click Moment: Seizing Opportunity in an Unpredictable World,* tells the story of what happened next:

> "In 1986, once the secret was out, King re-released all of Bachman's published works under his real name and they skyrocketed up bestseller lists. The first run of *Thinner* had sold 28,000 copies—the most of any Bachman book and above average for an author. The moment it became known that Richard Bachman was Stephen King, however, the Bachman books took off with sales quickly reaching 3 million copies."

This phenomenon isn't exclusive to Stephen King either. J.K. Rowling published a book called *The Cuckoo's Calling* under the pen name Robert Galbraith only to be outed by someone performing advanced text analytics.[89]

Shortly after the public discovered Galbraith was Rowling, *The Cuckoo's Calling* increased in sales by over 150,000%, shooting to the #3 on Amazon's bestseller list after previously being ranked 4,709th.[90]

Both King and Rowling's foray into undercover writing reveals a harsh truth about the role of luck in success. While King and Rowling's achievements aren't solely the result of chance, it's hard to explain how they sold millions while Bachman and Galbraith didn't, despite being of similar quality. Luck plays an important role.

Unfortunately, the same mysterious forces that can make or break your career can also have an outsized impact on your investment results as well.

How Your Birth Year Affects Your Investment Returns

You might think that something as random as the year you are born would have little impact on your ability to build wealth, but you'd be wrong. If you were to look throughout history, you'd see that equity markets tend to go through fits and starts that aren't easy to predict.

To illustrate this, consider the S&P 500's annualized return by decade since 1910 (including dividends and adjusted for inflation).

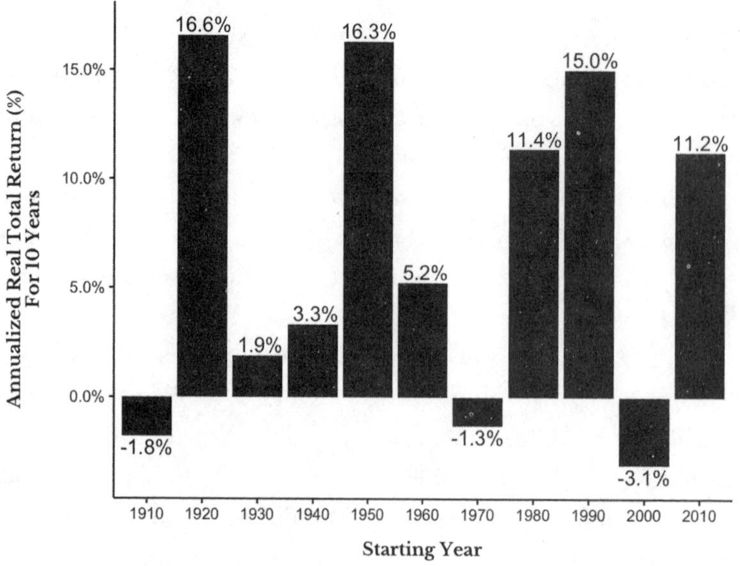

As you can see, depending on which decade you were investing in, you could have received annual returns of positive 16.6% or *negative* 3.1% over a 10-year timeframe. This is an annualized return spread of 20 percentage points that has nothing to do with your investment choices.

However, this is just the tip of the investment iceberg. Because if you look over 20-year periods, the variance in annualized returns is still large.

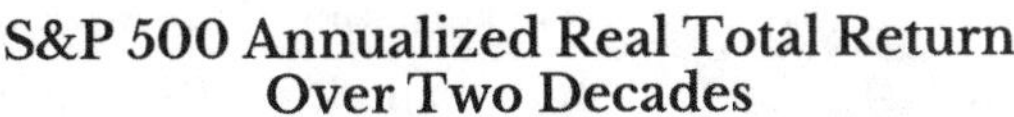

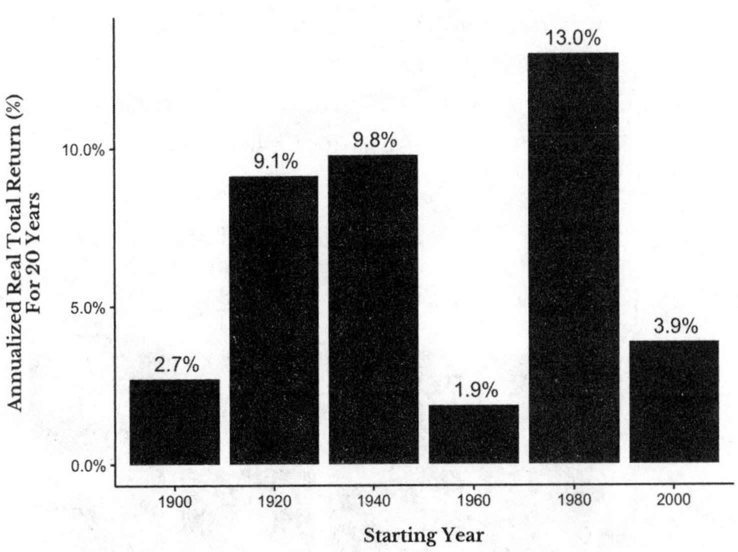

Over 20 years, depending on which period you were investing in, you could have received 13.0% annual returns at best, or 1.9% annual returns at worst.

Due to this variation in returns over time, even investors with legitimate skill can still underperform those who just got lucky.

For example, if you had beaten the market by 5% each year from 1960–1980, you would have made *less money* than if you had underperformed the market by 5% each year from 1980–2000. This is true since the annualized real total return from 1960–1980 was 1.9%, while it was 13% from 1980–2000 (and 1.9% + 5% < 13% – 5%).

Think about that. Someone who was an incredible investor (who beat the market by 5% annually) would have made less money than a terrible investor (who underperformed by 5% annually) simply because of *when* they started investing. This example is cherry-picked, but demonstrates how skilled investors (outperformers) can lose to unskilled investors (underperformers) simply because they were invested during a difficult market environment.

The only good news here is that, over 30-year periods, the differences in annualized returns are far less pronounced.

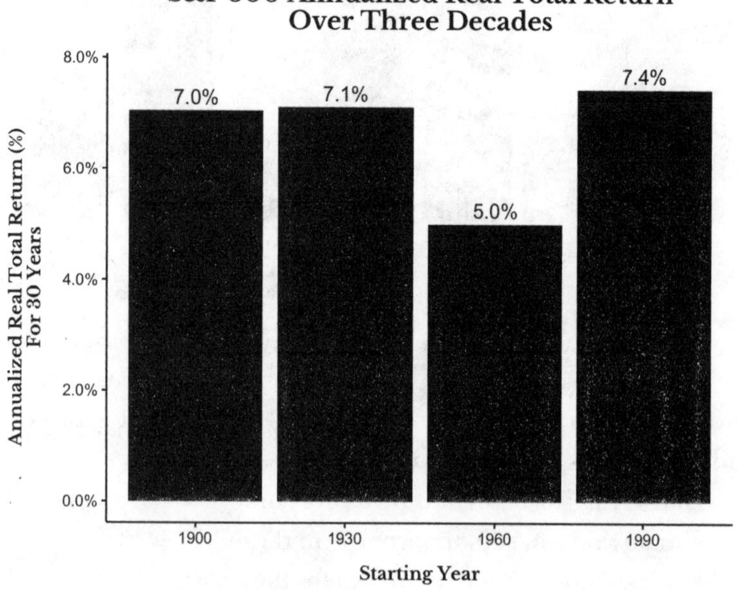

Though we are only looking at four non-overlapping periods of data, it suggests that long-term investors in U.S. equities are typically rewarded for their efforts. Though this may not hold in the future, based on the record of history, I think it will.

Now that we have examined how luck can impact your total investment return over time, we also need to consider *the order* of your investment returns and why they matter.

Why the Order of Your Returns Matters

Suppose you put $10,000 into an investment account that experienced the following returns over the next four years:

- +25% in year 1
- +10% in year 2
- −10% in year 3
- −25% in year 4

Would you have been better off if you had gotten the returns in a different order? For example, imagine you got the same returns as above but in reverse order:

- −25% in year 1
- −10% in year 2
- +10% in year 3
- +25% in year 4

Will that affect the final portfolio value of your initial $10,000 investment?

The answer is no.

When making a single investment, without adding or subtracting additional funds, the order of your returns does not matter. If you don't believe me, spend a minute trying to prove how 3 × 2 × 1 is not equal to 1 × 2 × 3.

But what if you add (or subtract) money over time? Does the return order matter then?

Yes. When you are adding money *over time* you are placing more emphasis on your future returns since you have more money at stake at a later period in time. As a result, the importance of your future returns increases as you add more money. This means that, after adding funds, a negative return will cost you more *in absolute dollar terms* than if that negative return had occurred before you added those funds.

And since most individual investors add assets over time, the ordering of investment returns matters more than almost any other financial risk you will face. This is formally known as *sequence of return risk* and can be explained with the following thought experiment.

Imagine saving $5,000 a year for 20 years under two different scenarios:

1. **Negative Returns Early**: You receive –10% returns for 10 years followed by +10% returns for 10 years.
2. **Negative Returns Late**: You receive +10% returns for 10 years followed by –10% returns for 10 years.

Both scenarios have the same returns and the same total contributions of $100,000 over a 20-year period. The only difference is *the timing* of the returns relative to the invested funds.

Let's see in the next chart how you would end up by looking at the final value of your portfolio under each scenario. Note that I included a vertical line at the 10-year mark to highlight when the return sequence flips from –10% to +10% (and vice versa).

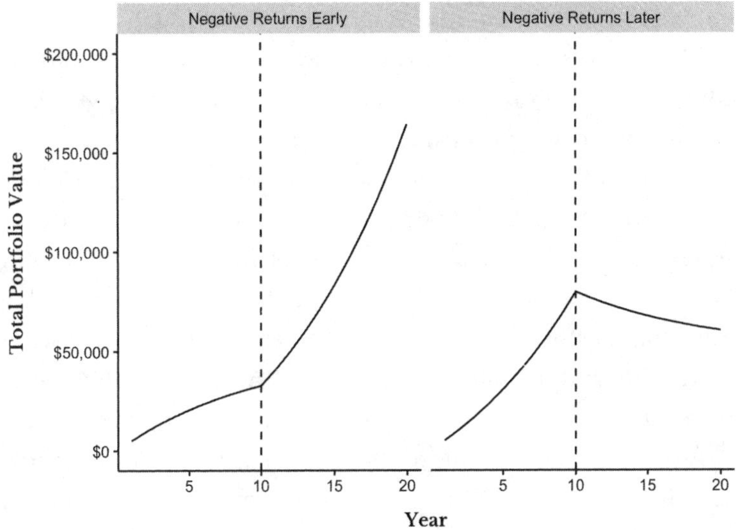

As you can see, though you invested $5,000 each year, your final portfolio value differs significantly based on *the order* of your returns. The Negative Returns Early scenario ends with over $100,000 more than the Negative Returns Late scenario, even though both invested the same amount of money over time.

Getting the negative returns later in life (when you have the most money in play) leaves you far worse off than if you experienced those negative returns when you first started investing. In other words, the end is everything.

The End is Everything

Given that you (like most investors) will be accumulating assets for most of your life, this means that your most important investment returns will occur as you approach and enter retirement. If you were to experience large negative returns during this time, your nest egg could be reduced significantly, and you may not live long enough to see it recover.

What makes this scenario even worse is that you could be subtracting money during retirement, which would deplete your nest egg at an even faster rate.

Fortunately, the research suggests that a bad year or two in the markets isn't likely to have a significant impact on your retirement. As financial expert Michael Kitces discovered, "In fact, a deeper look at the data reveals that there is remarkably little relationship between returns in the first year or two of retirement, and the safe withdrawal rate that can be sustained in the portfolio... even if retirement starts out with a market crash."[91]

But what Kitces did find was that *the first decade* of returns (specifically inflation-adjusted returns) can have a significant impact. While one or two bad years is no big deal, a bad decade can cause serious financial harm. This illustrates why the investment returns during your first decade of retirement are so important.

Given this information, below is the decade when your investment returns will matter most based on your year of birth (assuming you retire at 65):

- Born 1960 => 2025–2035
- Born 1970 => 2035–2045
- Born 1980 => 2045–2055
- Born 1990 => 2055–2065
- Born 2000 => 2065–2075

Since I was born in 1989, this implies that I need my best returns from 2055–2065 (when I should have the most money invested). But even if I don't get the stellar returns that I desire, I know that there are ways to lessen the impact of luck on my finances.

How to Mitigate Bad Luck as an Investor

Despite the importance of luck in investing, your financial future is more in your control than you might realize. This is because no matter what markets do, you always get to decide how much you save/invest, which assets you invest in, and how often you invest. Investing isn't just about the cards that you are dealt in life, but how you play your hand.

As much as I respect the importance of luck in both investing and in life, I am not powerless to it. You shouldn't be either. There is almost always something you can do to counteract bad luck both before and after it occurs.

For example, if you are on the verge of retirement and you are worried about a bad decade for markets, here are a few ways in which you can limit your downside:

- **Adequately diversify with enough low-risk assets (e.g., bonds)**. Having a large bond portion as you enter retirement may be able to provide enough income to prevent you from selling equities at depressed prices.
- **Consider withdrawing less money during market downturns**. If you had originally planned on withdrawing 4% a year, temporarily lowering your withdrawal rate could help mitigate the damage done by a market crash.
- **Consider working part-time to supplement your income**. One of the benefits of retirement is that you get to decide what you want to do with your time. This means you could start working on something new to generate income instead of selling down your existing assets.

Even if you aren't on the verge of retirement, using proper diversification and making temporary changes to your income/spending can be incredibly helpful during difficult financial times.

And if you are a younger investor, the best way to mitigate bad luck is time itself. Since most markets go up most of the time, as we saw in chapter 13, this means that time is a young investor's friend.

Regardless of your financial situation, you will always have options to combat bouts of bad luck. More importantly, bad luck isn't always as bad as it seems. Sometimes it's just a part of the game. This is why the subject of our next chapter is market volatility and why you have no reason to fear it.

16. WHY YOU SHOULDN'T FEAR VOLATILITY

The price of admission for successful investing

FRED SMITH WAS at his wit's end. He had already sunk most of his net worth into starting a package delivery company called Federal Express (later FedEx) and he had just been denied additional funding from General Dynamics, his previous funding partner.

It was Friday and Smith knew that he had to make a payment of $24,000 the following Monday for the coming week's jet fuel. There was just one problem—Federal Express only had $5,000 in its bank account.

Smith did the only rational thing he could think of—he flew to Vegas and gambled the remaining $5,000 playing blackjack.

When Monday morning arrived, Roger Frock, Federal Express's General Manager and Chief of Operations, checked the company bank account and was in shock. Immediately Frock confronted Smith and asked what had happened.

Smith confessed, "The meeting with the General Dynamics board was a bust and I knew we needed money for Monday, so I took a plane to Las Vegas and won $27,000."

That's right. Smith had gambled the company's last $5,000 playing blackjack and won big.

Still in shock, Frock asked Smith how he could risk the company's last $5,000 in such a way. Smith responded, "What difference did it make? Without the funds for the fuel companies, we couldn't have flown anyway."[92]

Smith's story illustrates an important lesson about risk and the cost of inaction—sometimes the biggest risk you can take is taking no risk at all.

The is especially true in investing. Though the financial media will often mention when a hedge fund blows up or a lottery winner goes bankrupt, how often do they discuss the person sitting in cash for decades who fails to build wealth? Almost never.

The issue is that those who play it safe don't see the consequences of their actions for many years. But those consequences can be just as damaging as the consequences of taking too much risk.

Nowhere is this more evident than when examining market volatility and those who try to avoid it. Because avoiding too much downside can severely limit your upside.

Therefore, if you want the upside—building wealth—you have to accept volatility and periodic declines that come with it.

It's the price of admission for long-term investment success. But how much should you accept? And what is the price of admission?

This chapter uses a simple thought experiment to address this.

The Price of Admission

Imagine there exists a market genie who approaches you every December 31st with information about the U.S. stock market for the next year.

Unfortunately, this genie cannot tell you which individual stocks to buy or how the market will perform. However, the genie does know how much the stock market will be down *at its worst point* in the next 12 months (the maximum intrayear drawdown).

My question to you is: How much would the market have to decline in the next year for you to forgo investing in stocks altogether to invest in bonds instead?

For example, if the genie said the market would be down 40% at some point next year, would you stay invested or sit it out? What about down 20%? Where's your limit?

Before you answer the question, let me provide you with some data so that you are better informed. Since 1950, the average maximum intrayear drawdown for the S&P 500 has been 13.7%, with a median drawdown of 10.6%.

This means that if you had bought the S&P 500 on January 2 of any given year since 1950, half the time the market would be down by 10.6% (or more) from the start of the year and half the time it would decline by less than 10.6%. On average, the market declines by about 13.7% at some point within a given year.

The first plot illustrates the maximum intrayear drawdown for the S&P 500 since 1950.

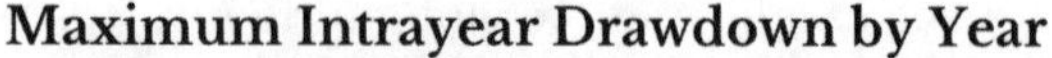

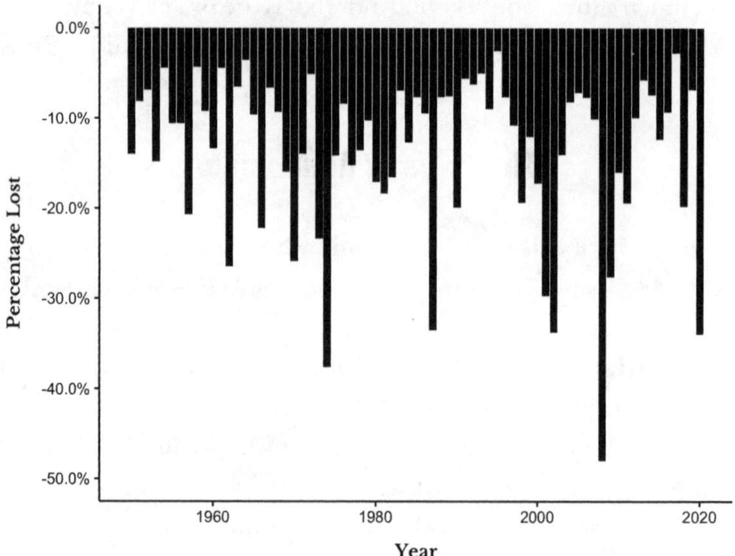

As you can see, the worst decline occurred in 2008 when the S&P 500 was down 48% on the year in late November.

After seeing this data, at what level of decline would you choose to sit things out?

Let's start by assuming you go ultra-conservative with your money. You tell the genie that you would avoid stocks in any year where there was a drawdown of 5% or more and invest in bonds instead.

We will call this the Avoid Drawdowns strategy because it invests all of its money in bonds in years when stock drawdowns are too high (in this case 5% or more) and moves that money to stocks in all other years. The Avoid Drawdowns strategy is either entirely in bonds or entirely in stocks in any given year.

If you had invested $1 in the Avoid Drawdowns strategy from 1950–2020 (while avoiding all years with 5% drawdowns or greater), it would have cost you dearly. By 2018 you would have

90% less money than if you had owned stocks the whole time ("Buy & Hold"). The following chart illustrates this situation (note: the y-axis is a logarithmic scale to better illustrate changes over time).

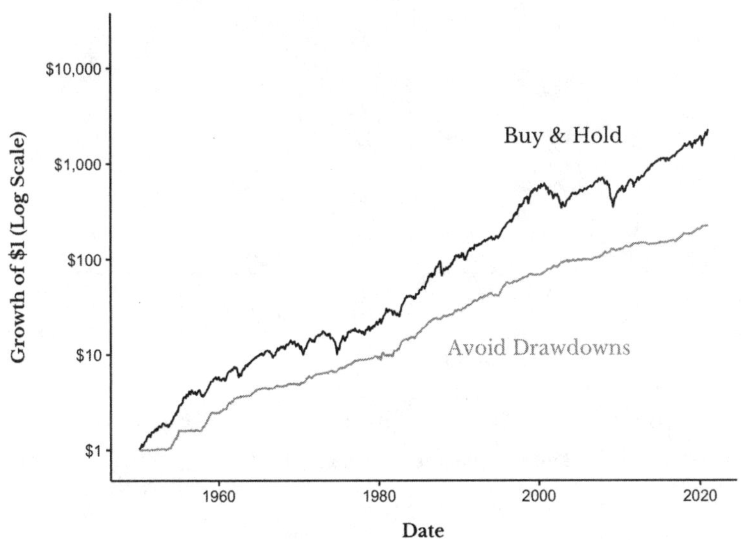

The reason you underperform Buy & Hold is simply because you are out of the market too often. In fact, you would spend 90% of all years (all but seven since 1950) in bonds.

You can see this by looking at the next plot which highlights (in gray) when the Avoid Drawdowns strategy is in bonds. Note that this plot is identical to the previous plot except I've included gray shading when the Avoid Drawdowns strategy is invested in bonds.

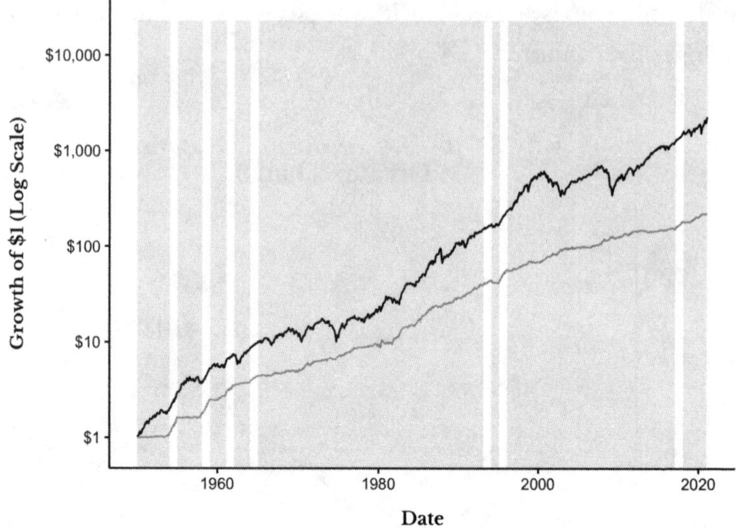

As you can see, since you are in bonds so often, you rarely participate in the growth of the stock market. By taking no risk at all you end up underperforming Buy and Hold by a significant amount.

Avoiding drawdowns of 5% or more is obviously too safe of a route to take, so what if we went to the other extreme and only avoided drawdowns bigger than 40%?

If you did so, the only year you would have been out of the market since 1950 was 2008. This is the exact point when the Avoid Drawdowns strategy differs from Buy and Hold, as shown in the next chart.

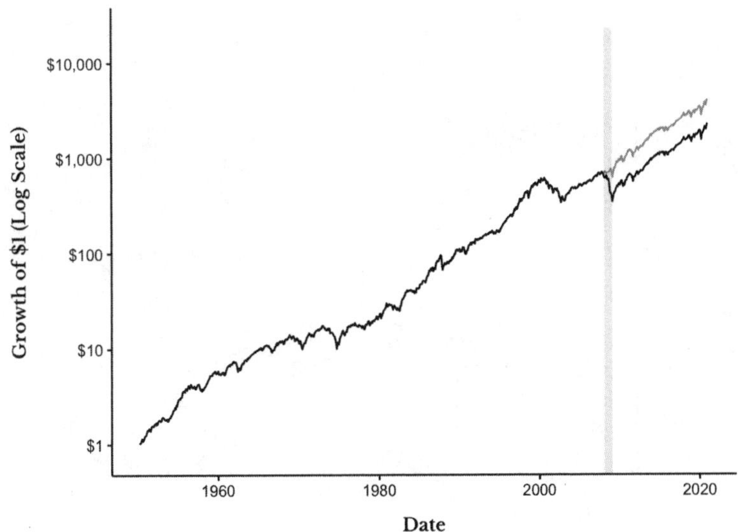

While the Avoid Drawdowns strategy (gray line) does beat Buy and Hold (black line) over time, it doesn't beat it by much. It can do far better if it was more conservative.

How conservative should it be? What size drawdown should you avoid if you want to maximize your wealth?

The answer is 15% and above.

Investing in bonds in years when the market declines by 15% (or more) and investing in stocks in all other years would maximize your long-term wealth.

In fact, if you were to be in bonds in each year when the market declined by 15% (or more), you would outperform Buy and Hold by over 10x from 1950–2020.

The next plot shows Buy and Hold versus the Avoid Drawdowns strategy when the Avoid Drawdowns strategy avoids drawdowns of 15% or greater.

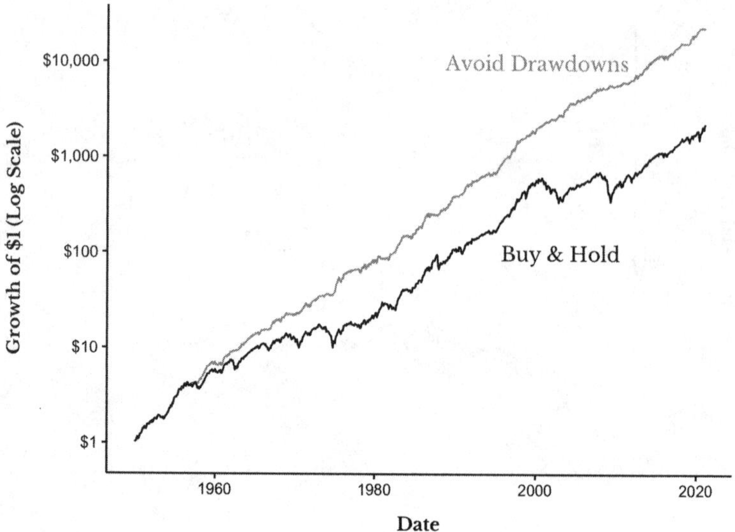

This is the Goldilocks zone of drawdown avoidance. It's not too risky, but it's not too timid either. In fact, this strategy spends about one-third of its time in bonds when avoiding intrayear drawdowns of 15% or more. The next plot illustrates the time in bonds with gray shaded areas.

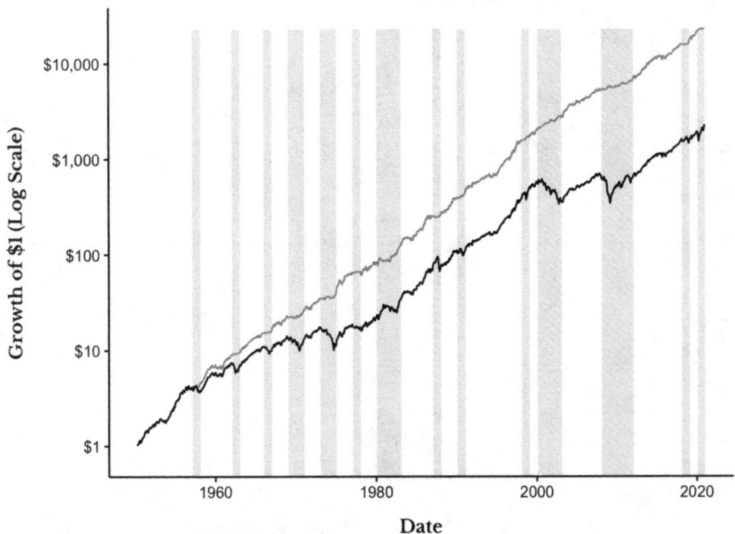

Increasing the drawdown threshold above 15% (e.g., 20%, 30%, etc.) gives you worse performance because you spend more time in stocks when they are more likely to lose money.

Why?

Because larger intrayear drawdowns for the S&P 500 are generally correlated with worse return performance by year end. Looking at a plot of annual returns against intrayear drawdowns for the S&P 500 illustrates this well.

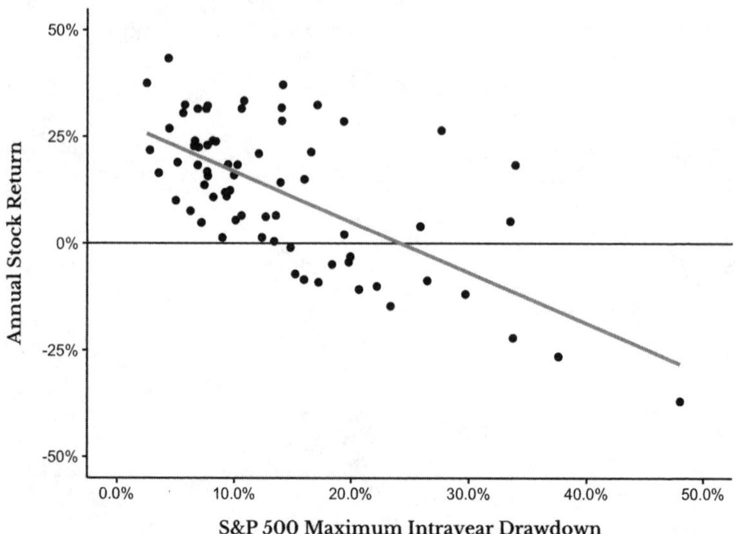

As you can see, there is a negative relationship between intrayear drawdowns and annual returns. Those years that have big declines don't usually end well for the stock market.

However, not all declines are bad. In fact, the S&P 500 has had a positive return in every year since 1950 with an intrayear drawdown of 10% or less.

There is No Magic Genie

This analysis implies that there is some level of intrayear decline we want to accept (0%–15%) and some level which we should avoid (>15%) if we want to maximize our wealth.

This is the price of admission for an equity investor. Because markets won't give you a free ride without some bumps along the way. You have to experience some downside in order to earn your upside.

And, as the plots above illustrate, avoiding these bumps can be beneficial, though knowing when they will occur is impossible. Unfortunately, there is no magic genie.

What do we have instead?

We have the ability to diversify. We can diversify what assets we own and we can diversify when we own them. Buying a diverse set of income-producing assets *over time* is one of the best ways to combat volatility when it rears its ugly head.

More importantly, you have to accept that volatility is just a part of the game. It comes with the territory of being an investor. You don't have to just take it from me, though. Consider the wisdom of Charlie Munger, Warren Buffett's long-time business partner:

> "If you're not willing to react with equanimity to a market price decline of 50% two or three times a century, you're not fit to be a common shareholder and you deserve the mediocre result you're going to get."

Munger, like many other great investors, was willing to stomach market volatility. What about you?

If you still fear volatility, then you might need to reframe your thinking on market crashes. For that, we turn to our next chapter.

17.
HOW TO BUY DURING A CRISIS

Why you should stay calm in a panic

I WILL NEVER FORGET what I was doing on the morning of March 22, 2020. It was a Sunday and I was on my way to get groceries from my local Fairway at 30th Street and 2nd Avenue in Manhattan.

Less than 48 hours earlier, the S&P 500 had finished the week down 3.4% and was now 32% off its highs from a month prior. I only remember this because I was struggling to justify to myself how the market could recover with the global economy grinding to a halt as a result of the pandemic.

Indoor dining had been shut down in New York City, the NBA season had been suspended, and the news of canceled weddings had just started to trickle into my inbox. I knew others were panicking as well because I was receiving an increasing amount of worried texts from friends and family:

> Is the bottom in?
> Should I sell my stocks?
> How much worse could it get from here?

To be honest, I had no clue. But I had to find a way of thinking about this crisis to keep myself (and those that had reached out to me) sane.

As I took the escalator down into the atrium of the store, I saw a huge assortment of flowers for sale. The flowers were always there at the base of the escalator, but on this particular Sunday morning I happened to notice that a man was taking his time to arrange them.

This was the moment when I realized that everything was going to be okay. Even as the world was crumbling all around me, somehow, the flower guy was still there trying to sell his flowers.

Something about that moment stuck with me. Maybe it was because of how audacious it seemed. Why would I need flowers at a time like this? I need canned goods and toilet paper.

But it wasn't audacious. It was a moment of normalcy. If the flower guy still has hope, why shouldn't I? I never told anyone about this private realization, but it lifted my spirits when I needed it most.

What happened next was a train of thought that allowed me to come up with a new framework for investing amid a financial panic. What follows is that framework, which I hope will change the way you think about buying assets during *future* market crashes.

I wrote this chapter as a guide for you to refer back to when the financial world looks most uncertain. When the perfect storm hits, as it inevitably will at some point in the future, I want you to return to this chapter and read it again. If you get it right, it will be worth what you paid for this book, many, many times over. May the investment gods have mercy upon your soul.

Why Market Crashes are Buying Opportunities

The 18th century banker Baron Rothschild reportedly said, "The time to buy is when there's blood in the streets." Rothschild made a small fortune using this motto in the panic that followed the Battle of Waterloo. But how true is it?

In chapter 14 I did everything in my power to convince you that it would be unwise to hold cash in hopes of buying during a market correction (i.e., when there's blood in the streets). The *infrequency* of these events makes hoarding cash unprofitable for most investors most of the time.

However, the data suggests that if you find yourself with investable cash during a market correction, it might be one of the best investment opportunities you will ever get.

The reasoning is simple—every dollar invested during the crash will grow to far more than one invested in months prior, *assuming that the market eventually recovers.*

To demonstrate this, let's imagine that you decided to invest $100 every month into U.S. stocks from September 1929 to November 1936. This period covers the 1929 crash and the recovery that followed.

If you were to follow such a strategy, the first chart shows what each $100 monthly payment would have grown to by the time U.S. stocks recovered in November 1936 (including dividends and adjusting for inflation).

Final Growth of Each $100 Payment into U.S. Stocks

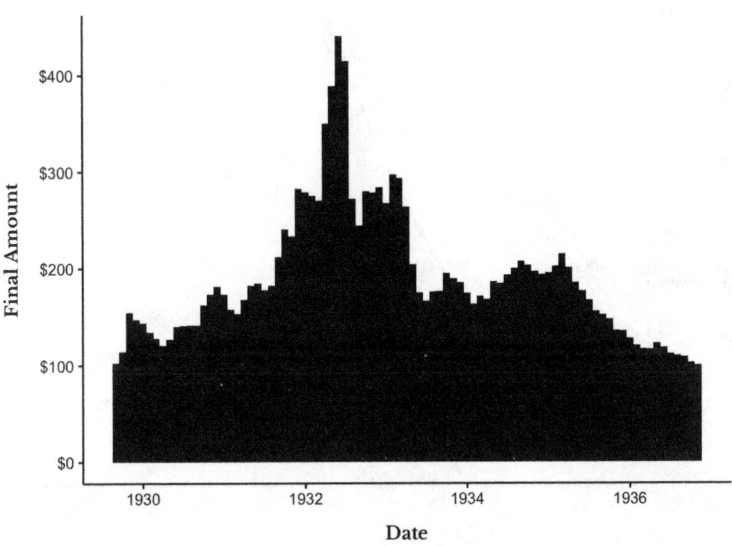

As you can see, the closer you bought to the bottom in the summer of 1932, the greater the long-term benefit of that purchase. Every $100 invested at the lows would grow to $440 by November 1936, which is roughly *three times greater* than the growth of a $100 purchase made in 1930 (which grew to $150 by 1936).

Most market crashes won't provide such 3x opportunities, but many of them do provide a 50%–100% upside.

Where does this upside come from?

It comes from a simple mathematical fact—every percentage loss requires an even larger percentage gain to get back to even.

Losing 10% requires an 11.11% gain to recover, losing 20% requires a 25% gain to recover, and losing 50% requires a 100% gain (a doubling) to recover. You can see this exponential relationship more clearly in the next chart.

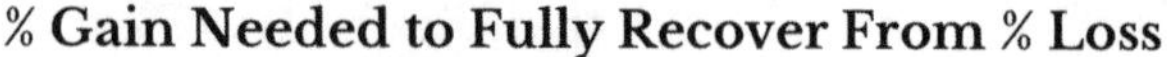

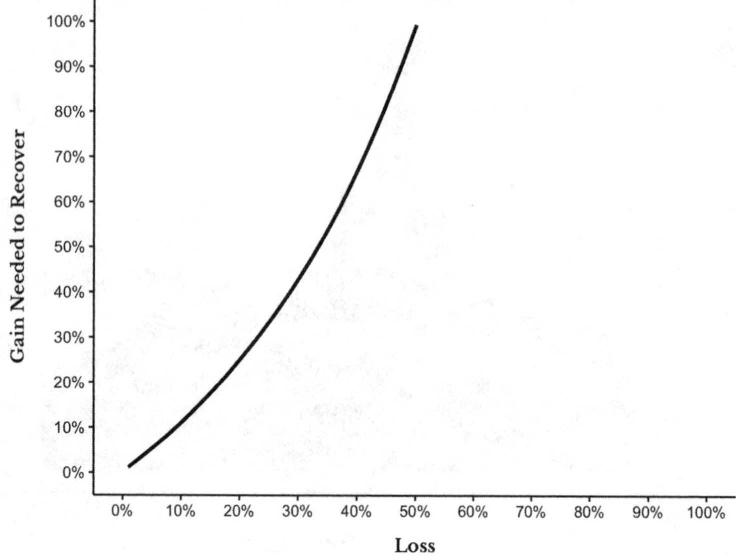

On March 22, 2020, when I had the realization that the world was going to make it through the COVID-19 pandemic, the S&P 500 was down about 33%.

From the previous chart, this implied that the market would have to gain 50% to get back to even. Every dollar invested on March 23, 2020 (the next trading day) would eventually grow to $1.50, assuming the market recovered to its previous level at some point in the future.

Thankfully, the market did recover and in record time. Within six months the S&P 500 was making all-time highs once again. Those who had bought on March 23 had a 50% gain within half a year.

However, even if the recovery had taken years longer, buying on March 23, 2020 would still have been a great decision. All you had to do was to reframe how you thought about the upside.

Reframing the Upside

Despite the seemingly obvious upside to buying on March 23, 2020, many investors were afraid to do so. Unfortunately, the problem seemed to be how they thought about the issue.

For example, if I had asked you on March 22, 2020, "How long do you think it will take for the market to recover from its 33% loss?" what would you have said?

Will it take a month before it hits a new all-time high?

A year?

A decade?

Based on your answer, we can then back out your expected annual return for the market going forward.

How?

Well, we know that a 33% loss requires a 50% gain to get back to even. So, once I know how *long* you expect the recovery to take, I can turn that 50% upside into an annualized number.

The formula for this is:

Expected Annual Return = (1 + % Gain Needed to Recover)^(1/Number of Years to Recover) – 1

But since we know that the "% Gain Needed to Recover" is 50%, we can plug in this number and simplify this equation to:

Expected Annual Return = (1.5)^(1/Number of Years to Recover) – 1

So, if you think the market recovery will take:

- 1 year, then your expected annual return = 50%
- 2 years, then your expected annual return = 22%
- 3 years, then your expected annual return = 14%
- 4 years, then your expected annual return = 11%
- 5 years, then your expected annual return = 8%

At the time, I thought the market would take one to two years to recover, meaning that every dollar I invested on March 23, 2020 was likely to grow by 22% (or more) annually for that two-year period.

More importantly, even those who expected the market to recover in five years would receive an 8% annual return if they bought on that day. This 8% return is very similar to the long-term average return of U.S. stocks.

This is why buying during this crisis was such a no-brainer. Even in the scenario where the market took half a decade to recover, you would still earn an 8% return while you waited.

This logic can be used during *any* future market crisis as well. Because if you had bought anytime the market was down by *at least* 30%, your future annualized returns would usually have been quite good.

The next chart illustrates this. It shows the distribution of your annualized returns if you were to buy during any month when U.S. stocks were down by 30% (or more) from 1920–2020. The returns shown are from when stocks first were down 30% (or more) until their next all-time high.

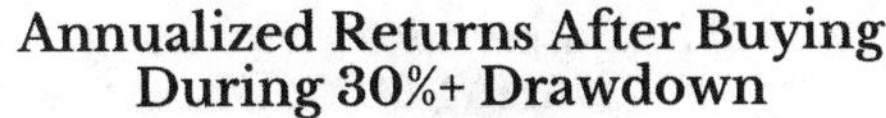

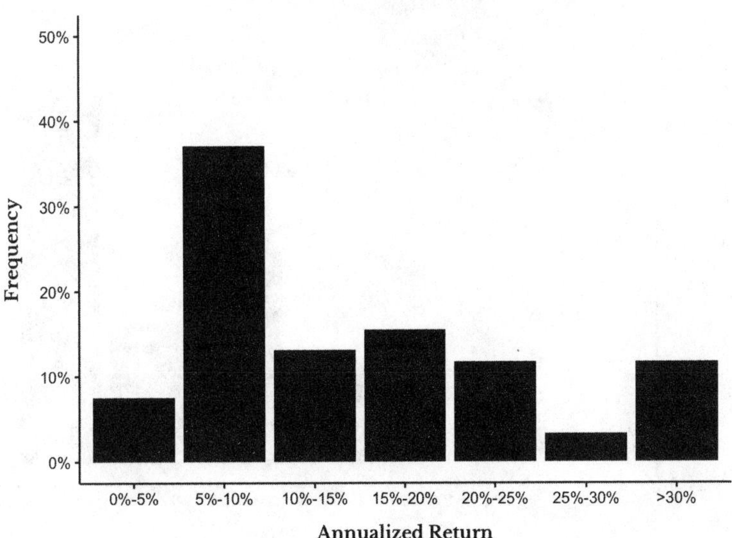

This chart implies that there is a less than 10% chance that you would have experienced 0%–5% annualized returns (including dividends and adjusting for inflation) when buying while the market was down at least 30%. In fact, more than half the time, your annualized return during the recovery would have exceeded 10% per year. You can see this if you add the 0%–5% bar and the 5%–10% bar together, which totals less than 50%.

But wait, there's more. If we subset the data to include only those periods where the market was down 50% (or more) from 1920–2020, your future returns would look even *more* attractive.

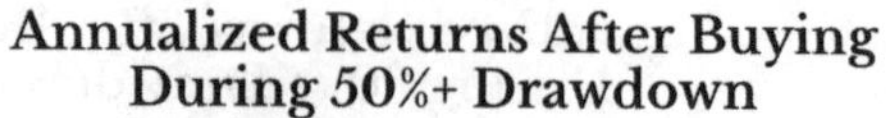

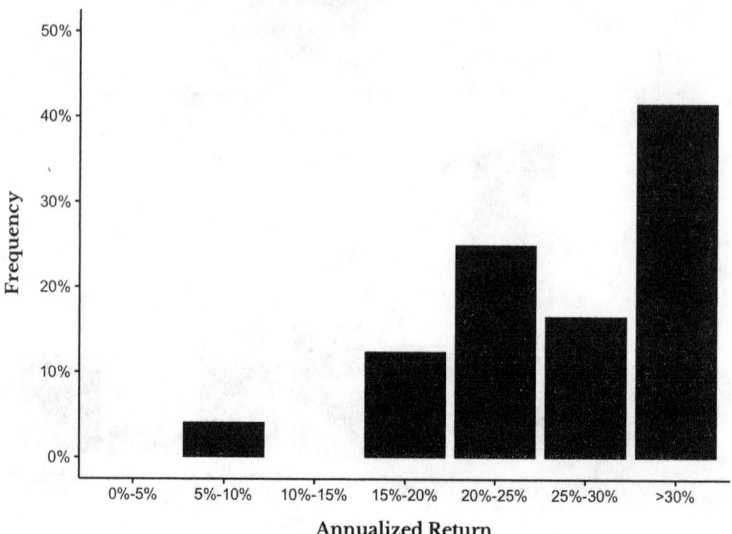

As you can see, when U.S. equity markets have gotten cut in half, the future annualized returns usually exceed 25%. This implies that when the market is down by 50%, it's time to back up the truck and invest as much as you can afford.

Of course, you may not have a lot of investable cash to take advantage of these rare occurrences when the market is in turmoil, because of wider economic uncertainty. However, *if you do* have the cash to spare then the data suggests that it would be wise to take advantage of this buying opportunity.

What About Markets That Don't Recover Quickly?

The analysis in this chapter has assumed that equity markets recover within a few years to a decade from a major crash. And while this is true most of the time, there have been notable exceptions.

For example, the Japanese stock market was still below its December 1989 highs over 30 years later at the end of 2020, as shown in the next chart.

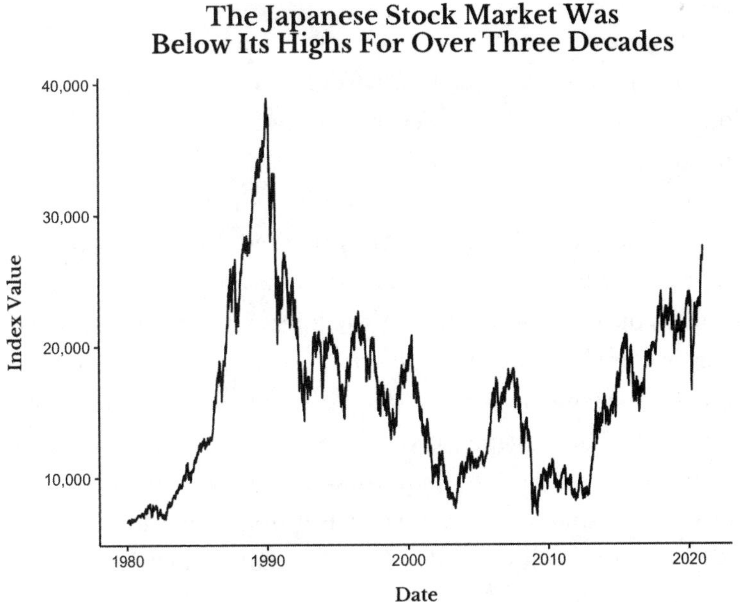

Anytime I discuss the importance of long-term investing, Japan is the primary counter example.

But there are others too. For example, at the end of 2020, Russian stocks were down 50% and Greek stocks were down

98% from their 2008 highs. Will these markets ever recover? I have no idea.

However, we shouldn't let the exceptions overwrite the rule—most equity markets go up most of the time.

Yes, there will be occasional periods of poor performance over longer time periods. After all, even U.S. stocks had their lost decade from 2000–2010.

But how likely is it that an equity market will lose money over a multi-decade time frame?

After analyzing developed equity market returns across 39 countries from 1841 to 2019, researchers estimated that the probability of losing relative to inflation over a 30-year investment horizon was 12%.[93]

This means that there is roughly a 1 in 8 chance that you could expect an investor in a particular equity market to see a loss of purchasing power over three decades. The Japanese stock market is one example of this.

However, as frightening as this may seem, this research gives me *more confidence* in global equity markets, not less. Because it implies that there is a 7 in 8 chance that an equity market will grow its purchasing power over the long run. I like those odds.

More importantly though, the researchers' estimates are based on a single investment into an equity market, not periodic purchases. For example, if you invested *all* of your cash at the Japanese market peak in 1989, you would have been underwater on that investment 30 years later. But how often do individual investors make these kinds of one-off big financial decisions? Almost never.

Most people are buying income-producing assets *over time,* not just once. If you control for these periodic purchases instead of using single investments, then the probability of losing money over multiple decades is smaller.

For example, if you had invested $1 into the Japanese stock

market on *every trading day* from 1980 until the end of 2020, your portfolio would still have earned you a slightly positive return over that 40-year period.

As the next chart illustrates, there were some periods over these four decades where your portfolio value exceeded your cost basis (how much you put in) and there were some periods where it didn't.

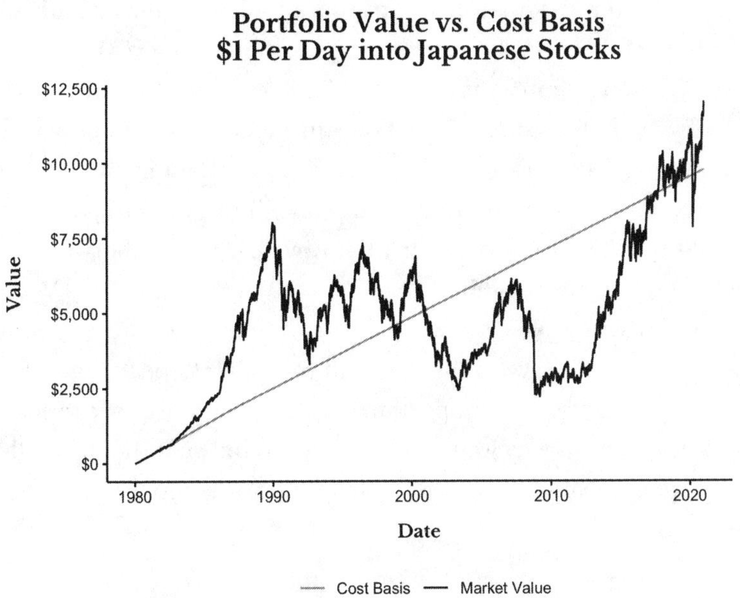

Anytime the market value (black line) is above the cost basis (gray line), this means that you had earned a positive return on your money. And anytime the market value is below the cost basis, you had earned a negative return on your money.

As you can see, by the end of 2020, the total return over this 40-year period was slightly positive. Not a great result, but also not bad considering Japan had one of the worst stock market performances on earth over the last 30 years.

Ultimately, the example of Japan illustrates that while you can lose money in some equity markets over multiple decades, the chances are lower if you are investing your money over time (as most individual investors are).

Nevertheless, some people will use Japan and other examples as an excuse to sit in cash until the dust settles during the next crisis. However, by the time the dust has settled, the market is typically already on its path upward.

Those timid souls who were too afraid to jump in end up getting left behind. I saw this happen with my own eyes in March 2020 and I am quite confident that I will see it again in the future.

If you are still too scared to buy during a crisis, I don't blame you though. It's easy to find examples throughout history where doing so would have been foolish in hindsight. But we can't invest based on exceptions or what *might* happen. Otherwise, we would never invest at all.

As Friedrich Neitzsche once said, "Ignore the past and you will lose an eye. Live in the past and you will lose both."

Knowing history is important, but obsessing over it can lead us astray. This is why we must invest based on what the data tells us. Jeremy Siegel, the famed financial author, summarized it best when he wrote:

> "Fear has a greater grasp on human action than does the impressive weight of historical evidence."

It's my favorite investing quote of all time and the only one fitting enough to end this chapter. I can only hope that it provides you with the mental fortitude to just keep buying the next time there's blood in the streets.

Now that we have spent time reviewing how to buy assets, even during the darkest of times, we turn out attention to an even more difficult question—when should you sell?

18. WHEN SHOULD YOU SELL?

On rebalancing, concentrated positions, and the purpose of investing

DESPITE OUR INVESTING philosophy to *Just Keep Buying*, there will inevitably come a point in your investment journey when you will need to sell. Unfortunately, choosing when to sell can be one of the most difficult decisions you ever make as an investor.

Why?

Because selling forces you to face off against two of the strongest behavioral biases in the investment world—fear of missing out on the upside and the fear of losing money on the downside. This emotional vice can make you question every investment decision that you make.

To avoid this mental turmoil, you should come up with a set of conditions under which you would sell *beforehand* instead of relying on your emotional state when you are thinking of getting out of a position. This will allow you to sell your investments on your own terms, to a predefined plan.

After coming up with a list of reasons myself, I can only find three cases under which you should consider selling an investment:

1. To rebalance.
2. To get out of a concentrated (or losing) position.
3. To meet your financial needs.

If you aren't rebalancing your portfolio, getting out of a concentrated (or losing) position, or trying to meet a financial need, then I see no reason to sell an investment—ever.

I say this because selling can have tax consequences, which is something we should avoid as much as possible. But before we dig into this and the three conditions listed above, let's discuss the overarching strategy as to *when* you should sell an investment.

Sell Right Away or Over Time?

In chapter 13 we examined why it's usually better to buy immediately rather than over time. The reasoning was simple: since most markets go up most of the time, waiting to buy usually means losing out on upside.

When it comes to *selling* an asset, we can use the same set of reasoning, but come to the opposite conclusion. Since markets tend to go up over time, the optimal thing to do is to sell *as late as possible*. Therefore, selling over time (or as late as possible) is usually better than selling right away.

Of course, there are circumstances where you would be better off if you sold immediately, but if you have the option, waiting as long as possible before selling or averaging out of your position will typically net you more money.

In other words, *buy quickly, but sell slowly.*

I raise this point because it can help guide all your future timing decisions around buying and selling investments. Unfortunately, even with this framework, nowhere in investing is there more confusion around timing than when it comes to rebalancing.

As we saw above, rebalancing is one of the three times it's acceptable to sell an investment. Let's look at that now.

What's Rebalancing Good for Anyways?

"Perfectly balanced, as all things should be."

Not only is this one of the more popular lines from Thanos, the leading villain in the Marvel Cinematic Universe, but it also has some practical applications when it comes to managing your portfolio.

In chapter 11 we discussed what assets you should invest in—however, we never discussed how that mix of assets will change over time. The solution to this problem in the investment world is *rebalancing.*

As a reminder, when you first set up your portfolio it should be according to your target allocation (the mix of assets that you believe will reach your financial goals). For example, you might have a target allocation of 60% U.S. stocks and 40% U.S. bonds. If you invested $1,000, this means that $600 would be in U.S. stocks and $400 would be in U.S. bonds.

However, without rebalancing, your portfolio would drift from its target allocation to be dominated by its highest returning assets. For example, if we made a single investment into a 60/40

U.S. stock/bond portfolio and never rebalanced it over 30 years, it would be mostly stocks by the end of the period.

As you can see in the first plot, over the period from 1930–1960, a single investment into a 60/40 portfolio that was never rebalanced would end up holding 90% stocks after 30 years.

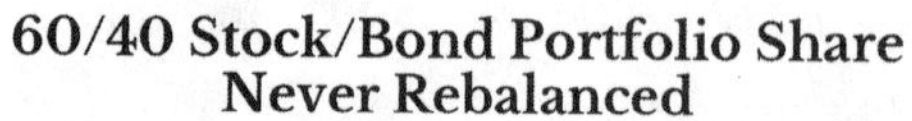

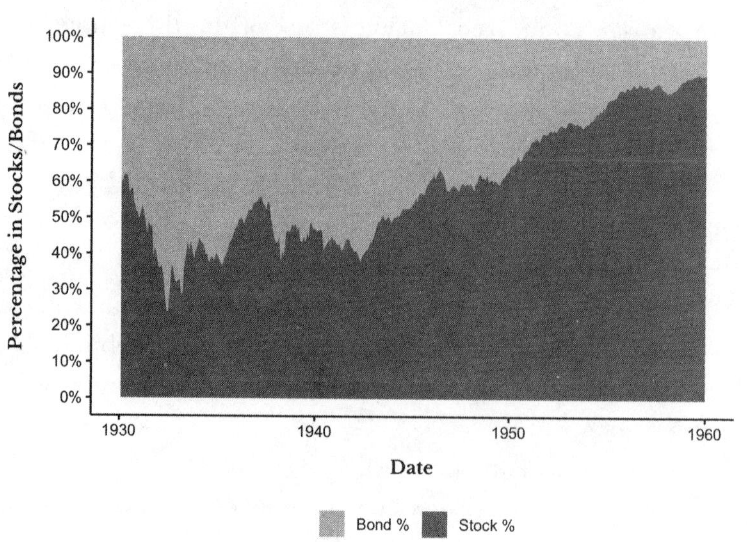

And it's not just the 1930s that exhibit this either. If we extend this analysis to every 30-year period from 1926–2020, we see similar results.

The next plot shows the final percentage that is in stocks for a 60/40 U.S. stock/bond portfolio after 30 years for two different rebalancing strategies—one that rebalances annually and one that never rebalances.

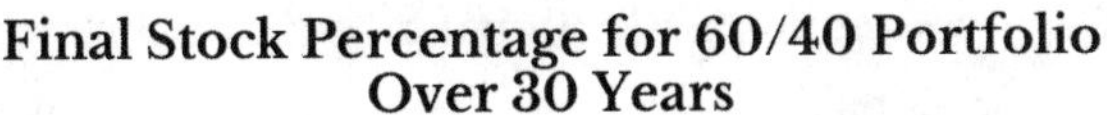

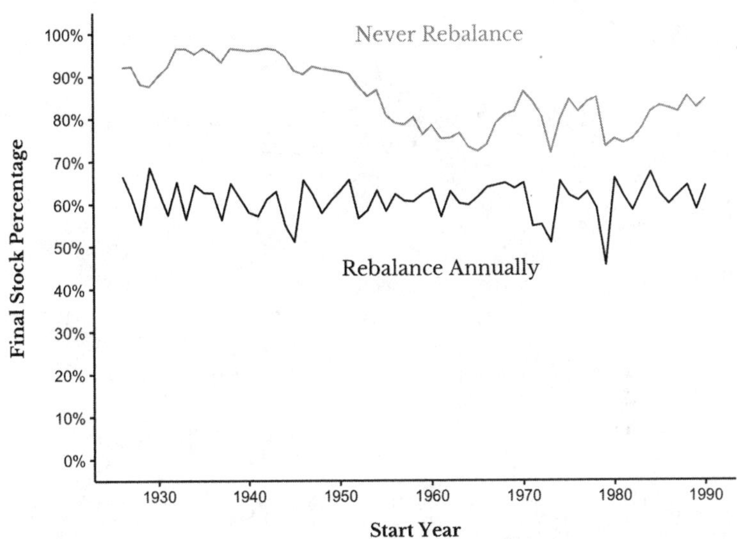

As you can see, the Rebalance Annually strategy tends to have portfolios with about 60% stocks at the end of the 30-year period. This makes logical sense as this strategy rebalances its stock holdings back to 60% of the portfolio each year.

On the other hand, the Never Rebalance strategy tends to have portfolios that end up with 75%–95% in stocks after 30 years. This occurs because U.S. stocks tend to outperform U.S. bonds over longer periods of time. As a result, they take over the portfolio.

From this simple fact we can then infer that the portfolio that never rebalances generally outperforms the one that rebalances annually. Why? Because nearly every time you rebalance you usually end up selling a higher-growth asset (stocks) to buy a lower-growth asset (bonds). This process inherently detracts from your total return over time.

We can see this more clearly by comparing the growth of

a $100 investment in the Rebalance Annually strategy versus the Never Rebalance strategy over 30 years. This is shown in the next plot.

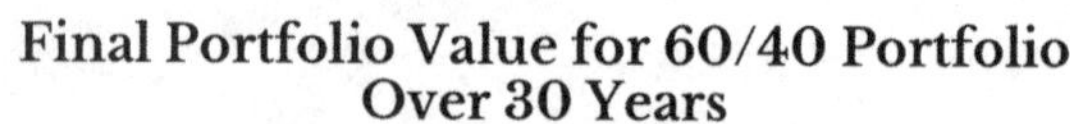

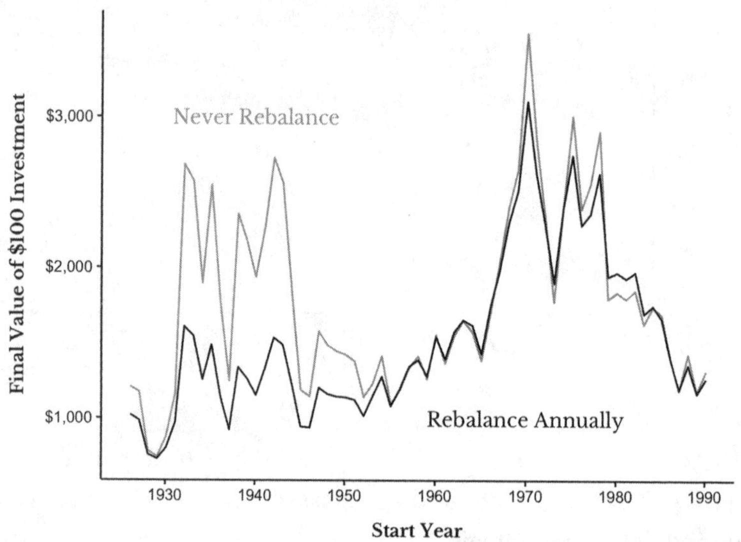

This plot illustrates that, most of the time, rebalancing between a higher-growth asset and a lower-growth asset in your portfolio tends to lower overall performance. The major exception to this occurred from 1980–2010, where U.S. bonds performed well and U.S. stocks got hammered in the final decade (2000–2010).

Given that rebalancing doesn't typically enhance returns, why do people still do it?

To reduce risk.

Rebalancing is all about controlling risk. If your target portfolio is a 60/40 U.S. stock/bond portfolio, without rebalancing you could end up moving towards a 75/25 portfolio or even a 95/5 portfolio within a few decades. As a result, your portfolio will have ended up taking on far more risk than you initially set out to take.

A simple illustration of this is considering the maximum drawdown of each of these strategies over a 30-year period. As a reminder, the maximum drawdown is the point at which the portfolio is down the most within a given period of time. So if you started with $100 and at your worst point were down to $30, that would be a maximum drawdown of 70%.

As the next plot illustrates, throughout most periods, never rebalancing leads to much larger drawdowns than a strategy that rebalances each year.

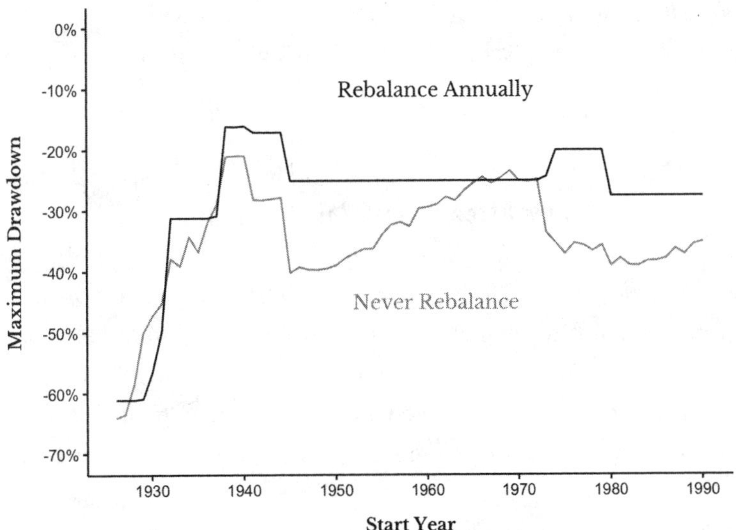

For example, if you had invested $100 in a 60/40 U.S. stock/bond portfolio in 1960 and never rebalanced it over 30 years, at its worst point your portfolio would be down by about 30% from its highest value. This is its maximum drawdown over the 30-year time frame and is represented in the plot above as the point on the gray line above 1960.

But, if you had rebalanced your portfolio each year back to its target allocation, you would have only seen a maximum decline of 25% instead. This is represented in the plot above as the point on the black line above 1960.

From this plot we can see that, most of the time, rebalancing reduces risk by shifting money from your higher-volatility assets (stocks) to your lower-volatility assets (bonds). However, during extended declines in equities (e.g., early 1930s and 1970s), it can do the opposite. In these instances, rebalancing actually *increases* volatility by selling bonds to buy stocks that continue to decline.

Though these circumstances are rare, they illustrate how periodic rebalancing is an imperfect solution to risk management. Nevertheless, I do recommend that most individual investors rebalance on some schedule. But figuring out the *right* schedule is the hard part.

How Often Should You Rebalance?

While I would love to give you the definitive answer on how often you should rebalance your portfolio, the truth is… no one knows. I've examined rebalancing periods ranging from once a month to once a year, yet I never been able to find a clear winner. Unfortunately, no rebalancing frequency consistently outperformed all the others.

Researchers at Vanguard came to a similar conclusion after analyzing the optimal rebalancing frequency for a 50/50 global stock/bond portfolio. Their paper states, "The risk-adjusted returns are not meaningfully different whether a portfolio is rebalanced monthly, quarterly, or annually; however, the number of rebalancing events and resulting costs increase significantly."[94]

And though their analysis examined rebalancing between assets with *different* risk characteristics (e.g., stocks and bonds), the same logic also holds when rebalancing between assets with *similar* risk characteristics. For example, the famed financial writer William Bernstein concluded that, "No one rebalancing period dominates," after examining rebalancing frequencies between pairs of global equities.[95]

All of these analyses illustrate the same thing—it doesn't matter when you rebalance, just that you do it on some periodic basis. As a result, I recommend an *annual* rebalance for two reasons:

1. It takes less time.
2. It coincides with our annual tax season.

Both of these are important for different reasons.

First, taking less time to monitor your investments each year allows you to spend more time doing the things you enjoy. This is why I am not a fan of rebalancing based on tolerance bands. Tolerance band rebalancing is when you rebalance your portfolio after the allocation gets too far away from your target allocation.

For example, if your portfolio is 60% stocks with a 10% tolerance band, you would rebalance it back to 60% every time the stock allocation was above 70% or below 50%. This method works fine, but also requires more monitoring than a periodic rebalance.

Second, annual rebalancing is also ideal because you can do it when you make other tax-related financial decisions. For example, if you sold an investment that you owed capital gains taxes on, you might find it helpful to rebalance your overall portfolio at the same time to save yourself the extra effort.

Whatever you decide to do when it comes to rebalancing frequency, avoiding unnecessary taxation is a must. This is why I don't recommend rebalancing frequently in your taxable accounts (i.e., brokerage account). Because every time you do, you have to pay Uncle Sam.

But what if we could rebalance without paying Uncle Sam? Is there a better way than selling?

A Better Way to Rebalance

While selling an asset to rebalance isn't the worst thing in the world, there is a way to rebalance your portfolio that involves no tax consequences at all—Just Keep Buying. That's right. You can buy your way back into a rebalanced portfolio. I call this an *accumulation rebalance* because you are rebalancing by buying your most underweight asset over time.

For example, imagine that your portfolio is currently 70% stocks and 30% bonds, but you really want it to be 60% stocks and 40% bonds. Instead of selling 10% of the stocks and buying 10% more in bonds, you would keep buying bonds until your allocation is back to 60/40.

Unfortunately, this method only works for those who are still in the accumulation phase of their investment journey. Once you can't save anymore, you have to sell to rebalance.

I like the accumulation rebalance strategy because it can reduce how much your portfolio draws down during market crashes. By adding money over time, you are constantly offsetting losses that develop in your portfolio. For example, going back to our 60/40 portfolio simulations, if you added money consistently over 30 years, you would have seen a much smaller maximum drawdown in most periods compared to not adding money.

As the next plot illustrates, rebalancing while adding funds each month can reduce your maximum drawdown by as much as half in some cases. Once again, this plot shows the maximum decline in your portfolio over a 30-year time frame. However, in this case it compares one portfolio that never adds funds to one that adds funds every month for 30 years using an accumulation rebalance strategy.

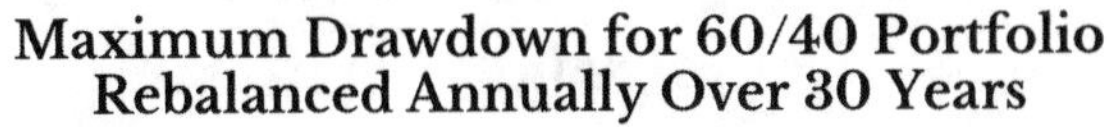

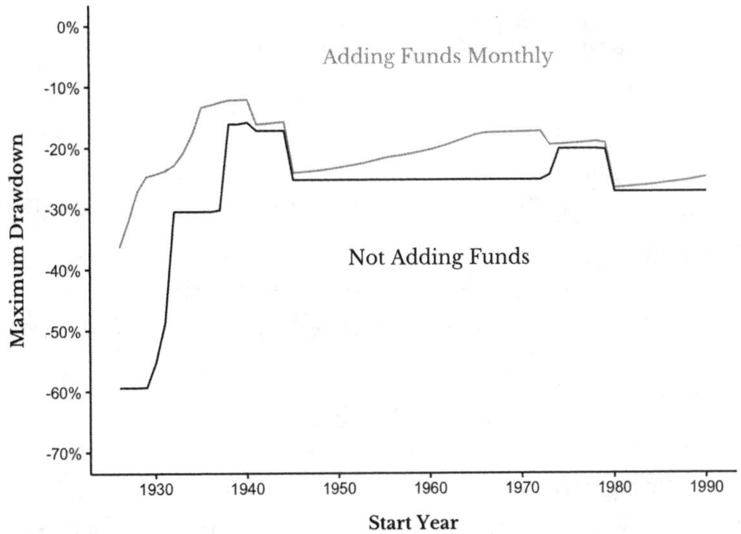

In both of these simulations I rebalance annually, but by adding funds over time you would see your portfolio decline by less in percentage terms.

The only difficult thing about the accumulation rebalance strategy is that it becomes harder to pull off as your portfolio increases in size. While it's easy to add money to rebalance your portfolio when it is small, as it gets bigger you may not have enough cash to keep up. In those instances, selling in your taxable account can make sense from a risk perspective. Just try not to do it too often.

Now that we have discussed why you might need to sell when

it comes to rebalancing, let's look at how to sell to get out of a concentrated (or losing) position.

Getting Out of a Concentrated (or Losing) Position

As I discussed in chapter 12, I am not a big fan of getting into concentrated positions in individual securities. However, sometimes life doesn't give you a choice. For example, if you work at (or start) a company that provides equity compensation, you may one day find that a significant portion of your wealth is in a single security.

In this case, congratulations on your gains! However, you will probably want to sell at least *a portion* of this position down over time. How much should you sell? It depends on your goals.

For example, if you have mortgage debt and a large, concentrated position in one security, it may make sense to sell down enough of this security to pay off your mortgage. From a return perspective this is probably sub-optimal since your concentrated asset will probably rise in value more quickly than your home.

However, from a risk perspective this can make lots of sense. After all, while the future returns in your concentrated position are only a possibility, your future mortgage payments are guaranteed. Sometimes it's better to trade maybes for certainties.

How exactly should you do this?

Find a selling methodology and stick to it. Whether that means selling 10% chunks every month (or every quarter), selling half and letting the rest ride, or selling most of it right away, find something that allows you to sleep at night. You can also sell based on price levels (on the upside and the downside) as well, as long as they are determined *beforehand*. Using a set of predetermined rules will allow you to remove the emotion from your selling process.

Whatever you decide to do, don't sell all of it at once. Why? Because of the tax consequences and the possibility of regret if the price skyrockets. If you sell it all right away and it goes up 10x, you will feel far worse than if you sell 95% of it and the remaining 5% goes to $0. It's this regret minimization framework that you should employ when deciding on how much to sell.

Nevertheless, I do need to remind you that your concentrated position is *likely* to underperform the overall stock market. If you look at the universe of individual stocks in the U.S. going back to 1963, the median one-year return is 6.6%, including dividends. This means that if you grabbed an individual stock at random at any point in time since 1963, you would've earned roughly 6.6% over the next year. However, if you did the same thing with the S&P 500, you would've earned 9.9% instead.

This illustrates the real risk of holding a concentrated position—underperformance. While some people may be okay with this risk, others won't be. Find what level of risk you are willing to accept with your concentrated positions and then sell accordingly.

In addition to selling a concentrated position, you may also need to sell a losing position at some point in your investment life. Whether your beliefs around an asset class change or one of your concentrated positions keeps going down, sometimes you just have to get out.

I experienced this after doing some analysis on gold that made me realize that I shouldn't own it as a long-term holding. Since my beliefs on the asset class changed based on fundamental analysis (and not emotion), I sold the position. This was true even though my gold holdings had increased in value. While this position wasn't a losing one on monetary terms yet, I believed it eventually would be, so I sold.

Since losing positions tend to be rare, especially over longer time periods, this shouldn't be a common occurrence. And don't mix up a period of underperformance with a losing position. Every asset class goes through periods of underperformance, so you shouldn't use these periods as an excuse to sell.

For example, from 2010–2019 U.S. stocks gained 257% in total return compared to only 41% for emerging market stocks. However, from 2000–2009, the opposite was true with emerging market stocks appreciating 84% while U.S. stocks were up less than 3%! The point is that underperformance is inevitable and not a good reason to sell.

Now that we have discussed selling to get out of a concentrated (or losing) position, there is still one other reason why you might need to sell your investments.

The Purpose of Investing

The final reason why you should consider selling an investment is the most obvious—to live the life that you want to live. Whether that means funding your lifestyle in retirement or raising cash for a big purchase, selling assets is one way to get there. After all, what's the point of investing if you never get to enjoy the results?

This is especially true for someone who has the vast majority of their wealth in a large, concentrated position. This person has won the game, yet they don't want to stop playing. Why take that risk? Why not take some money off the table, diversify your wealth, and create a minimum standard of living that you can't fall below?

You could establish a safety net for you and your loved ones, fund your children's 529 education accounts, and pay off your mortgage. Hell, you could even buy your dream car if you want. I don't care what you do with your money, just take it.

Fund the life you need before you risk it for the life you want.

I only recommend this approach because human psychology suggests that it's the wise thing to do. As first discussed in chapter 3, each additional unit of consumption provides less happiness than the unit before. The same is true for wealth.

This is why going from $0 to $1 million in wealth provides a much bigger boost to someone's happiness than going from $1 million to $2 million. Though both changes in wealth are equal in absolute terms, the person going from $0 to $1 million experienced a much bigger change in relative terms. It's this diminishing relationship between wealth and happiness that should convince you that, sometimes, it's okay to sell.

Now that we have discussed when you should consider selling your assets, we turn to *where* your assets should be located.

19. WHERE SHOULD YOU INVEST?

On taxes, Roth vs. traditional, and why you probably shouldn't max out your 401(k)

"WAIT... WHERE'S THE rest of it?" I said in shock. In my hands was my first paycheck ever. As I stared blankly at the page, I was sure that there had been a mistake. My mother, who was standing nearby, overheard me and started to laugh.

But it wasn't my mother's normal laugh. No, this was a laugh that came with a sense of wisdom. She had known something for a long time that I was about to learn.

"Taxes, honey. Taxes," she said with a grin.

I'm guessing you had a similar experience after getting your first paycheck as well. The moment of confusion followed by disappointment. "Wait… where's the rest of it?" is a universal reaction.

So far we have ignored how taxes can affect your investment decisions, but this chapter changes that. In the following pages we will examine some of the most important tax-related investment questions including:

- Should I contribute to a Roth (post-tax) or a traditional (pre-tax) retirement account?
- Should I max out my 401(k)?
- How should I organize my assets?

These questions will provide general guidance on *where* you should be investing your money. Though the account types covered in this chapter will focus on those found in the U.S. (401(k), individual retirement account (IRA), etc.), the *principles* discussed apply anywhere where investing and taxation cross paths.

The Changing Nature of Taxes

Benjamin Franklin once said, "There are only two things that are certain in life—death and taxes." Unfortunately, Franklin's popular phrase is less true than it initially seems. You only need study the history of income taxes in the U.S. to see why.

Though the modern iteration of the U.S. income tax started in the early 1900s, income taxes in the U.S. have a much more complicated history. The first proposed income tax in the U.S. occurred during the War of 1812, but was never enacted.

The next time an income tax appears is in the Revenue Act of 1862 as a relief measure during the Civil War. This one passed, but was abolished a few years after the war in 1872.

Over two decades later, Congress imposed a peacetime income tax with the Revenue Act of 1894. Unfortunately for Congress, the tax was ruled unconstitutional by the Supreme Court a year later in *Pollock v. Farmers' Loan & Trust Co.*

Despite these setbacks, popular support for the income tax continued. And in 1909, the 16th Amendment was passed. When ratification occurred in 1913, Congress officially had the power to "lay and collect taxes on incomes, from whatever source derived."

Before the 16th Amendment, Congress could only legally receive revenue from tariffs and excise taxes on specific items, like alcohol or tobacco. However, with the 16th Amendment, they could now tax individual incomes as well. The modern version of the U.S. income tax was born.

However, it still was nothing like the income tax we know today. Not only were the rates lower (only 1% in 1913), but the exemption limit was so high that only 2% of American households paid the income tax.[96] As you can see, we've come a long way since then.

I tell you the history of income taxes in the U.S. to illustrate the *changing nature* of U.S. tax policy. Unfortunately, this constant evolution in tax policy is what makes it so difficult to write about. As laws change in the future, the optimal decisions around those laws will change as well.

This is why I recommend getting professional help from a tax advisor. Why? Because, when it comes to taxes, individual circumstances matter a lot. Your age, family structure, state of residence, and much more will impact how you make investment-related tax decisions. Unfortunately, there is no one-size-fits-all solution when it comes to taxes.

Even so, the discussion that follows should provide a useful framework for thinking about taxes.

To start, we look at the age-old question: Should I contribute to a Roth or traditional retirement account?

To Roth or Not to Roth?

One of the most asked questions in personal finance is whether to sign up for a 401(k) or a Roth 401(k) retirement plan through your employer. As a reminder, a 401(k)—also called a *traditional* 401(k)—is funded with pre-tax money while a Roth 401(k) is funded with post-tax money. The only difference between these account types is *when* you decide to pay your taxes.

To illustrate this, below I will do a simple walk-through on how each of these account types work. Before we do that though, I should remind you that while I am discussing traditional vs. Roth 401(k)s, the same logic can generally be applied to 403(b)s and IRAs as well.

Let's begin.

- **Traditional 401(k)**: Kate earns $100 which she contributes directly into her traditional 401(k) without paying any income taxes. Over the next 30 years let's assume that the $100 grows by 3x to $300. In retirement, Kate withdraws the $300 but has to pay 30% of it in income taxes. The final (post-tax) money that she can spend in retirement is $210 (or 70% of $300).
- **Roth 401(k)**: Kevin earns $100 and pays a 30% tax rate on it today to have $70 after tax. He contributes the $70 directly into his Roth 401(k) where, over the next 30 years, it grows by 3x to become $210. In retirement, Kevin is able to spend all $210 without having to pay any additional income taxes.

Both Kate and Kevin end up with $210 in retirement spending because they had the same contributions, the same investment growth, and paid the same effective tax rates over time. Mathematically this makes sense because when multiplying a bunch of numbers together, the ordering of the numbers doesn't matter.

$3 \times 2 \times 1 = 1 \times 2 \times 3$

Or in Kate and Kevin's case:

$(100 \times 3) \times 70\% = (100 \times 70\%) \times 3$

The only difference between the two of them was when they paid their taxes, with Kate paying her taxes at the end while Kevin paid his at the beginning. This is why the traditional 401(k) vs. Roth 401(k) decision is irrelevant if your *effective* income tax rate is the same in your working years and in retirement.

Note that I say effective tax rate for simplicity's sake, because in the real world marginal tax rates are what matter. For example, if Kate had taxable income greater than $9,875 in 2020, her tax rate would only be 10% for the first $9,875 in earned income and would increase to more than 10% for every dollar afterwards. For the rest of this chapter, you can assume that any mention of a tax rate is an effective rate (the average rate of tax across all income) unless specified otherwise.

To reiterate, it won't make a difference whether you choose a traditional or a Roth if your *effective* tax rate is the same over time. However, if you do expect some variation in your income tax rate, then we can simplify the decision.

Simplifying the Traditional vs. Roth Decision

Given that *the timing* of taxes is the most important thing when deciding between a traditional 401(k) and a Roth 401(k), we can reduce this problem down to answering a single question:

Will your effective income tax rate be higher now (while working) or later (in retirement)?

All else equal, if you think your income taxes will be higher now, then contribute to a traditional 401(k), otherwise contribute to a Roth 401(k).

Yes, this answer is simple, but it ain't easy. It's simple because the goal when making retirement contributions is to avoid paying taxes when your tax rate is highest. However, this isn't an easy question to answer because you have to consider how your federal, state, and local income taxes might change over time.

Thinking About Future Tax Rates

Given that future tax rates are what's important when choosing between a traditional 401(k) and a Roth 401(k), your next question might be, "So Nick, what will future tax rates be?"

Unfortunately, I have no idea!

But neither does anyone else. You can try to use historical trends to think about whether federal or state tax rates will be higher or lower over the next few decades, but this is harder than it seems.

For example, in 2012, I was under the impression that U.S. federal income tax rates were likely to increase in the future to be somewhat closer to that of their European counterparts. But then, to my surprise, the Tax Cuts and Jobs Act of 2017 passed and *lowered* U.S. federal income tax rates. Predicting the future is hard.

Though I am not expecting you to forecast the future path of income tax rates in the U.S., I do think that taking time to think about your retirement situation can help clarify the traditional vs. Roth decision.

For example, let's assume that you expect your federal effective tax rate to increase from 20% while working to 23% during retirement. All else equal, this implies that the Roth

401(k) would be the better option, as you would pay a lower tax rate now (20%) than you would expect to pay in retirement (23%).

But what if all else isn't equal? What if you are working in a state with high income taxes now (e.g., California) and you plan on retiring in a state with low income taxes later (e.g., Florida)? In that case, using a traditional 401(k) would be preferred as the expected savings in state income tax today are likely to exceed the expected increase in federal income taxes in the future.

However, this will vary from state to state. For example, New York State residents who are aged at least 59.5 are entitled to a state income tax deduction of up to $20,000 if that money comes from a qualified retirement plan and meets some other criteria. I understand this complicates the calculus surrounding your retirement contributions, but it is worth noting.

Though we cannot predict future tax rates, what we can do is estimate how much income we will need in retirement and where we plan on taking that retirement. Having these two pieces of information can do a lot to clarify whether you should be contributing to a traditional 401(k) or a Roth 401(k).

When is a Traditional 401(k) Better?

Though there are a few scenarios where a Roth 401(k) would be preferred to a traditional 401(k), I generally prefer the traditional 401(k). Why? Because it has one thing that a Roth doesn't have—optionality.

With a traditional 401(k) you have far more control over *when* and *where* you pay your taxes. If you couple this with the ability to convert a traditional 401(k) into a Roth IRA, you can play some interesting tax games.

For example, if you experience a year of low (or no) income, you can use this time to convert your traditional 401(k) into a Roth IRA at a lower tax rate.

I have friends who used this tactic while they were in business school because they knew they would be temporarily earning next to nothing. The taxes they paid on their conversions were far lower than what they would have paid had they made Roth 401(k) contributions while working.

But you don't have to go to business school to use this strategy. Any prolonged period of low income (such as taking a year off to raise your children, going on sabbatical, etc.) can be utilized for greater tax efficiency.

Note that this assumes that your 401(k) balance is not greater than a year of your income. If it is, then you will be paying the same (or higher tax rates) when converting. Keep this in mind before converting your traditional 401(k) to Roth IRA.

Besides timing decisions, you can also change where you retire in order to avoid those cities/states that impose larger income taxes. This is why it probably doesn't make sense to contribute to a Roth 401(k) while living in a high tax area like New York City, unless you know you are going to retire in an area with similarly high taxes.

Lastly, though we have been using effective tax rates throughout this chapter, marginal tax rates are what matter. For example, when you take traditional 401(k) distributions in retirement (as a single person), you pay only 10% on the first $9,875, 12% on the next $9,876 to $40,125, and so forth. This means that if you plan on taking distributions in retirement *that would be lower than your current income,* then a traditional 401(k) is the way to go.

For example, if you earn $200,000 while working but only plan to withdraw $30,000 a year in retirement, then the traditional 401(k) allows you to avoid the higher marginal rate while working and then pay the lower marginal rate when retired.

At 2020 tax rates for single filers this would mean avoiding a 32% marginal rate to pay a 12% marginal rate instead.

Though I don't know which of these tax tactics will be most useful to you in the future, I do know that none of these options are available with a Roth 401(k). The added flexibility associated with a traditional 401(k) is what makes it my go-to choice when it comes to employer-sponsored retirement vehicles.

When is a Roth Better?

Despite the lack of optionality in a Roth 401(k), there are a few special cases where a Roth might be the way to go. One of these cases is for people who are high savers.

Why is this true? Because maxing out a Roth 401(k) places more total dollars into a tax-sheltered account than maxing out a traditional 401(k). A little math will demonstrate this.

Imagine Sally and Sam max out their 401(k)s in 2020 by each contributing $19,500. While Sally places her $19,500 contribution into a Roth 401(k), Sam places his $19,500 into a traditional 401(k). After 30 years, let's assume both of their accounts have tripled in value to $58,500. Unfortunately, Sam still has to pay income taxes. Assuming that he pays 30% in taxes, he will be left with only $40,950 to spend in retirement.

How did Sally end up with more in retirement than Sam? Sally placed more total dollars into her tax-sheltered account to begin with. For Sam to have $58,500 after taxes in retirement using his traditional 401(k), he would have had to contribute $27,857 into his account initially. However, since the maximum annual contribution amount into a traditional 401(k) was $19,500 in 2020, Sam is out of luck.

This simple example demonstrates that the Roth 401(k) is

probably the better choice for high savers, as you get more total tax-deferred benefits.

In addition, as mentioned previously, the Roth is also better if you are reasonably certain that your tax rate in retirement will exceed your tax rate while working. If this is the case, then it is clearly better to use a Roth and pay your taxes now while they are relatively lower.

Why Not Both?

So far I have pitted the traditional 401(k) and Roth 401(k) against each other, as if they were a part of some sort of ancient rivalry. But they aren't. There is nothing stopping you from relying on *both* of these account types in retirement.

In fact, for anyone who contributes to a Roth 401(k), if your employer matches contributions then you have a traditional 401(k) component in your account automatically, so you will have to get used to both. However, this isn't a bad thing. Using both account types could allow for even more optionality than using either account by itself.

For example, I spoke with some retirement professionals who recommend utilizing a Roth 401(k) early in your career when your earnings may be lower and then switching to a traditional 401(k) later as your earnings increase.

This strategy is great because it avoids the highest tax brackets in your highest earning years and provides additional flexibility when making retirement withdrawals. And, as I mentioned previously, because the tax treatment of retirement withdrawals varies by state, a dual strategy might be the best solution to effectively navigate such a complex landscape.

Now that we have discussed the costs and benefits of a

traditional vs. a Roth, let's quantify how much tax benefit you get from using these accounts in the first place.

Quantifying the Benefit of a Retirement Account

When it comes to taxes and investing, there are two layers of taxation that you have to worry about. The first layer is the *income* tax, which we just discussed, and the second layer is *capital gains* tax. It's the avoidance of the capital gains tax that makes retirement accounts so attractive.

For example, if you bought $100 of an S&P 500 index fund and sold it two years later at $120, you would have to pay long-term capital gains taxes on the $20 gain. However, when using retirement accounts (e.g., 401(k), IRA, etc.) there are no taxes on these gains, assuming you are of retirement age.

How much of a benefit do you get in a retirement account by avoiding these capital gains taxes? Let's find out.

To do this we can simulate a one-time $10,000 investment into three different account types:

1. **No Tax**: A nontaxable account (e.g., Roth 401(k), Roth IRA, etc.) where all relevant income taxes have already been paid.
2. **Taxed Once**: A taxable account (e.g., brokerage) where capital gains taxes are only paid at account liquidation. Assume that there are no dividends to be paid and that all gains are realized at the end.
3. **Taxed Annually**: A taxable account (e.g., brokerage) where capital gains taxed are paid every year. Imagine that the entire portfolio is sold and re-bought once a year. This generates realized gains at the long-term capital gains rate.

All accounts will experience a 7% annual growth rate (over 30 years) and the taxable accounts will pay the 2020 long-term capital gains rate of 15% when applicable. Also, I am using a Roth 401(k)/IRA here because I only want to compare the effect of taxation that occurs *after* income taxes have been paid.

I have removed the first layer of taxation (income taxes) from this simulation to focus on the second layer of taxation (capital gains) explicitly. The point of this exercise is to quantify the long-term benefit of avoiding capital gains (No Tax vs. Taxed Once) and the benefit of not buying/selling annually (Taxed Once vs. Taxed Annually).

If we were to plot the growth of $10,000 for the No Tax and Taxed Once accounts over 30 years, after all applicable capital gains taxes had been paid, it would look like this:

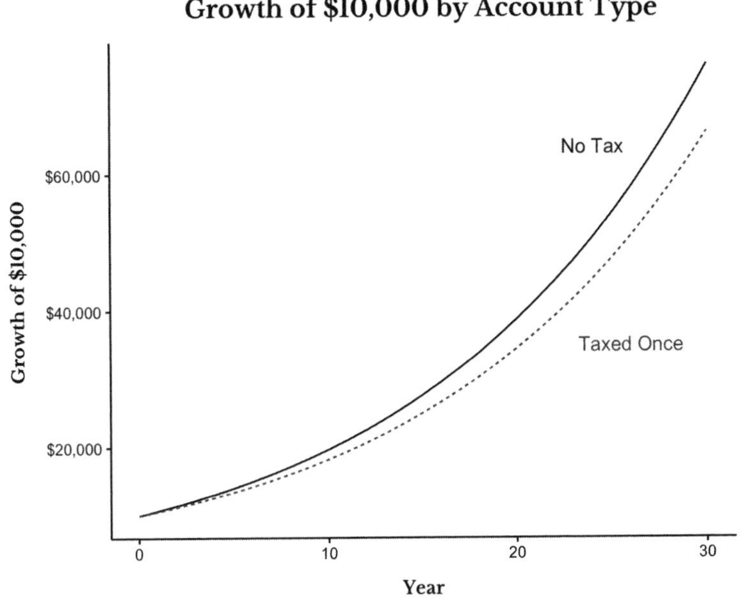

After 30 years, the No Tax account ends up with $76,000 while the Taxed Once account ends up with $66,000. In percentage terms, the No Tax outperforms the Taxed Once account by 15% in total or by 0.50% annually over 30 years.

In other words, the benefit of avoiding capital gains taxes by using a nontaxable retirement account like a 401(k) is about 0.50% a year (assuming a 7% growth rate and 15% long-term capital gains rate). All else equal, this means that a 401(k) provides about half a percent more in after-tax return than a well-managed brokerage account.

But this comparison assumes that you will be able to buy and hold in your taxable brokerage account for 30 years. If you don't have this level of discipline, then the calculus changes significantly. For example, if you were to trade in/out of your positions annually and pay long-term capital gains taxes along the way (i.e., the "Taxed Annually" strategy), you would lose an additional 0.55% in annual return to Uncle Sam.

Going back to our simulation, a $10,000 investment following the Taxed Annually strategy would only grow to $57,000 instead of $66,000 with the Taxed Once strategy. Trading too frequently costs you 17% in total, or about 0.55% a year.

When you combine this with the 0.50% lost by using a taxable account instead of a nontaxable account, that's over 1% a year you lose to capital gains taxes. About half of that loss comes from using a brokerage account (instead of a retirement account) and the other half comes from trading in and out of that taxable account too often.

Why is the Taxed Annually strategy so disastrous for your investment returns? Because frequently trading in and out of your taxable account prevents your gains from compounding on themselves. Mathematically you only get 85% of your expected return when you realize gains annually at the 15% rate [1 – 0.15 = 0.85]. This is equivalent to compounding your wealth at 5.95%

a year instead of at 7% a year because of the annual tax hit [0.85 × 7% = 5.95%].

For people who are too tempted to trade in and out of their positions each year, having that money in a 401(k) can boost after-tax returns by over 1% annually. This can be significant over longer periods of time.

However, for those who are more disciplined, putting as much money as possible into a retirement account may not be your best option. This is why, counter to mainstream financial advice, you probably shouldn't max out your 401(k).

Why You Probably Shouldn't Max Out Your 401(k)

I know that you've heard the advice many times before—if you can, max out your 401(k). It's an almost universal recommendation among personal finance experts. In fact, I used to preach this advice as well.

However, since running the numbers, I've changed my tune. Maxing out your 401(k) is far less beneficial than it initially seems. Don't get me wrong though. You should always contribute to your 401(k) *up to the employer match.* The employer match is basically free money that you do not want to miss out on. However, anything *beyond* the employer match needs to be considered more carefully.

As I highlighted in the prior section, the annual tax benefit of having your money in a nontaxable account compared to a well-managed taxable account is about 0.5% per year. However, that comparison assumed that you only make a single contribution into your account, and you earn no annual dividends. But we know that both of these assumptions aren't likely to be true.

Most people will add money over time and will have to pay

taxes on their dividends in their brokerage account. If we make these adjustments by using a 2% annual dividend and annual contributions for 30 years, then the after-tax benefit of a 401(k) increases to 0.73% per year.

While this is a somewhat sizeable premium, it doesn't adjust for 401(k) plan fees. So far we have assumed that you would pay the same fees in a 401(k) as you would in a taxable account. But we know that this isn't always the case. Because the investment options are limited in a 401(k) and there are administration and other plan fees, you will probably have to pay more in your 401(k) than in a taxable account.

And with the calculation above, if the investment options in your employer's 401(k) plan are just 0.73% more expensive than what you would pay in a taxable brokerage account, then the annual benefit of your 401(k) would be completely eliminated.

This isn't a high bar to hit. For example, if we assume that you would have to pay 0.1% per year in fund fees to get a diversified portfolio in a brokerage account, then paying anything more than 0.83% [0.73% + 0.1%] per year in your 401(k) would eliminate its long-term tax benefit entirely.

TD Ameritrade found that the average all-in cost for the typical 401(k) plan in the U.S. was 0.45% in 2019.[97] This means that the average American gets a 0.38% annual benefit [0.83% – 0.45%] from their 401(k) plan (beyond the employer match).

Unfortunately, that's not a lot considering that you have to lock up your capital until you are 59.5 years of age. While you can withdraw your money from a Roth 401(k) in certain circumstances, for all practical purposes you should act as if the money inside your 401(k) is inaccessible.

And what if your plan fees are higher than 0.45%? If you happen to be at a smaller company where the all-in 401(k) fees typically exceed 1%, then the long-term benefit of contributing beyond the match would be negative! Every dollar you contribute beyond the match would actually cost you money relative to putting that dollar in a well-managed taxable account.

On the other hand, if the all-in costs of your employer's 401(k) plan are low (0.2% or less), then there is still some monetary benefit to maxing out.

But, before you do, you should ask yourself: is an extra 0.6%–0.7% a year worth locking up a decent part of your wealth until old age? I'm not necessarily sure.

I ask this question because I feel like I made a financial mistake by contributing *too much* to my 401(k) when I was younger. While my retirement projections look great now, I also placed some limits on what I can do with my money.

For example, because I maxed out my 401(k) throughout most of my 20s, I can't currently afford the sizable down payment required to buy a place in Manhattan. I'm not even sure if I want to buy anytime soon, but if I did, it would take me a few extra years to get there because of my excessive 401(k) contributions. This is partially my fault for not planning ahead, but it's also because I was seduced by the "max out your 401(k)" advice when I was younger.

This is why it's hard for me to support maxing out your 401(k) for an extra half a percent a year (or sometimes less). That illiquidity premium is just too small to be worth it, even if you don't need the money for something like a down payment on a house.

Of course, if you change any of the assumptions I've made so far, the decision around whether to max out your 401(k) would change as well. For example, if the long-term capital gains tax rate were to increase from 15% to 30%, the annual benefit of a 401(k) over a brokerage account would increase from 0.73% to 1.5% per year. That's a big difference that could tip the scales in favor of maxing out your 401(k).

In addition, there are strong behavioral reasons for why you might want to max out. For example, if you are someone who finds it difficult to manage their own money, then the automation and illiquidity provided by a 401(k) could be exactly what you need to stay the course. You won't find these benefits in a spreadsheet, but they definitely matter.

Ultimately, the decision to max out your 401(k) will be dependent on your individual circumstances. Factors such as your temperament, financial goals, and the cost of your employer's 401(k) plan will all play a role in this decision. Make sure you have considered these factors carefully before moving forward.

Now that we have discussed the pros and cons of maxing out your 401(k), we can conclude our discussion of taxes by addressing the best way to organize your assets.

The Best Way to Organize Your Assets

It's not about what you own, but where you own it. What I'm talking about is *asset location*, or how you distribute your assets across different account types. For example, do you have your bonds in your taxable accounts (e.g., brokerage), your nontaxable accounts (e.g., 401k, IRA, etc.), or both? What about your stocks?

The conventional wisdom suggests that you should put your bonds (and other assets that pay frequent distributions) into your nontaxable accounts and your stocks (and other high-return assets) into your taxable accounts. The logic is that, if you have more bond income (i.e., interest) than stock income (i.e., dividends), you should shelter that income from taxes.

More importantly though, since the tax rate on bond income is higher than the tax rate on stock income (ordinary income vs. capital gains), having your bonds in your nontaxable accounts would avoid these higher rates.

Historically, this strategy would have made sense when

bond yields were much higher than dividend yields on equities. However, when bonds have lower yield/growth, shielding them from taxes may not be the best choice.

In fact, if you want to maximize your after-tax wealth, then you should put your highest-growth assets in tax-sheltered accounts (e.g., 401k, IRA, etc.) and your lowest-growth assets in taxable accounts.

This is true even though tax rates on ordinary income (and interest) exceeded those on capital gains in 2020. If you want to understand why high-growth assets are better off in nontaxable accounts, let's use an example.

Imagine you put $10,000 into two different assets (Asset A and Asset B). Asset A earns 7% a year and pays no dividends/interest while Asset B pays 2% each year in interest. After one year, the account for Asset A will have $10,700 (before taxes) and the account for Asset B will have $10,200 (before taxes).

Assuming a 15% long-term capital gains rate and a 30% tax rate on interest income, the taxes owed from Asset A would be $105 [$700 gain × 15%] while the taxes owed from Asset B would be $60 [$200 interest × 30%]. Since we want to minimize our taxes paid, it would be better to have Asset A in a nontaxable account, even though it doesn't pay any interest/dividends.

This example illustrates why you need to consider the expected growth rate of your assets *in addition to* the tax rates on income/capital gains before making an asset location decision.

Additionally, by placing your high-growth (and likely higher-risk) assets into a nontaxable account, you may be less tempted to sell them during a market crash because they are harder to access.

The other added benefit of this strategy is that your low-growth assets (bonds) are likely to maintain their value and provide you with extra liquidity when you need it most. Having your low-growth (and lower-risk) assets in your taxable accounts means that they are more easily accessible than if they were in a nontaxable account. So, when the market crashes, the assets that are most likely to maintain their value are the ones that are also most accessible.

However, separating high-growth and low-growth assets between taxable and nontaxable accounts could make it harder to rebalance across accounts. For example, if you have all your stocks in your 401(k)/IRAs and then they get cut in half, you can't add money from your brokerage account to these accounts to rebalance. Though it might be mathematically optimal to put your higher-growth assets into your nontaxable accounts, I don't like it because of the difficulty this creates for rebalancing.

This is why I prefer having *the same allocation* across all my accounts. This means that my brokerage account, IRAs, and 401(k) all hold similar assets in similar proportions. They are carbon copies of each other.

I prefer this method because it's easier for me to manage them than having stocks in one account, REITs in another, and bonds somewhere else. It's not the most tax-efficient solution, but it's the solution that I prefer.

In full, if you are someone who needs to get a bit more return, then sheltering your higher-growth assets in nontaxable accounts is the way to go. However, if this isn't as important to you, then having similar allocations across account types may allow for easier management of your investments.

Now that we have examined how to optimize where you store your wealth, let's discuss why that wealth will never make you feel rich anyways.

20. WHY YOU WILL NEVER FEEL RICH

And why you probably already are

IT'S CHRISTMAS DAY 2002 and across the state of West Virginia people are spending money like it is going out of style. But, instead of gifts or eggnog, what are they buying?

Lottery tickets.

At 3:26 PM the ticket buying frenzy peaks with 15 people buying a ticket EVERY. SINGLE. SECOND. Tick. Tick. Tick. 45 new hopefuls catch the lottery fever.

Jack Whittaker was one of these hopefuls. He doesn't play the lottery normally, but with over $100 million at stake, how can he say no? Jack buys his ticket and heads home to see Jewell, his wife of 40 years.

At 11 PM that night the winning Powerball numbers are announced. Jewell wakes up Jack who had fallen asleep. It's a miracle. They got four out of the five numbers correct. It's not the jackpot, but they both know a six-figure payday awaits them as they head to bed.

The next morning Jack turns on the TV before heading to work and makes a startling discovery. One of the numbers from last night's drawing was announced incorrectly. Jack checks his ticket against the correct numbers and is speechless.

He has just won the largest single ticket lottery jackpot in American history—$314 million. Jack decides to take the money immediately and receives $113 million after taxes.[98]

But you already know that this doesn't end well, don't you?

Within two years of taking the $113 million lump sum, Jack's granddaughter is found dead (likely from a drug overdose), his wife is estranged, and Jack divides his time between high roller gambling, propositioning women to have sex for money, and driving intoxicated. Jack would eventually lose all his winnings.

I already know what you're thinking, "Oh Nick, another story about a lottery winner gone wrong. How original."

Well, there's one small detail I left out about Jack Whittaker—he was already rich.

That's right. Jack had a net worth greater than $17 million *before* he ever bought the ticket that would change his life forever. How did he get wealthy? He was a successful businessman as the president of Diversified Enterprise Construction, a contracting firm in West Virginia.

I tell this story because it illustrates how even those with the best intentions, the best background, and the best judgment can succumb to the life-altering effects of money.

Jack Whittaker wasn't a bad man. He supported his wife and granddaughter. He went to church. He even donated tens of millions of dollars to start a non-profit foundation *immediately after* winning the lottery.

Yet, he couldn't shake temptation's wings when they presented themselves. Money has that way of changing people.

Ironically, none of this would've happened had Jack realized how rich he already was.

How do I know that Jack didn't feel rich? Because he was still playing the lottery even though he was worth $17 million! While it's easy to conclude that Jack was just a greedy man, I know from experience that recognizing your wealth is always harder than it seems.

I'm Not Rich, They Are

In the mid-2010s my friend John (not his real name) and I got into a discussion about what it means to be rich in the United States. John had grown up in one of the wealthiest cities in the Bay Area with two parents who had graduate degrees and distinguished careers in medicine and education. However, John said that he wasn't that rich and he told me why.

When John turned 16, his father gave him $1,000 to open a brokerage account and learn about the stock market. Later that night John told his best friend Mark about the gift and asked Mark what he had gotten for his birthday, since they were both born around the same date. Mark said he had gotten the exact same gift from his father.

John was shocked to hear this. He knew that his dad and Mark's dad were good friends, so it seemed plausible that they had planned to gift their sons the same thing. However, John also knew that Mark's family was far wealthier than his. In fact, Mark's family was loaded.

Mark's grandfather had founded a famous investment firm and Mark's father was on the board of a major technology company. On paper Mark's family were billionaires, so it confused John when he heard that Mark had only gotten $1,000.

When John asked Mark, "So you got $1,000 too?" Mark replied hesitantly, "Well no. It was $100,000. But it's basically the same gift."

There's rich and then there's *rich*.

From 2002 to 2007, I thought I was rich too. Or at least kind of rich.

My family owned a big screen TV (it was 2 and a 1/2 feet deep). We had a dune buggy and a sports car. We lived in a three-story house in a gated community that kids at my school simply called "The Gates." I later found out that this life of luxury was only temporary.

In 2002, when my Mom and Stepdad bought our three-story house, it cost $271,000. By early 2007, the house reached a peak value of $625,000. The entire ride up my family refinanced the mortgage over and over, extracting increasing amounts of home equity. We could keep living high off of this equity as long as house prices kept going up.

Unfortunately, they didn't. As house prices started to crash in late 2007, everything came undone. We lost the house and were forced to sell the dune buggy, the TV, and the sports car. The Gates we once called home were now a barrier to a life that was no longer ours. We weren't rich after all.

But it wasn't until college that I realized just how un-rich we were. I'll never forget during my first week of school when I found out that I was one of two kids, out of the 20 in my freshman hall, that had never been to Europe. In fact, at that point in time the furthest I had ever flown from California was New Mexico, and that flight had been paid for by a science grant. Looking back, I now understand why I thought I was rich from 2002 to 2007. It was because I knew what it was like to live under worse conditions.

Right before living in The Gates my family and I lived in a condominium that had an infestation of roaches under the oven. Anytime we went to bake something they would come out and bask on the oven's control panel like little lizards in the sun. They constantly invaded our pantry and left behind little brown specs of you know what. It was disgusting. To this day I can't stand roaches.

However, as bad as that situation was, I had a lot of nice things going for me. I never went hungry, I had an incredibly supportive family, and I even had my own computer (back in 2001!). Yet, I couldn't see how well I had it because it was all I knew.

This was just like my friend John who couldn't see his wealth because all *he knew* growing up was being relatively poorer than his high school friends. Unfortunately, this feeling doesn't seem to go away even as you move further up the wealth spectrum.

Why Even Billionaires Don't Feel Rich

You would think that by the time you became a billionaire you would realize that you are rich, but that's not always the case. For example, consider a February 2020 interview with ex-Goldman Sachs CEO and current billionaire Lloyd Blankfein. In the interview he claims that, despite his immense wealth, he isn't rich:

> "Blankfein insists that he is 'well-to-do,' not rich. 'I can't even say rich,' he insists. 'I don't feel that way. I don't behave that way.'
>
> He says he has an apartment in Miami as well as New York. But he abjures most of the trappings. 'If I bought a Ferrari, I'd be worried about it getting scratched,' he jokes."[99]

As shocking as this sounds, I get where Blankfein is coming from.

When you regularly hang out with people like Jeff Bezos and David Geffen and look at Ray Dalio and Ken Griffen as your peers, having only $1 billion doesn't seem like much.

However, on a completely objective basis, Blankfein is in the top 0.01% of U.S. households, or the 1% of the 1%. According to Saez and Zucman, the top 0.01% of U.S. households (~16,000 families) had a net worth of at least $111 million in 2012.[100] Even if you adjust for the increase in asset prices since 2012, Blankfein would easily be in the top 0.01%.

But it's not just Blankfein who has this perception problem. Most people at the upper end of the income spectrum think they are less well off than they actually are.

For example, research in *The Review of Economics and Statistics* illustrates that most households in the upper half of the income spectrum don't realize how good they have it.[101] As the following chart illustrates, households above the 50th percentile in income tend to underestimate how well they are doing relative to others.

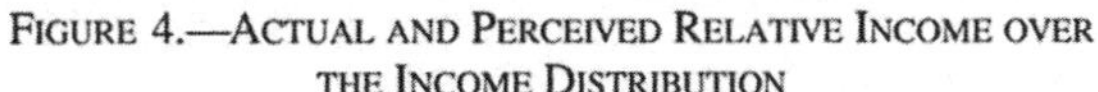

FIGURE 4.—ACTUAL AND PERCEIVED RELATIVE INCOME OVER THE INCOME DISTRIBUTION

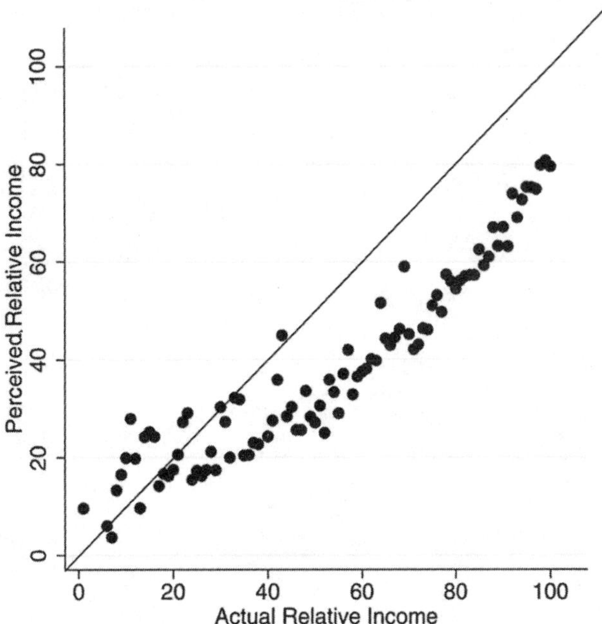

The figure displays the relation between perceived and actual relative income among the respondents of the first round. We construct 100 equally sized bins of actual relative income and display mean perceived relative income in each bin. The solid 45 degree line illustrates the no-bias case. The number of observations is 1,242.

As we can see in the chart, even households at the 90th percentile and above in actual income believe that they are in the 60th–80th percentile range.

While this result might seem surprising at first glance, if you think about wealth perception as a network problem, it makes a lot of sense. Matthew Jackson explained this concept well in *The Human Network*, when discussing why most people feel less popular than their friends:

> "Have you ever had the impression that other people have many more friends than you? If you have, you are not alone. Our friends have more friends on average than a typical person in the population. This is the friendship paradox… The friendship paradox is easy to understand. The most popular people appear on many other people's friendship lists, while the people with very few friends appear on relatively few people's lists. The people with many friends are overrepresented on people's list of friends relative to their share in the population, while the people with few friends are underrepresented."[102]

You can apply this same thinking within your social networks to illustrate why most people feel less rich than they actually are.

For example, you can probably think of at least one person who is wealthier than you are. Well, that wealthier person likely has some wealthier friends, so they can think of someone wealthier than themselves as well. And if they can't, then they can easily reference a celebrity (e.g., Gates, Bezos, etc.) who is.

If you extend this logic to its natural conclusion, you will realize that everyone (besides the world's richest person) can point to someone else and say, "I'm not rich, they are rich."

That's how filthy rich billionaires like Blankfein can feel like they are just "well-to-do."

Well, guess what? You probably don't act all that different.

How do I know? Because you are likely far richer than you think. For example, if your net worth is greater than $4,210, then you are wealthier than half of the world, according to the 2018 Credit Suisse Global Wealth Report.[103]

And if your net worth exceeds $93,170, which is similar to the median net worth in the U.S., that puts you in the top 10% globally. I don't know about you, but I would consider someone in the top 10% to be rich.

Let me guess, you disagree? You don't think it's fair to compare yourself with random people across the globe like rural farmers in the developing world?

Well guess what? Lloyd Blankfein probably doesn't think it's fair to compare himself with people like you and me!

Yes, Blankfein's claim of not being rich is objectively more outlandish than the claim that being in the top 10% globally isn't rich. However, they are fundamentally the same argument. We are just splitting hairs.

After all, is the top 10% rich?

The top 1%?

The top 0.01%?

And at what aggregation level? Globally? Nationally? City-wide?

There is no right answer, because being rich is a *relative* concept. Always has been and always will be. And that relativity will be present throughout your life.

For example, you would need a net worth of $11.1 million to be in the top 1% of U.S. households in 2019. However, after controlling for age and educational attainment, the top 1% varies from as little as $341,000 to as much as $30.5 million.

For example, to be in the top 1% of households under 35 that are also high school dropouts you would only need $341,000. However, to be in the top 1% of college educated households aged 65–74 years, you would need $30.5 million.

The next chart illustrates this by breaking out the net worth of the top 1% of U.S. households in 2019 by educational attainment (in each panel) and by age (across the x-axis).

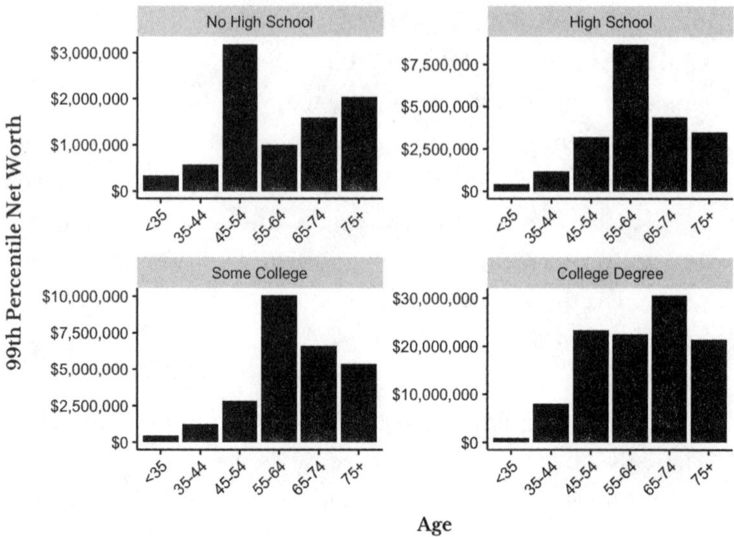

This is why no one feels rich. Because it's always easy to point at someone who is doing better.

The trick is not to forget all the people who could be pointing at you.

Now that we have discussed why you'll probably never feel rich, we turn our attention to the one asset that could make you feel richer than all the rest.

21. THE MOST IMPORTANT ASSET

And why you'll never get any more of it

PETER ATTIA, A physician and longevity expert, did a talk in 2017 on how to increase your lifespan where he proposed the following thought experiment to his audience:

> "I would be willing to bet that not one of you, if you were offered every dollar of Warren Buffett's fortune, would trade places with him right now… And I would also bet, by the way, that Buffett would be willing to be 20 years old again if he was broke."[104]

Consider Attia's trade for a moment. Imagine having Buffett's wealth, fame, and status as the greatest investor on earth. You can go anywhere you please, meet anyone you want, and buy anything that can be sold. However, you're now 87 years old (Buffett's age at the time). Would you make the trade?

I know it sounds cryptic, but I bet you wouldn't. You intuitively understand that, in some circumstances, time is worth far more than money. Because you can do some things with time that you could never do with money. In fact, with enough time you could even move mountains.

The Mountain Man

One of the most remarkable tales of perseverance in human history is one that you probably have never heard before.

The story starts in 1960 in the town of Gehlaur in the north-eastern part of India. Back then Gehlaur was isolated. In fact, it was so isolated that villagers would have to walk a treacherous 30-mile (50km) path around a mountain ridge if they ever needed supplies or medical treatment.

One such villager was walking along the ridge one day when she fell and injured herself. Her husband, Dashrath Manjhi, learned of her injuries and decided that the villagers of Gehlaur had walked around that mountain ridge for long enough. That same night Manjhi made a vow that he would carve a path through the mountain.

The next day, using only a hammer and chisel, Manjhi started cutting away at the ridge. When the local villagers heard about Manjhi's mission they mocked him saying that it was impossible. However, he never gave up.

Over the course of the next 22 years Manjhi chipped away at the mountain by himself. Day by day and night by night. He eventually carved a path that was 360 feet long (110m), 30 feet wide (9.1 m), and 25 feet deep (7.6m).

In total he moved over 270,000 cubic feet of rock by the

time he finished the path in the early 1980s, earning himself the nickname "Mountain Man."

In creating this path, Manjhi was able to reduce the travel distance between the neighboring villages from 34 miles (55km) to 9 miles (15km). If you search "Dashrath Manjhi Passthrough" on Google Maps and go to Street View you can find the final product of his two decades of work. Sadly, Manjhi's wife, who was the inspiration for his mission, died a few years before his work was complete.

Manjhi's story illustrates the incredible *unseen* value that time has. Though Manjhi didn't have the money to pay a construction crew to carve a path through that mountain, he did have the time.

This is why time is, and always will be, your most important asset. How you use that time in your 20s, 30s, and 40s will have huge impacts on your life in your 50s, 60s, and 70s. Unfortunately, it can take a while to learn this lesson. I know from personal experience.

I started this book by discussing my money worries as a young college graduate and I will end it by telling you about a goal I set for myself at around the same age. It wasn't the goal that was important, but what pursuing that goal taught me about the value of time and how we judge our lives.

We Begin Our Lives as Growth Stocks and End Our Lives as Value Stocks

When I was 23 years old I told myself that I wanted to have half a million dollars by the age of 30. At that point in time I had less than $2,000 to my name. I chose $500,000 as my end goal after reading that Warren Buffett had $1 million by the time he was 30.

Note that Buffett had his $1 million back in 1960, which would be over $9 million today. Since I'm no Warren Buffett, I cut the goal in half and didn't adjust it for inflation either.

When I turned 31 in November 2020 my net worth still hadn't hit half a million dollars. I came up short. How short? Far more than I would have wanted.

But that's not really important. As Dominic Toretto, Vin Diesel's character in *The Fast and the Furious*, once said, "It don't matter if you win by an inch or a mile. Winning's winning."

Well, losing is losing too, whether by one figure or six figures. But what makes this loss particularly unfortunate is that it occurred during a raging bull market. I can't blame the S&P 500 for my shortcoming, only my own behavior.

Where did I slip up? Well, it wasn't for a lack of trying. I had been working full-time for over eight years and had put in 10 hours a week on my blog for almost four years. Though I didn't really monetize my blog until 2020, even if I had monetized it earlier I still would have come up short.

I also don't think I can blame my spending either. Though I could have traveled and dined out less often (experiences I thoroughly enjoyed), those purchases wouldn't have moved the needle enough to make a difference.

But you know what would have made a difference? Making better decisions earlier in my career. It wasn't my money I should have optimized, *but my time.*

While many of my friends went off to big tech firms (Facebook, Amazon, Uber, etc.) and got that sweet, sweet equity compensation, I worked at the same consulting firm for six years where I was paid generously, but had no such upside. I didn't realize how much I was missing out until it was a bit too late.

Now many of those friends are millionaires (or at least half millionaires) after exercising their stock options following the massive growth in tech valuations. Yes, it's easy to write my friends off as lucky, which is partially true, but I also know that's just an excuse. Because I had many opportunities to board the big tech boat as it passed by, but I declined them all.

And it's not that I wanted to work in big tech specifically (I didn't). It's that I didn't spend any significant time thinking about my career until I was 27 years old. Researchers at the Federal Reserve Bank of New York have shown that an individual's income grows most rapidly in their first decade of work (ages 25–35).[105] Given this information, you can see why my focus at age 23 should've been on my career and *not* my investment portfolio.

The reason for my mistake is that I incorrectly believed that money was a more important asset than time. I only later realized why this was false.

Though you can always earn more money, nothing can buy you more time.

As harsh as this sounds, I promise that I am not as hard on myself as it might seem. I know that I currently have a much better life than what I would've expected given my upbringing. In addition, I doubt I would have had the opportunity to write this book had I joined a big tech company. So there's that.

But more importantly, I know that even if I had reached my $500,000 goal, it likely wouldn't have changed my life in any meaningful way. I know this because affluence increases in steps, roughly by factors of 10. This is why someone who increases their wealth from $10,000 to $100,000 will probably see a bigger life impact than someone going from $200,000 to $300,000. So even if I had been a half millionaire at age 30, it wouldn't have made a difference.

I understand how tone deaf it sounds when I complain about not reaching an exorbitant financial goal while many U.S. households struggle to make ends meet. But, as I explained in the prior chapter, wealth isn't an absolute game, it's a relative game.

For better or for worse, I will compare myself relative to my own aspirations and my own peer group just like you will. I wish it wasn't like this, but it is. You can argue with me all you want—however, overwhelming research suggests otherwise.

For example, in the book *The Happiness Curve*, Jonathan Rauch describes how happiness in most people starts declining in the late 20s, bottoms at age 50, and then increases after that. When plotted, lifetime happiness ends up looking like a U-curve (or a little smile).

Visually, you can see this in empirical research from Hannes Schwandt, an economist and assistant professor at Northwestern University, when he plots the *expected* life satisfaction five years in the future by age and the actual life satisfaction at that same age.[106]

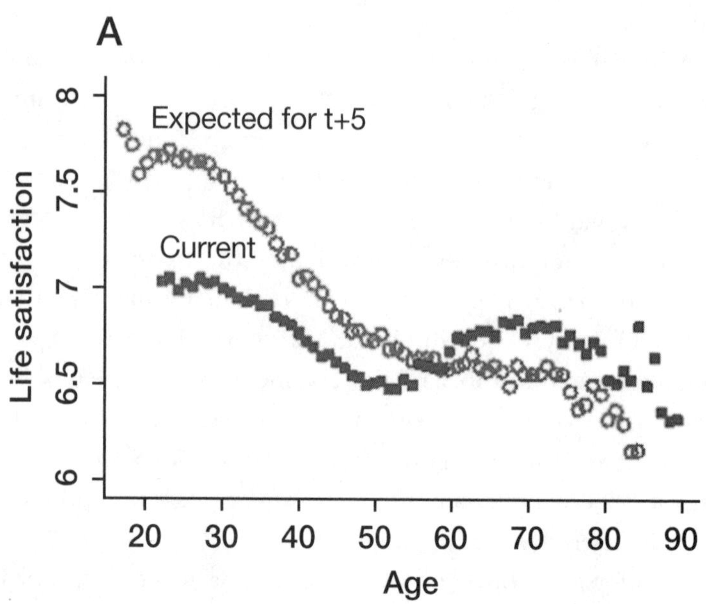

For example, 30-year-olds have a current life satisfaction of 7 (out of 10). And they expect their life satisfaction to be 7.7 (out of 10) five years from now, when they reach age 35. However, looking at the chart you can see that 35-year-olds have *lower* life satisfaction than 30-year-olds—their actual life satisfaction at age

35 is 6.8, rather than the 7.7 they predicted at age 30. On average, 30-year-olds expect a 0.7 point increase in their life satisfaction but are actually likely to experience a 0.2 point *decrease* over the next five years.

If you look just at the dots representing current life satisfaction, it forms the famous happiness U-curve from ages 25–70.

But why does happiness start to decline in the late 20s? Because, as people age, their lives usually fail to meet their high expectations. As Rauch states in *The Happiness Curve*:

> "Young people consistently overestimate their future life satisfaction. They make a whopping forecasting error, as nonrandom as it could be—as if you lived in Seattle and expected sunshine every day… Young adults in their twenties overestimate their future life satisfaction by about 10 percent on average. Over time, however, excessive optimism diminishes… People are not becoming depressed. They are becoming, well, realistic."[107]

This research explains why I was a bit bummed about not reaching the audacious financial goal I set for myself when I was 23 years old. However, it also explains why I was unlikely to reach that goal in the first place (i.e., it was probably too optimistic).

You may find this same pattern in your life too. You may have set your expectations rather high while you were young, only to be let down later. However, as the research suggests, this is completely normal.

What's also normal is lowering your expectations over time, probably too much, to the point where, as you head into old age, pleasant surprises will provide you with additional happiness. We begin our lives as growth stocks, but end our lives as value stocks.

Growth stocks are priced similarly to how we think of ourselves when we are young. There are high expectations and high hopes for the future. However, many of us, like many growth stocks, eventually fail to meet these high expectations.

Over time we lower our expectations so much that we doubt that things could be better in the future. This is similar to how investors price value stocks. However, things usually go better than expected and we, like value stock investors, can experience pleasant upside surprises.

Of course, this is only on average. Everyone's life is different with its own twists and turns. We all must make decisions based on what we know at the time. That's all we can ever do.

Now that we have discussed the most important asset in your portfolio, let's wrap up by bringing everything together with a game.

CONCLUSION: THE JUST KEEP BUYING RULES

How to win the time traveler's game

IMAGINE YOU ARE approached by a time traveler who has a keen interest in learning how to get rich. To this end, the time traveler has devised a game that they want you to play, which goes as follows.

Tomorrow you will wake up at some point in the last 100 years with no knowledge of your current life and no knowledge of what the future will hold. However, you will be allowed to give yourself a specific set of financial instructions to follow. Assuming that you want to maximize the probability of building wealth, what would you tell yourself?

While it's tempting to say things like "Buy Apple" or "Avoid the stock market from September 1929–June 1932," let's assume that history won't repeat itself in the same way. You could go back to 1929 and never experience The Great Depression or to 1976 and Apple never makes it out of the garage.

Given this limited information, what instructions would you give yourself today to take with you into the past? How would you win the time traveler's game?

My answer to this question has been this book. Given that I don't know anything about you, my goal has been to maximize the probability of your financial success, regardless of your background. With this in mind, let's review the specific set of financial instructions I would tell myself to win the time traveler's game.

These are the *Just Keeping Buying* rules.

Saving is for the Poor, Investing is for the Rich

Find where you are in your financial journey before deciding where to focus your time and energy. If your expected savings are greater than your expected investment income, focus on savings; otherwise focus on investing. If they are similar, focus on both. (Ch. 1)

Save What You Can

Your income and spending are rarely fixed, so your savings rate shouldn't be fixed either. Save what you can to reduce your financial stress. (Ch. 2)

Focus on Income, Not Spending

Cutting spending has its limits, but growing your income doesn't. Find small ways to grow your income today that can turn into big ways to grow it tomorrow. (Ch. 3)

Use The 2x Rule to Eliminate Spending Guilt

If you ever feel guilty about splurging on yourself, invest the same amount of money into income-producing assets or donate to a good cause. This is the easiest way to have worry-free spending. (Ch. 4)

Save at Least 50% of Your Future Raises and Bonuses

A little lifestyle creep is okay, but keep it below 50% of your future raises if you want to stay on track. (Ch. 5)

Debt Isn't Good or Bad, It Depends on How You Use It

Debt can be harmful in some scenarios and helpful in others. Use debt only when it can be most beneficial for your finances. (Ch. 6)

Only Buy a Home When the Time Is Right

Buying a home will probably be the biggest financial decision you ever make. As a result, you should only do it when it fits into both your finances and your current lifestyle. (Ch. 7)

When Saving for a Big Purchase, Use Cash

Though bonds and stocks may earn you more while you wait, when saving for a wedding, home, or other big purchase, cash is the way to go. (Ch. 8)

Retirement is About More Than Money

Before you decide what to retire *from*, make sure you know what you want to retire *to*. (Ch. 9)

Invest to Replace Your Waning Human Capital with Financial Capital

You won't be able to work forever, so replace your human capital with financial capital before it's too late. Investing is the best way to accomplish this. (Ch. 10)

Think Like an Owner and Buy Income-Producing Assets

To really grow your income, think like an owner and use your money to buy income-producing assets. (Ch. 11)

Don't Buy Individual Stocks

Buying individual stocks and expecting to outperform is like flipping a coin. You might succeed, but even if you do, how do you know it wasn't just luck? (Ch. 12)

Buy Quickly, Sell Slowly

Since most markets are expected to rise over time, buying quickly and selling slowly is the optimal way to maximize your wealth. If you don't feel comfortable with this, then what you are buying/selling might be too risky for you. (Ch. 13, 18)

Invest As Often As You Can

If you think you can time the market by saving up cash, think again. Even God couldn't beat dollar-cost averaging. (Ch. 14)

Investing Isn't About the Cards You Are Dealt, but How You Play Your Hand

You will experience periods of good and bad luck throughout your investing career. However, the most important thing is how you behave over the long term. (Ch. 15)

Don't Fear Volatility When It Inevitably Comes

Markets won't give you a free ride without some bumps along the way. Don't forget that you have to experience some downside if you want to earn your upside. (Ch. 16)

Market Crashes Are (Usually) Buying Opportunities

Future returns are usually the highest following major crashes. Don't be afraid to take advantage of these crashes when they periodically occur. (Ch. 17)

Fund the Life You Need Before You Risk it for the Life You Want

Though this book is called *Just Keep Buying*, sometimes it's okay to sell. After all, what's the point of building your wealth if you don't do anything with it? (Ch. 18)

Don't Max Out Your 401(k) Without Considerable Thought

The annual benefit of a 401(k) can be less than you think. Before you lock up your money for multiple decades, consider what else you might need it for instead. (Ch. 19)

You'll Never Feel Rich and That's Okay

No matter how successful you get with your money, there will always be someone with more. If you win the financial game, make sure you don't lose yourself in the process. (Ch. 20)

Time is Your Most Important Asset

You can always earn more money, but nothing can buy you more time. (Ch. 21)

The Financial Game That We Are Already Playing

Fortunately, we don't need a time machine to play the time traveler's game, because *we are already playing it.* In fact, we've been playing it for our entire adult lives.

Every day we have to make financial decisions without knowing what the future holds. And though we don't have a specific set of instructions to follow, we are constantly searching to find the best information that we can. The fact that you've read this book demonstrates that you are trying to find the set of instructions that will work for you.

I can only hope that *Just Keep Buying* has made the list. Thank you for reading.

ACKNOWLEDGMENTS

MY LIFE HAS been a series of lucky events. The creation of *Just Keep Buying* is no different. This book would not exist without guidance from hundreds of people over the years. Among those that have been particularly supportive include:

Gherty Galace, for inspiring me to write long, long ago.

Michael Batnick, for believing in me before anyone else.

Morgan Housel, for showing me the way without saying a word.

Craig Pearce, for providing clarity and confidence when I need it most.

I would also like to thank Ben Carlson, James Clear, Carl Joseph-Black, and Jim O'Shaughnessy for their invaluable feedback when putting together this book. Shout out to my wonderful friends, especially the Boston Boiz (Justin, Tyler, and Sam), for their ongoing encouragement.

To the Maggiulli and Montenegro families, they say it takes a village to raise a child and I know I wouldn't be here without my villagers. I love you all.

Lastly, to everyone who has ever shared or supported my work over the years, thank you. From the depths of my soul, thank you. You have no idea what it means to me.

ENDNOTES

1 Miller, Matthew L., "Binge 'Til You Burst: Feast and Famine on Salmon Rivers," Cool Green Science (April 8, 2015).

2 Nichols, Austin and Seth Zimmerman, "Measuring Trends in Income Variability," Urban Institute Discussion Paper (2008).

3 Dynan, Karen E., Jonathan Skinner, and Stephen P. Zeldes, "Do the Rich Save More?" *Journal of Political Economy* 112:2 (2004) 397–444.

4 Saez, Emmanuel, and Gabriel Zucman, "The Distribution of US Wealth: Capital Income and Returns since 1913." Unpublished (2014).

5 "Stress in America? Paying With Our Health," American Psychological Association (February 4, 2015).

6 "Planning & Progress Study 2018," Northwestern Mutual (2018).

7 Graham, Carol, "The Rich Even Have a Better Kind of Stress than the Poor," Brookings (October 26, 2016).

8 Leonhardt, Megan, "Here's How Much Money Americans Say You Need to Be 'Rich'," CNBC (July 19, 2019).

9 Frank, Robert, "Millionaires Need $7.5 Million to Feel Wealthy," *The Wall Street Journal* (March 14, 2011).

10 Chris Browning et al., "Spending in Retirement:

Determining the Consumption Gap," *Journal of Financial Planning* 29:2 (2016), 42.

11 Taylor, T., Halen, N., and Huang, D., "The Decumulation Paradox: Why Are Retirees Not Spending More?" *Investments & Wealth Monitor* (July/August 2018), 40–52.

12 Matt Fellowes, "Living Too Frugally? Economic Sentiment & Spending Among Older Americans," unitedincome.capitalone.com (May 16, 2017).

13 Survey of Consumer Finances and Financial Accounts of the United States.

14 19th Annual Transamerica Retirement Survey (December 2019).

15 The 2020 Annual Report of the Board of Trustees of the Federal Old-Age and Survivors Insurance and Federal Disability Insurance Trust Funds (April 2020).

16 Pontzer, Herman, David A. Raichlen, Brian M. Wood, Audax Z.P. Mabulla, Susan B. Racette, and Frank W. Marlowe, "Hunter-gatherer Energetics and Human Obesity," *PLoS ONE* 7:7 (2012), e40503.

17 Ross, Robert, and I.N. Janssen, "Physical Activity, Total and Regional Obesity: Dose-response Considerations," *Medicine and Science in Sports and Exercise* 33:6 SUPP (2001), S521–S527.

18 Balboni, Clare, Oriana Bandiera, Robin Burgess, Maitreesh Ghatak, and Anton Heil, "Why Do People Stay Poor?" (2020). CEPR Discussion Paper No. DP14534.

19 Egger, Dennis, Johannes Haushofer, Edward Miguel, Paul Niehaus, and Michael W. Walker, "General Equilibrium Effects of Cash Transfers: Experimental Evidence From Kenya," No. w26600. National Bureau of Economic Research (2019).

20 Stanley, Thomas J., *The Millionaire Next Door: The Surprising Secrets of America's Wealthy* (Lanham, MD: Taylor Trade Publishing, 1996).

21 Corley, Thomas C., "It Takes the Typical Self-Made

Millionaire at Least 32 Years to Get Rich," Business Insider (March 5, 2015).

22 Curtin, Melanie, "Attention, Millennials: The Average Entrepreneur is This Old When They Launch Their First Startup," Inc.com (May 17, 2018).

23 Martin, Emmie, "Suze Orman: If You Waste Money on Coffee, It's like 'Peeing $1 Million down the Drain'," CNBC (March 28, 2019).

24 Rigby, Rhymer, "We All Have Worries but Those of the Rich Are Somehow Different," *Financial Times* (February 26, 2019).

25 Dunn, Elizabeth, and Michael I. Norton, *Happy Money: The Science of Happier Spending* (New York, NY: Simon & Schuster Paperbacks, 2014).

26 Pink, Daniel H, *Drive: The Surprising Truth about What Motivates Us* (New York, NY: Riverhead Books, 2011).

27 Matz, Sandra C., Joe J. Gladstone, and David Stillwell, "Money Buys Happiness When Spending Fits Our Personality," *Psychological Science* 27:5 (2016), 715–725.

28 Dunn, Elizabeth W., Daniel T. Gilbert, and Timothy D. Wilson, "If Money Doesn't Make You Happy, Then You Probably Aren't Spending It Right," *Journal of Consumer Psychology* 21:2 (2011), 115–125.

29 Vanderbilt, Arthur T, *Fortune's Children: The Fall of the House of Vanderbilt* (New York, NY: Morrow, 1989).

30 Gorbachev, Olga, and María José Luengo-Prado, "The Credit Card Debt Puzzle: The Role of Preferences, Credit Access Risk, and Financial Literacy," *Review of Economics and Statistics* 101:2 (2019), 294–309.

31 Collins, Daryl, Jonathan Morduch, Stuart Rutherford, and Orlanda Ruthven, *Portfolios of the Poor: How the World's Poor Live On $2 a Day* (Princeton, NJ: Princeton University Press, 2009).

32 "The Economic Value of College Majors," CEW Georgetown (2015).

33 Tamborini, Christopher R., ChangHwan Kim, and Arthur Sakamoto, "Education and Lifetime Earnings in the United States," *Demography* 52:4 (2015), 1383–1407.

34 "The Economic Value of College Majors," CEW Georgetown (2015).

35 "Student Loan Debt Statistics [2021]: Average + Total Debt," EducationData (April 12, 2020).

36 Radwin, David, and C. Wei, "What is the Price of College? Total, Net, and Out-of-Pocket Prices by Type of Institution in 2011–12," Resource document, National Center for Education Statistics (2015).

37 Brown, Sarah, Karl Taylor, and Stephen Wheatley Price, "Debt and Distress: Evaluating the Psychological Cost of Credit," *Journal of Economic Psychology* 26:5 (2005), 642–663.

38 Dunn, Lucia F., and Ida A. Mirzaie, "Determinants of Consumer Debt Stress: Differences by Debt Type and Gender," Department of Economics: Columbus, Ohio State University (2012).

39 Sweet, Elizabeth, Arijit Nandi, Emma K. Adam, and Thomas W. McDade, "The High Price of Debt: Household Financial Debt and its Impact on Mental and Physical Health," *Social Science & Medicine* 91 (2013), 94–100.

40 Norvilitis, J.M., Szablicki, P.B., and Wilson, S.D., "Factors Influencing Levels of Credit-Card Debt in College Students," *Journal of Applied Social Psychology* 33 (2003), 935–947.

41 Dixon, Amanda, "Survey: Nearly 4 in 10 Americans Would Borrow to Cover a $1K Emergency," Bankrate (January 22, 2020).

42 Kirkham, Elyssa, "Most Americans Can't Cover a $1,000 Emergency With Savings," LendingTree (December 19, 2018).

43 Athreya, Kartik, José Mustre-del-Río, and Juan M. Sánchez, "The Persistence of Financial Distress," *The Review of Financial Studies* 32:10 (2019), 3851–3883.

44 Shiller, Robert J., "Why Land and Homes Actually

Tend to Be Disappointing Investments," *The New York Times* (July 15, 2016).

45 Bhutta, Neil, Jesse Bricker, Andrew C. Chang, Lisa J. Dettling, Sarena Goodman, Joanne W. Hsu, Kevin B. Moore, Sarah Reber, Alice Henriques Volz, and Richard Windle, "Changes in US Family Finances from 2016 to 2019: Evidence From the Survey of Consumer Finances," *Federal Reserve Bulletin* 106:5 (2020).

46 Eggleston, Jonathan, Donald Hayes, Robert Munk, and Brianna Sullivan, "The Wealth of Households: 2017," U.S. Census Bureau Report P70BR-170 (2020).

47 Kushi, Odeta, "Homeownership Remains Strongly Linked to Wealth-Building," First American (November 5, 2020).

48 "What is a Debt-to-Income Ratio? Why is the 43% Debt-to-Income Ratio Important?" Consumer Financial Protection Bureau (November 15, 2019).

49 Bengen W.P., "Determining Withdrawal Rates Using Historical Data," *Journal of Financial Planning* 7:4 (1994), 171–182.

50 Kitces, Michael, "Why Most Retirees Never Spend Their Retirement Assets," Nerd's Eye View, Kitces.com (July 6, 2016).

51 Bengen, William, Interview with Michael Kitces, *Financial Advisor Success Podcast* (October 13, 2020).

52 "Spending in Retirement," J.P. Morgan Asset Management (August 2015).

53 Fisher, Jonathan D., David S. Johnson, Joseph Marchand, Timothy M. Smeeding, and Barbara Boyle Torrey, "The Retirement Consumption Conundrum: Evidence From a Consumption Survey," *Economics Letters* 99:3 (2008), 482–485.

54 Robin, Vicki, Joe Dominguez, and Monique Tilford, *Your Money or Your Life: 9 Steps to Transforming Your Relationship with Money and Achieving Financial Independence* (Harmondsworth: Penguin, 2008).

55 Zelinski, Ernie J., *How to Retire Happy, Wild, and Free:*

Retirement Wisdom That You Won't (Visions International Publishing: 2004).

56 O'Leary, Kevin, "Kevin O'Leary: Why Early Retirement Doesn't Work," YouTube video, 1:11 (March 20, 2019).

57 Shapiro, Julian, "Personal Values," Julian.com.

58 Maggiulli, Nick, "If You Play With FIRE, Don't Get Burned," Of Dollars And Data (March 30, 2021).

59 "Social Security Administration," Social Security History, ssa.gov.

60 Roser, M., Ortiz-Ospina, E., and Ritchie, H., "Life Expectancy," ourworldindata.org (2013).

61 Hershfield, Hal E., Daniel G. Goldstein, William F. Sharpe, Jesse Fox, Leo Yeykelis, Laura L. Carstensen, and Jeremy N. Bailenson, "Increasing Saving Behavior Through Age-Progressed Renderings of the Future Self," *Journal of Marketing Research* 48 SPL (2011), S23–S37.

62 Fisher, Patti J., and Sophia Anong, "Relationship of Saving Motives to Saving Habits," *Journal of Financial Counseling and Planning* 23:1 (2012).

63 Colberg, Fran, "The Making of a Champion," Black Belt (April 1975).

64 Seigel, Jeremy J., *Stocks for the Long Run* (New York, NY: McGraw-Hill, 2020).

65 Dimson, Elroy, Paul Marsh, and Mike Staunton, *Triumph of the Optimists: 101 Years of Global Investment Returns* (Princeton, NJ: Princeton University Press, 2009).

66 Biggs, Barton, *Wealth, War and Wisdom* (Oxford: John Wiley & Sons, 2009).

67 U.S. Department of the Treasury, Daily Treasury Yield Curve Rates (February 12, 2021).

68 Asness, Clifford S., "My Top 10 Peeves," *Financial Analysts Journal* 70:1 (2014), 22–30.

69 Jay Girotto, interview with Ted Seides, Capital Allocators, podcast audio (October 13, 2019).

70 Beshore, Brent (@brentbeshore). 12 Dec 2018, 3:52 PM. Tweet.

71 Wiltbank, Robert, and Warren Boeker, "Returns To Angel Investors In Groups," SSRN.com (November 1, 2007); and "Review of Research on the Historical Returns of the US Angel Market," Right Side Capital Management, LLC (2010).

72 "Who are American Angels? Wharton and Angel Capital Association Study Changes Perceptions About the Investors Behind U.S. Startup Economy," Angel Capital Association (November 27, 2017).

73 Altman, Sam, "Upside Risk," SamAltman.com (March 25, 2013).

74 Max, Tucker, "Why I Stopped Angel Investing (and You Should Never Start)," Observer.com (August 11, 2015).

75 Wiltbank, Robert, and Warren Boeker, "Returns To Angel Investors in Groups," SSRN.com (November 1, 2007).

76 Frankl-Duval, Mischa, and Lucy Harley-McKeown, "Investors in Search of Yield Turn to Music-Royalty Funds," *The Wall Street Journal* (September 22, 2019).

77 SPIVA, spglobal.com (June 30, 2020).

78 Bessembinder, Hendrik, "Do Stocks Outperform Treasury Bills?" *Journal of Financial Economics* 129:3 (2018), 440–457.

79 West, Geoffrey B., *Scale: The Universal Laws of Life, Growth, and Death in Organisms, Cities, and Companies* (Harmondsworth: Penguin, 2017).

80 Kosowski, Robert, Allan Timmermann, Russ Wermers, and Hal White, "Can Mutual Fund 'Stars' Really Pick Stocks? New Evidence from a Bootstrap Analysis," *The Journal of Finance* 61:6 (2006), 2551–2595.

81 "The Truth About Top-Performing Money Managers," Baird Asset Management, White Paper (2014).

82 Powell, R., "Bernstein: Free Trading is Like Giving Chainsaws to Toddlers," The Evidence-Based Investor (March 25, 2021).

83 Stephens-Davidowitz, Seth, *Everybody Lies: Big Data, New Data, and What the Internet Can Tell Us About Who We Really Are* (New York, NY: HarperCollins, 2017).

84 Rosling, Hans, *Factfulness* (Paris: Flammarion, 2019).

85 Buffett, Warren E., "Buy American. I Am," *The New York Times* (October 16, 2008).

86 "Asset Allocation Survey," aaii.com (March 13, 2021).

87 This is the median outcome for investing every month for a decade into U.S. stocks from 1926–2020.

88 For more detail see: ofdollarsanddata.com/in-defense-of-global-stocks.

89 Zax, David, "How Did Computers Uncover J.K. Rowling's Pseudonym?" Smithsonian Institution, Smithsonian.com (March 1, 2014)

90 Hern, Alex, "Sales of 'The Cuckoo's Calling' surge by 150,000% after JK Rowling revealed as author," *New Statesman* (July 14, 2013).

91 Kitces, Michael, "Understanding Sequence of Return Risk & Safe Withdrawal Rates," Kitces.com (October 1, 2014).

92 Frock, Roger, *Changing How the World Does Business: FedEx's Incredible Journey to Success – The Inside Story* (Oakland, CA: Berrett-Koehler Publishers, 2006).

93 Anarkulova, Aizhan, Scott Cederburg, and Michael S. O'Doherty, "Stocks for the Long Run? Evidence from a Broad Sample of Developed Markets," ssrn.com (May 6, 2020).

94 Zilbering, Yan, Colleen M. Jaconetti, and Francis M. Kinniry Jr., "Best Practices for Portfolio Rebalancing," Valley Forge, PA: The Vanguard Group.

95 Bernstein, William J., "The Rebalancing Bonus," www.efficientfrontier.com.

96 Brownlee, W. Elliot, *Federal Taxation in America* (Cambridge: Cambridge University Press, 2016).

97 Leonhardt, Megan, "Here's What the Average American Typically Pays in 401(k) Fees," CNBC (July 22, 2019).

98 Witt, April, "He Won Powerball's $314 Million Jackpot. It Ruined His Life," *The Washington Post* (October 23, 2018).

99 Luce, Edward, "Lloyd Blankfien: 'I Might Find It Harder to Vote for Bernie than for Trump'," *Financial Times* (February 21, 2020).

100 Saez, Emmanuel, and Gabriel Zucman, "Wealth Inequality in the United States Since 1913: Evidence from Capitalized Income Tax Data," *The Quarterly Journal of Economics* 131:2 (2016), 519–578.

101 Karadja, Mounir, Johanna Mollerstrom, and David Seim, "Richer (and Holier) Than Thou? The Effect of Relative Income Improvements on Demand for Redistribution," *Review of Economics and Statistics* 99:2 (2017), 201–212.

102 Jackson, Matthew O., *The Human Network: How Your Social Position Determines Your Power, Beliefs, and Behaviors* (New York, NY: Vintage, 2019).

103 "Global Wealth Report 2018," Credit Suisse (October 18, 2018).

104 Petter Attia, "Reverse Engineered Approach to Human Longevity," YouTube video, 1:15:37 (November 25, 2017).

105 Guvenen, Fatih, Fatih Karahan, Serdar Ozkan, and Jae Song, "What Do Data on Millions of US Workers Reveal About Life-cycle Earnings Dynamics?" FRB of New York Staff Report 710 (2015).

106 Schwandt, Hannes, "Human Wellbeing Follows a U-Shape over Age, and Unmet Aspirations Are the Cause," British Politics and Policy at LSE (August 7, 2013).

107 Rauch, Jonathan, *The Happiness Curve: Why Life Gets Better After 50* (New York, NY: Thomas Dunne Books, 2018).